THE FIVE
GIFTS

Advance Praise

"When she was a journalist in the 1970s, Laurie Nadel covered Chile following the military coup that brought General Augusto Pinochet to power. That experience—combined with her deep compassion—led her to help create the Committee to Protect Journalists, an organization which since 1981 has fought for the right of journalists around the world to report the news. In this book, Nadel draws from her experience surviving Hurricane Sandy while huddled in her attic and taps into her enormous reservoir of empathy to offer guidance to all those who have experienced trauma. There is no one in the world who cares more than Laurie Nadel."

—**Joel Simon**,
Executive Director, CPJ

"This is a fantastic book. I always like to quote that 'The problem is not the problem; the problem is how you deal with the problem.' Dr. Nadel guides you through adversities using other cultures' wisdom to transform the 'problem' into a growth opportunity—her last gift. This book is the gift that American society needs now to reassess its values and to reconquer its wisdom."

—**Dr. G. Clotaire Rapaille**,
Author of *The Culture Code*

"This is a fine teaching for anyone in this human condition."

—**Zen Monk Dai-en Friedman**

"If the reader can't find some strength, courage, hope, peace, and/or healing in this work then they are not paying attention."

—**Alan Clyne**,
US Marine Corps (Ret.)

"Learning the Five Gifts was the most important healing journey of my life. They have helped me in ways I could not have possibly imagined."

—**Frank Smyth**,
Founder and Executive Director of
the Global Journalist Security

"In these unusual times of our human existence, Dr. Laurie Nadel's new book is an elixir for the soul. A guide to finding the power and direction to reclaim your life when all is lost. *The Five Gifts* is the ultimate bible to survival. A spiritual and wisdom filled journey by one of America's great thinkers. This is a book we need to read before tragedy strikes. The life it saves could be our own."

—**Harris Salomon**,
President/Producer, Atlantic Overseas Pictures Television

"Thanks to Dr. Laurie for these important first steps into the future that we now face in our wounded world. Her book is a necessary companion to all those who are becoming professionals in service to others instead of self."

—**Leslie McTyre**,
UNICEF ambulance driver during the Rwandan genocide

"My fire service is dedicated to the memory of my best friend, FDNY Captain Patrick J. Brown LADDER-3, who was killed on 9/11/01. He said, 'You can do everything right and still be killed on the job.' To understand this reality and still perform one's duty speaks to the humility, courage, and inherent calling of first responders. This book speaks to how trauma invariably batters itself against these most human qualities. And it reinforces what Patrick believed: 'When they need help, they call us, but when we need help we call each other. It's a brotherhood.'"

—**Robert John Burke**,
Captain, Ocean Beach, New York Fire Department

"There are five things you should know about author Dr. Laurie Nadel: she is a kick-ass writer; she has more guts than most people I know; she is intimately connected to human nature at its core; she is a meticulous researcher; and she is a great alchemist. *The Five Gifts* clearly demonstrates how to transform serious human trauma into silver linings and golden dreams for our future."

—**Nancy du Tertre, Esq.**,
Remoter Viewer and Author, *Psychic Intuition: Everything You Ever Wanted to Ask But Were Afraid to Know*

"In *The Five Gifts*, Dr. Laurie helps the reader find ways to move from devastation to hopefulness. She shows how NLP protocols and presuppositions reframe disaster as an opportunity for new learning and creative applications for recovery and healing."

—**Rachel Hott, PhD**,
Co-director of The NLP Center of New York

THE FIVE
GIFTS

Discovering Hope, Healing,
and Strength When Disaster Strikes

Laurie Nadel, PhD
Foreword by Dan Rather

Health Communications, Inc.
Deerfield Beach, Florida

www.hcibooks.com

**Library of Congress Cataloging-in-Publication Data
is available through the Library of Congress**

The Five Gifts: Discovering Hope, Healing, and Strength When Disaster Strikes
© 2018 Laurie Nadel, PhD

ISBN-13: 978-07573-2044-6 (Paperback)
ISBN-10: 07573-2044-9 (Paperback)
ISBN-13: 978-07573-2045-3 (ePub)
ISBN-10: 07573-2045-7 (ePub)

Publisher: Health Communications, Inc.
    3201 S.W. 15th Street
    Deerfield Beach, FL 33442–8190

Cover and interior design by Lawna Patterson Oldfield

For Megan and Lisa

CONTENTS

PART FOUR: *Renewal*

Welcoming the Five Gifts

ACKNOWLEDGMENTS

*A*lthough writing is a solitary activity, this book would not have come into being without the unconditional support of many people. While I cannot thank everyone by name, I owe deep thanks to my patient family and friends—especially James—who put up with me as I carved chapters out of thin air while balancing research, interviews, and organization.

My deepest thanks to Dan Rather, who has never stopped believing in my work and who continues to encourage me to write. I have been privileged to work with him, and his values, strength, and work ethic always inspire me to go the course.

For their generous endorsements, thanks to Dr. Larry Dossey, Nancy du Tertre, Dr. and Mrs. Clotaire Rapaille, Harris Salomon, and Joel Simon of the Committee to Protect Journalists.

As Dorothy Parker wrote, "Writing is a tough and lonely job." Megan Marshack, Lisa Hagan, and PJ Dempsey held my hand every step of the way. Sakura Amend, thanks for believing in this book from the beginning. You are the best!

Working with the editorial and publicity team at Health Communications, Inc. has surpassed all previous experiences with publishers. In addition to their creativity and support for *The Five Gifts*, they bring an exceptional level of professionalism to the complex process of editing, producing, and promoting a new book. A deep bow to my amazing editor Allison Janse, book designer Lawna Oldfield, copy editor David Tabatsky, and my media soul sister Kim Weiss.

At News and Guts Media, thanks to the ever-patient Alex van Amson, Phil Kim, and Wayne Nelson. At MindBodyNetwork.com, my gratitude to Tore Kesicki, Mark Callipari, and James Retza. At the *New York Times*, thanks to Pat Lyons, Phil Coffin, Dean Toda, and Marcelle Fischler.

Going above and beyond the call of friendship, a shout out to: my Sarah Lawrence BFFs Amy Nicholls, Bernice Green (okay, we go back to high school), Teresa Oster, and Vern Oster; Patty Harris; Barbara Vettell; CBS News alums Ted Data, Haig Tufankjian, Jack Smith, Laurie Singer, and Nell Donovan (and Bill Frolisch); in Long Beach City Hall, Robin Lynch and Izzy; and the congregation at St. James of Jerusalem. At the WTC Family Center, thanks to Dr. Tom Demaria, Dr. Minna Barrett, Margie Miller, Carole Sankary Cullens, and the Comfortos.

Special thanks to Kathy Michaels, Marcia Isman, Anna Ervolina, Laura Manno, Sue Hecht, Barbara Fischkin, Marianne Weinstein, Jane Finnegan, Carol and Sandy Denicker, Eileen and Denis Kelly, Jenny Rivera, and Dr. Sergey Kulikov's indefatigable office team.

My appreciation to Paul Schweinler for inviting me to join his CISM team, Dr. George Everly and Dr. Jeff Mitchell of ICISF, and Sean Starbuck at the UK Fire Brigade Union.

To those of you whom I do not have space to mention, please know you are in my heart.

 FOREWORD

*J*n the shank of many an evening after covering some horrific event—a natural or man-made disaster—I, and other reporters, have often pondered together the question, "After what we have just witnessed, how can those still living, who have suffered most, cope?" Hurricanes, tsunamis, tornadoes and earthquakes, wars, revolutions and riots, starvations, epidemics, and genocides always make news. The people left suffering in their wake frequently do not, or at best, don't make news for long. The news cycle moves on; so do the journalists. Thus the question goes unanswered among us. There are new stories to cover and, besides, we say to ourselves—excuse makers and "rationalizers" that we tend to be—"We're journalists not psychologists, sociologists, or philosophers." But sometimes, at the end of other evenings when we are by ourselves, alone with our thoughts, the question resurfaces in our memory; resurfaces and haunts.

For journalists and non journalists alike, these are the personal, trying times all of us face in our individual lives, when it is not someone else suffering—when it is you and yours wracked with loss and hurt. That's when the question of coping cuts deepest.

Dr. Laurie Nadel has spent years seeking to answer this question. Once a seasoned journalist and now a distinguished scholar and practicing psychotherapist, she has immersed herself in the academic study of suffering—in addition to the depth her own life story provides. She doesn't know it all, doesn't claim to, but she knows a lot and knows how to tell it. When it comes to dealing with personal struggle, she possesses infinite wisdom.

Dictionaries define a wise person as one who judiciously applies experience and knowledge; a person characterized by sound judgment, prudence, and practical sense. This fits Laurie Nadel like a bespoke suit. The good doctor earned her reservoir of uncommon wisdom for troubling times the old-fashioned way—through hard work, intense scholarship, and having an unusual variety of life experiences, good and bad. She knows the science and the literature, and not for nothing was her long, difficult slog to a PhD, but she also knows the realities of life from the bottom up. She was not born to privilege or place; she has been working since she was thirteen years old and has a firsthand knowledge of the Dickensian underside of life at home.

The common sense part of what became her wisdom was apparent when I first met her some thirty years ago at CBS when she was a beginning news writer and obituary producer for Newsfeed (formerly Syndication, now Newspath.) In the newsroom she stood out—at least to me and to others who observed her closely—because she was that rarity: a talented, dedicated young journalist who also was an unusually committed scholar. She cared about the news but also about continuing serious academic study. And she cared mightily about people, as evidenced by her volunteer work in professional organizations and community service, which included launching two groups to protect the human rights of journalists, the first being the Overseas Press Club in 1977–78 and the second the Committee to Protect Journalists.

Then there also was this: She was an exceptionally good listener. This unusual combination for a journalist so young, along with the seasoning of having to fight through her own multiple setbacks and suffering, eventually led her to pursue a doctorate in psychology.

All of that might not matter much for a book if she were not able to write well, but good writing is one of her strengths. Clarity and excellent storytelling skills are hallmarks of her writing and always have been, whether it's news copy, academic papers, blogs, or books. And it's always backed by deep-digging research—not just of the library and internet search kind but also in-the-field and person-to-person. Mark well that part of Laurie's teaching is a version of the ancient dictum that she, you, or anyone can be beaten but never defeated if you have the will and the spirit. Knowledge and advice of this kind are offered in these pages.

When it comes to teaching how to get up after being knocked down, how to not just survive life's hardest blows but eventually thrive, nothing beats a teacher who has learned through personal experience. I'll be surprised if you don't find this book highly readable and the information in it unusually accessible and easy to understand, digest, and put to use.

Dr. Laurie Nadel touches off many new sunbursts of thought as she guides us through what we need to know about the Five Gifts that are keys to coping with life's most troubling times.

—Dan Rather
New York, NY

INTRODUCTION

*F*or the past twenty-five years, I have made the same New Year's resolution: Throw out half of what you own and spend more time with friends. Little did I know how prescient that resolution would prove to be in 2012. Nor did I sense that before the year was out, I would receive a transformational opportunity to fully experience what it means to "let go, let God."

Swish! First, the storm broke through the back wall of the house where I was watching The Weather Channel. Ninety-mile-an-hour winds bashed tree branches against the triple-pane windows. *Glug-glug!* Mini-fountains began spouting up near the wall. Three hours to high tide.

Ever since childhood, my dream house had been a cottage with a view of the water. I used to have a painting of one in my bedroom. When my divorce was finalized in 1993, a joint custody clause required that I live within a fifty-mile radius of the Empire State Building. This led me to Long Beach, a barrier island community of some 35,000 residents about twenty-five miles from Manhattan. A family-oriented beach community where I never had to lock my door, it met the requirements of both the joint custody clause and my childhood dream. From my front garden, you could watch boats in the Reynolds Channel at the north end of the block. In 2011, when Hurricane Irene breached the seawall at the end of the block, a small river ran down the middle of the street at curb height until the tide receded, but the house was untouched.

After speaking to several first responders who advised me to put sand-bags in front of the doors and hunker down, I decided that, whatever happened, I needed to see it for myself. Better to take action immediately than to worry from a remote location. Like the captain of a ship, if the house was going to float away, I was going with it.

Team coverage! This just in! During my nearly two decades in TV newsrooms, I had committed multiple egregious acts of hurricane hype. No stranger to hyperbole masquerading as news, I checked the National Oceanic and Atmospheric Association (NOAA) website. The forecast called for a twenty-four-hour rain event with two to four inches of rain. This seemed to indicate that if the house flooded during high tide, the water would quickly recede when it ebbed. This turned out to be the case.

When you think of fountains, you probably think of spas, gardens, and meditative spaces. But the gentle sound of water bubbling up as it spread triggered an eerie cognitive dissonance. This sound was not refreshing, and the visuals were unforgettably disturbing, even more so because the ankle-deep water was not coming from the Reynolds Channel, which was just reaching the sidewalk. A quick look out the back door revealed a four-and-a-half-foot sheet of water extending to a smaller canal, about 200 yards west of the house.

As the flood surged to mid-calf level, my boyfriend and I began moving emergency supplies into the attic, along with Bogart the cat. Cat food, litter, water, blankets, first-aid kit, power bars, laptops, TV screen, and a backup drive were lifted to safety, along with candles, lanterns, matches, and an emergency radio/lantern that operated on electricity, batteries, solar power, and a crank. My boyfriend had laughed at me when I proudly unpacked this last item, having bought it from Macy's the previous May as a birthday present to myself. He was not laughing now.

Nor was he laughing at the ten gallons of water I had stockpiled after my father appeared to me in a dream six months earlier. "Buy water," he said. "You are going to need it." My dad died in 1989, but I figured if he had gone to the trouble of showing up in a dream I needed to pay attention. Each time I went to the supermarket, I would grab a gallon of water to take home. After I had stockpiled half a dozen gallons, I was forced to admit that I had, in fact, become something of a closet prepper.

Doomsday preparation suppliers were the network sponsors of Genesis Communications Network, where I hosted *The Dr. Laurie Show: Your Place to Explore the Unknown and Expect the Unexpected* from 2007 to 2009. We ran commercials for everything from gold to meals ready-to-eat to survivalseedsinacan.com. At the time, I'd thought of survivalists as a subculture, but during the past five years I had started to notice that high tides were covering all the marsh grass. The seas were visibly rising. I loved living near the water, but for the past few years it was looking like the ocean might someday pay me a visit. That day had now come—an hour and a half before high tide—when three and a half feet of water filled the entire house. The channel had overflowed the sandbags, pushing through the front door, leaving us completely surrounded.

"Guess we're not leaving now," I shrugged.

Crash! Gurgle! The refrigerator fell onto its side, floating near the back door. The washing machine and a ten-foot leather couch were floating, too.

Titanic! In my own home!

The flood was churning up books, manuscripts, potted plants, firewood, a loveseat, antique wooden chairs, and a legal bookcase. Wet clumps of paper towels and toilet paper smeared against the walls. Catching a whiff of natural gas, I called the gas company, only to have the phone go dead before I finished tapping out the emergency phone number. The smell dissipated, thanks to emergency shut-down valves in the water heater, furnace, and stove.

For nearly two decades, the little house had provided a place of safety and refuge to hundreds of individuals who came for therapy and support after life-shattering events. In the quiet of my back office, I had written three books and several hundred articles for magazines and the *New York Times, Times of London*, and *Huffington Post*. I had lived here for a decade as a single mom, and friends from around the world had come for vacations. It was all being taken, right in front of my eyes.

A strong wave pushed me from behind. Pulling myself up, I gripped the aluminum staircase to the attic and turned. A force far greater than I could comprehend was at work. My history and life as I knew it were being washed out from under me. Although I expected to feel shock and sorrow, in one sparkling moment an oceanic wave of tranquility washed over me from head to toe. My spirit released. What was gone was meant to be gone. What was over was meant to be over. An unmistakable spiritual presence was totally in charge. All I had to do was let go, and this Spirit would do whatever it meant to do. It was my choice and my privilege to be here at this moment, bearing witness to all this.

In the interest of full disclosure, I am a world-class worrier. But oddly, my worries were being lifted from my shoulders in that moment. A message whispered to my soul, assuring me that the tranquility of my home would not be lost. It was now imbued in me and I would carry it wherever I went. The words of a Brazilian prayer came back: "Let there be peace in the ocean. Let there be peace in my soul."

We spent the night in the attic, watching the flood slowly creep up the stairs. It stopped at the fourth step, right around the time that we lost our transmission from *CBS News* on the emergency radio. After a few hours' sleep, the first light woke us up. Downstairs, a thick film of dirty grease and raw sewage coated the tile floor, walls, and every item in the house.

Apparently, the main sewage pump had broken during the storm. The toxic smell of human feces made us cover our noses and mouths as we went into the street, where our neighbors had gathered, pointing cell phones at the sky, as if somehow that would help catch a signal. What were we supposed to do without power, phone service, or clean water? We were cut off from the rest of the world. Helpless. Confused. Yesterday's normal was completely gone.

Unnerving? Yes. But that deep sense of calm from the previous night was still present.

Curious about what my new world would be like, I gathered as many things as I could that were not contaminated and left for a month-long sojourn as a FEMA-certified, displaced person. After nearly twenty years in the same home, I left its ruins and moved six times in one month—to two different apartments in Brooklyn, to Washington DC, my brother's home in Dallas, and finally to a friend's basement close to a subway I could take to work, once the electricity had returned to lower Manhattan. When I charged my cell phone to call FEMA from a Starbucks in Park Slope, I yearned to go home, and then realized with a shock that I had no home. Once the power came back in Long Beach, I moved to a family member's apartment.

Along the way, I found that I had managed to pack fifteen pairs of socks and no underwear. How did that happen? I bought a really ugly purple suitcase to lug everything I owned: a laptop, computer backup, financial documents, jewelry, and safe deposit keys. I figured that people would look at the purple suitcase and think, "Anyone who has such lousy taste in luggage couldn't possibly have anything worth stealing." From the looks of pity I got from fellow passengers waiting at baggage claim, the strategy worked.

Walking through my old neighborhood, I realized that it had been a long time since I had hung out with lifelong friends. In some cases, years had slipped by without stopping for coffee or having dinner. In keeping busy, I had missed out on a lot of laughter. For years on end, I had failed to keep my New Year's resolution.

An author and Zen master once told me, "A friend helps you move. A real friend helps you move the body." In this case, the body was mine. By taking every "thing" away, Hurricane Sandy carried me into the arms of my real friends and my true family. I could not have wished for anything more beautiful.

That's why I made the same New Year's resolution this year: Less stuff, more friends.

In facing the ruins of my former life, I discovered Five Gifts that helped me persevere:

1) humility
2) patience
3) empathy
4) forgiveness
5) growth

I also discovered a considerable body of scientific research supporting the benefits of each trait. Trusting my spiritual instincts has become an organic process but finding research that backs up my intuition gives the Five Gifts a scientific seal of approval.

Anyone who has traveled this road knows how arduous and long it can be. We have to expect the unexpected and keep going, even without a map or direction. In uncharted territory, we need new thinking, new ways of processing intense emotions, and new behavioral choices. If you open the book to a random spot, don't be surprised to find a useful piece of information or a new idea that seems to be just what you need. It is my hope that the Five Gifts can serve as a beacon to shine light into the darkness so that you can navigate to a new place of hope and strength.

You can make it—one step at a time.

PART ONE

Prepping

Red skies at night,
sailors' delight.
Red skies in the morning,
sailors take warning.

—Anonymous

1

There Is No Change Without Loss, No Loss Without Change

The sky is red. You can't get away. From the moment you turn on your phone, you see faces of people whose day started off much like yours, with an expectation of going from point A to point B, to lunch, to point C, and then back home. But something happened. Someone drove a truck into a crowd. A bomb went off at a concert. Somebody got shot or got hit by a bus. A tornado touched down. Or maybe there was a seven-car pileup on the highway. Within seconds, life as usual got blown away.

It's in our faces and on our screens. Streaming images stab at us. We swipe them away. And so it goes, until it happens to you or someone you know and love.

Say it's early in the morning; you're drinking your coffee, and you swipe or click to make those upsetting faces go away. There is always last night's scores or today's cat video to distract you. Why get upset if you haven't had your breakfast yet?

It is human nature to move away from pain and toward pleasure. Thanks to the miracle of instant digital access, you can eliminate anything that reeks of unpleasantness in less than a second—however, this may reinforce an unrealistic assumption that when something painful happens you should be able to make it go away *right now*. If you can't, there must be something wrong with you. You must not be visualizing what you want to attract. Or you have "negative beliefs." Or perhaps you believe that God is punishing you.

It's Reality. Not Reality TV.

Practice in the art of swiping away whatever we don't want to face leaves us ill-prepared to face tragic events in our own lives. Not only does

Practice in the art of swiping away whatever we don't want to face leaves us ill-prepared to face tragic events in our own lives.

looking away make it harder for us to cope with our own emotional needs, it also leaves us with a deficit in compassion for others and ourselves when reality turns out to be a lot different from reality TV.

The unrealistic belief that we are somehow entitled to go through life unmoved by other people's suffering further limits our ability to cope with our own. Our capacity to disregard and discount viscerally painful experiences is so ingrained that we have come to believe that "moving forward" means not allowing ourselves to be moved at all.

Even first responders and military personnel can be deeply affected by what they see, smell, and hear on the job. It doesn't make them less effective. Nor do they consider themselves weak. It takes guts to wake up every day knowing you will be walking a knife's edge between life and death. As civilians, we can help ourselves become stronger in adversity by modeling some first responders' mindsets and coping strategies.

The Help Cycle Lasts Three Months

Forgetting what happened is not an option. It can take years before you stop thinking about it as soon as you wake up and throughout the day. That's right—*years*. After the initial rush of sending money to the American Red Cross, our collective attention wanders. Once the cameras leave, we tend to think that anyone affected should be "over it already." Nothing could be further from the truth.

Dr. Thomas Demaria is a psychologist specializing in trauma. He is the director of the Psychological Services Center in the doctoral program in clinical psychology at Long Island University's CW Post Campus. Dr. Demaria has consulted on more than 200 catastrophic events, including the Sandy Hook school shootings in Newtown, Connecticut; Hurricane Sandy; the 2008 earthquake in Haiti; the World Trade Center attacks of 1993 and 2001; and Hurricane Katrina.

"For the first three months, people want to donate time and money," he says. "Then they want to hear that the people who were traumatized are 'moving forward.' The hurt lasts longer than the public expects."

As a therapist specializing in helping people whose lives have been impacted by catastrophic events, I frequently hear that a few days, a few weeks, or maybe several months after a critical event, a survivor, loved one or eyewitness starts to get shamed and blamed for not "being over it." Messages from his or her partner, mother, best friend, or coworker frequently go something like this: "What's wrong with you? You're still dwelling on this. You should get over it. You need to go out more. Why don't you join Match.com? You should smile more. Why don't you go shopping?"

A Price for Everything

There is a price for forgetting *and* for remembering. Forgetting as a form of escape deprives us of what the Five Gifts can offer—humility, patience, empathy, forgiveness, and growth.

Forgetting as a form of escape deprives us of what the Five Gifts can offer—humility, patience, empathy, forgiveness, and growth.

Remembering in the form of flashbacks, second-guessing, and the head game called "could'a-should'a-would'a" comes with a heavy emotional price—remaining frozen in the initial stages of shock, hurt, and rage. You won't find the Five Gifts on anyone's wish list, but when your emotional tank is on empty, they will be there to help you replenish your energy.

The long and winding road to that place where we come to terms with our losses and begin to build our new sense of self demands that we give ourselves all the time we need to process the unthinkable, with compassion for ourselves and others. We need to unlearn the habits of impatience and take stock of those beliefs about life that no longer hold true.

Contrary to current mythology, everything does not happen for a reason that we can grasp. Some things are beyond human understanding. This doesn't jibe with our "Just Do It" mindset, but humility—the first gift—can help us surrender to an event outside our control, one we couldn't prevent and was not our fault.

Stop Trying to Fix It—or Him or Her or Yourself

Most of the people who have come forward to share their experiences in these pages have been to hell and back. I cannot thank them enough for the courage and raw honesty they are willing to offer so that *our* journeys can be less excruciating.

When someone we know is hurting, it's our instinct to want them to get better—first, for themselves, and also because our inability to assist leaves us feeling helpless. What happened to him or her could happen to any of us at any time. There is no such thing as "it can't happen here."

When somebody is emotionally injured in an unexpected and tragic event, that does not make him or her less of a person any more than our own vulnerability makes us "less than." It makes us "greater than."

No Timetable for Healing

I have never met anyone who decided that three weeks from today at 2:37 PM she would be "over it" and made it happen exactly like that. It's impossible to predict how the heart heals or how long it is going to take. Humility helps us come to terms with what we cannot know. Patience takes the edge off when the hurt continues.

Empathy is the gift that connects us with others. Although we might want to isolate, we need empathy during cycles of instability and loss, such as during war, epidemic, gas shortages, or seasons of drought and wildfires.

It's not uncommon to default to feeling like a failure when you are unable to will yourself to make the pain go away. Although you may be too shattered for a while to go to work or socialize or be a productive member of society, living with acute stress does not mean you have failed. Like breaking a leg, a serious injury to the psyche often gets us benched while the regular game of life goes on. It may seem strange that forgiving ourselves for having such perfectly human reactions is harder than forgiving whatever caused them.

The essence of the Five Gifts is elegantly expressed in this quote from Pope John Paul II: "See everything. Overlook a great deal. Improve a little."

Forgiveness Helps Us Let Go

Many of us feel "damaged" because we cannot fight off debilitating waves of emotion. "I don't know why I wake up worrying in the middle of the night," a woman who lost her home in a fire recently told me. Within the previous two years, she had also survived sexual assault, divorce, losing her job, and moving out of state.

"It feels like I was hit by a giant wave," she said. As we reviewed the events she had endured in a relatively short time, her responses made sense to her. Given the circumstances, they were normal and very human.

Finally, the gift of growth allows us to look back on those very painful events and say, "I never wanted to go through that nor would I wish it on someone else. But if I hadn't, I wouldn't have become the person I am today. And for that, I am grateful."

Three Cycles of Loss

Finding our balance in the aftermath of a big hit can be complicated by cycles of loss, which are rarely addressed. But recognizing what they are and how they affect us can protect us from slipping into depression and loss of self-worth.

The three cycles of loss center on our sense of control, safety, and identity.

1) *Loss of control, especially loss of control over physical symptoms.*

     In the wake of disaster, symptoms that include loss of appetite, difficulty sleeping, gastrointestinal pain, and headaches can become unsettling. Most of the time, they resolve on their own, but the key gift here is patience and paying attention to our basic needs—for food, water, and rest. If the discomfort continues, it is time to seek medical help. Conventional and homeopathic medication, as well as nutritional supplements, can alleviate psychogenic symptoms, such as headaches and insomnia.

     A couple of years after Rachelle Quiyara survived a shoot-out on a New York City bus, she was having so much trouble sleeping that she was unable to function at work.

     "I tried antianxiety medication but I couldn't tolerate the side effects," she says. "I created small comfort zones for myself, and whenever possible, my boyfriend and I took a drive. It felt calming to be around water."

2) *Loss of safety and an increase in vulnerability.*

     If anxiety is "the disease of the what-if's," imagining a plethora of life-threatening events can only serve to intensify anxiety. Eighteen months after she was hit by a bus while crossing the street, Margaret Sugarman became unable to leave her house.

     "I can't stop thinking that something horrible is going to happen again," she told me. "It's better if I just stay inside."

Margaret, who was blind, considered suicide because she felt too fragile to continue. As she came to understand that experiencing extreme vulnerability was a natural part of the healing process, she regained confidence in her ability to navigate outdoors.

"I thought there was something wrong with me," she said.

After I explained that anyone, sighted or blind, would be frightened after such an accident, she was able to stop blaming herself for being weak. Like Margaret, those who pride themselves on being self-reliant and independent often report that reframing their shame about feeling vulnerable in response to a loss of safety stops the spiral of negativity and helps them to reclaim their self-worth.

3) *Loss of identity.*

When life as we knew it gets ripped away and our ability to concentrate is impaired for months or years at a time, we can begin to question our identity. We find ourselves plagued by questions: Who am I, if I'm not a spouse? Or parent? Who am I if I can't work and take care of my family or balance my checkbook? What happened to the strong, independent person I used to be? Questioning our identity is an unsettling experience but it can open the way for a new appreciation for core strengths that no one can take away from us.

After one of my friends lost his restaurant in a fire, he discovered that what hurt the most was the loss of his professional identity. Multiple problems getting an insurance settlement and delays with building permits held up construction for more than a year.

"The restaurant was a neighborhood landmark. It bore my name and my sense of self, and pride in my work was a big part of who I was," he told me. "Then it dawned on me that I am not a place of business and my self-worth does not depend on my kitchen equipment. I realized that what I believe in is far more important. I'm loyal to those who matter and I value speaking the truth. That's who I am, and nothing, not even that fire, can take that away."

#Disturbing Trends

When I started working on this book full time, research in several fields of study showed potential future trends with regard to mass fatality events—natural, environmental, and intentional (human to human). But with each chapter, a surge in breaking news made evident the facts that climate change and random acts of violence are increasing in frequency and intensity. I can't help thinking that this surge in man-made and intentional disasters reflects a dangerous change in the emotional climate in our society.

The projected trends are no longer predictions.

The future is here.

If you are one of those millions of people who have been—or will be—directly affected by these trends, this book could well become your lifeline to emotional recovery.

As this book went to press, the *Washington Post* reported that "natural disasters caused $306 billion in US damage in 2017, the largest amount for one year." The hurricane trifecta—Harvey, Irma, and Maria—in combination with wildfires and various other natural disasters made 2017 the most expensive year since the National Oceanic and Atmospheric Administration started keeping records in 1980. Hurricane Harvey topped the list with $125 billion in damages, second only to Hurricane Katrina in 2005, which resulted in $215 billion in damages.[1]

- According to the National Institute of Mental Health in Bethesda, Maryland, 70 percent of us—approximately 223,400,000 people—will go through *at least* one traumatic event in our lives; some 17 percent of men and 13 percent of women will experience more than three.[2]

- In a nationwide Google survey that I commissioned for this book, 33 percent of those surveyed identified their greatest fear as a terrorist attack, followed by displacement from their homes. The third biggest fear was an auto accident, followed by fire or natural disaster.
- The likelihood of being shot increases each year. Since 2011, random shootings of three or more people have tripled, according to a Harvard School of Public Health Study. That is one mass shooting every 64 days. Between 1982 and 2011, there was one mass shooting every 200 days, perpetrated by killers who did not know their victims.[3] For the second year in a row, the Centers for Disease Control reported that 12 out of every 100,000 people died from gunshots in 2016; in 2015, it was 11 per 100,000. "It clearly shows an increase," the CDC's chief of mortality statistics, Bob Anderson, told the *New York Times*.[4]
- A 2012 report by the National Wildlife Foundation and the Robert Wood Johnson Foundation estimates that by 2025, as many as 200 million Americans will experience acute stress due to severe climate change. From super-storms to mega-droughts, acute stress caused by extreme weather events can lead to depression, substance abuse, and post-traumatic stress disorder.[5] The report published half a decade ago was based on research conducted in previous years. Its findings are no longer projections. We are living them today.

Okay, the numbers are frightening and depressing. We can stick our heads under the covers and refuse to come out. We can let fear and anger drive our personalities or we can channel the positive power of anger into healthy activism. With humility, patience, empathy, forgiveness, and growth, we can share necessary information about how to survive and take care of ourselves and each other, during and after a disaster. We can educate ourselves about the growing, real threat that environmental damage poses to our safety, health, and longevity. With the Five Gifts, we can solve our problems without shooting each other.

We have a lot of work to do. We could probably start a movement called #disturbingtrends and reach more people than we realize have a need to be part of a community like this.

Meanwhile, the Five Gifts can help us stay grounded when life as we knew it gets turned upside down and inside out.

Finding Hope

Two years after 9/11, I signed on to run an adolescent bereavement program at South Nassau Community Hospital's World Trade Center Family Center in Rockville Centre on Long Island. As a single mom who had survived raising a teenager, I knew reaching these kids would not be easy. Dr. Demaria, the program's executive director, told me that three experts in adolescent bereavement had already struck out. As I recall, he tried to set realistic expectations about my prospects for success. Unlike adults who had lost a loved one on 9/11, teenagers were not going to sit in a circle and share their feelings in a group. Nor would they be willing to paint, draw, or write letters to God, like the nine-year-old daughter of a New York City fireman, whose letter was posted near the counseling center's front door:

"Dear God," she had written. "Please give the people who hurt us a heart."

Finding a way to connect with thirty teens and young adults who did not want to be singled out as "9/11 kids" was challenging. Their moms described them as "shut down." They did not want to talk about anything related to September 11th and they were probably not going to show up at any events at the Family Center.

To my surprise, the keys to their opening up would be found at Yankee and Shea Stadiums. My indefatigable supervisor, Dr. Minna Barrett, who had logged months of service at Ground Zero, urged me to reach out to the NY Yankees and the NY Mets. I had never been a baseball fan, but Rocky

Halsey of the New York Yankees community relations team arranged for the kids to attend batting practice and meet Yankees' manager Joe Torre. My brother Eric, the Voice of the Texas Rangers, got special permission for me to bring the kids to the press box when the Rangers were in town, as the Yankee Stadium press box is normally off-limits to visitors. He also asked the Mets' general manager, Omar Minaya, to organize a day when 9/11 families could meet the players and watch the game.

We spent three baseball seasons together. Despite their initial dislike for the group bus nicknamed "The 9/11-mobile," the kids shared memories of going to games with their dads. They missed their fathers on Opening Day and remembered the Father's Day games when their favorite team won. Organically, the younger boys and girls confided to the older kids that they missed their fathers coming home from work to practice batting with them before dinner. A sixteen-year-old who had been quiet for nearly two years opened up about how his father had gone to work early that Tuesday just so that he would be home in time for Little League that night.

"It's hard because I'm different from my friends," he said. "I know that what you love can be taken away from you in an instant. So whatever you do, you have to seize the day and make it yours."

On the bus home from Yankee Stadium, a few of the older boys came over to talk about an idea they had developed among themselves. After sitting with the younger kids and listening to them talk about their fathers teaching them to play, my older kids were eager to start coaching and mentoring the little ones. This was the gift of empathy in action.[6]

Having disconnected emotionally to protect themselves from feeling helpless and scared, they found that they could reach each other through their shared love of baseball.

"That program made a huge difference to me," one of the young men told me recently. "Before, I was a wreck. I was really angry and I didn't know how I could go on. That helped me turn the corner because it showed me that 9/11 wasn't an end. It was a beginning."

As it says in *After the Fall: The Rise of a 9/11 Community Center*, a documentary film about this work we all did together, "There is no magic formula for healing the pain. Indescribable damage to the landscape of the heart and mind will forever remain invisible. The pioneers built their communities so that they could stand united against adversities. It is our American tradition to come together in times of tragedy. This is how we grow as a people and as a nation."[7]

KEYS FOR GETTING READY TO STAY STEADY

- FLEX YOUR MIND. Change one habit, such as holding the phone against your left or right ear, brushing your teeth with your left or right hand, or how you travel to and from home. Choose one habit to change and practice it for 30 days. Think of this simple exercise as mind training. It helps tune up the brain's ability to create new neural pathways for new patterns and choices.

- SPIRAL YOUR FEARS. This process was given to me in a Native American women's circle. It takes about 20 to 30 minutes. On a sheet of paper or cardboard, draw a large spiral. Starting from the innermost point, follow the curving line as you write your fears into the spiral. Stop when you are ready. As you look at your spiral, what stands out? Are there any repetitions or patterns? Date your work and file it somewhere safe. A few months or a year from now, when you look at the spiral, you will see that you have lived or worked through most of those fears.

- GIVE YOURSELF A NEWSBREAK. Take a break when the news gets to be too much. It's important to be informed about the world around us but it is up to each of us to decide when to step back for a while.

- ASK THE **"POWER QUESTION."** Certain people, places, and
  situations can be draining, especially during difficult times. If the
  issue is not urgent, you can choose to conserve your energy,
  which only you can do, by asking yourself the Power Question.

"IF I DO (X) WITH (Y) AT (Z), WILL IT":

    A. Give me energy

    B. Help me conserve my energy

    C. Drain my energy.

PUT ANSWER (C) ON YOUR NOT-TO-DO LIST.
Be ruthlessly honest with yourself. If the answer is
"C, drain my energy," please move that item from your
"To Do" list to your "*Not* to Do" list. Estimate how much time
you would have spent doing this task. Give that time to yourself.
Now that this question is no longer on your "To Do" list,
give yourself that half-hour or hour as a gift for something
enjoyable and relaxing.

2

When You Can't
Change the Channel

*n*ow you know. Life doesn't happen in chapters with neat beginnings, middles, and ends. Sheer survival doesn't work like that. Every signpost, every landmark, every little anchor that you trusted to help you mark your day is no longer accessible. You have been beamed up into this new God-awful reality, with no idea how you got here or where to go next.

Now you understand that the event was the opening scene in a disaster movie that goes on and on. Now you get it: Tom Cruise is not coming to rescue you. Every morning, you get up, wishing you didn't have to. You put one foot in front of the other. Every breath hurts. Throughout the day, surges of energy suddenly drop off, leaving you queasy and off-balance. Sudden noise makes you want to jump out of your skin.

When It Hurts to Be Alive

To others, you look the same. From the inside out, you no longer recognize yourself. It's impossible to remember "before" and even harder to conceive of an "after." This is all there is, all there ever was. You can't change the channel. It hurts to be alive.

"I never realized how physically painful it is to be so intensely affected by this. It hurts your gut," says Margie Miller, whose husband Joel was working at the insurance brokerage firm Marsh and McLennan on the 97th floor of Tower One at the World Trade Center on September 11, 2001. The hijacked jet with its load of fuel smashed through the upper floors of Tower One. Joel Miller was among those incinerated, although his family hoped against hope that was not so.

"If you had to die that day, that was probably the better way to go," says his widow. "I am grateful."

With 20/20 hindsight, it seems ironic that Joel Miller was an assistant vice-president for disaster recovery who was always in his office by 7:30 AM.

"He kissed me goodbye as he did every morning. I was half-asleep," she remembers.

The calls started coming in a few minutes before nine.

"My girlfriend, Jeannie, called and said, 'There's a fire on top of the World Trade Center. Where does he work?'"

Friends who gathered on her front lawn were invited inside.

"We sat on my bed and watched TV, trying to figure out what we were looking at," she says.

Within minutes, the second plane hit. After attempting to call, text, and page her husband, Margie started calling women whose husbands were Joel's colleagues.

"How is Paul? Have you heard from Harry?" she kept asking.

No one had heard from her husband.

"By 9:15, it was just catastrophic. I kept trying to zoom into the building and count floors from the top but you couldn't," she says.

Her sons and sister-in-law started calling to ask if Joel was at work.

"I didn't hear from him. I didn't hear from him," she kept chanting.

Then it hit her.

"Truly this is not going to be a good end."

New York City shut down.

"The bridges are closed. The city is closed. Please stay where you are," she remembers telling her sons. "I don't want to worry about any more people."

That evening, she called the police and reported that Joel was missing. When law enforcement officers came to her home, the first thing they asked was, "Where is his car?" She remembers them asking if maybe Joel could have gone somewhere else. "If he did, he would call me for directions first," Margie smiles sadly. "He has a poor sense of direction."

A neighbor's kids found the car where Joel had parked it at the train station before catching the 6:20 train to Penn Station that morning.

"At home, it was a mob scene," Margie says. "People needed to gather, to be supportive and process this together."

Getting Used to It? Not.

Margie cried every day.

"For months and months and months. You took a million showers to cry where the kids couldn't hear you," she says. "You get into the car to run errands so you don't upset people in the house. You don't know how to stop. If you lost a limb, you'd know it's missing. Every day, you get up and you put on your prosthetic and you function. But you can't help but notice that your leg is missing."

Now a professional speaker who addresses audiences on resilience and life lessons from September 11th, Margie says, "The important thing is I put my prosthetic on and I go out and function."

It Didn't End on September 11th

The unsettling process of mourning those who died on September 11th remains complicated by the problems involved in identifying fragments of human remains, even with advances in processing DNA.

"In 2016, a woman got the first piece of her husband," says Margie, who received two fragments of Joel's remains several years apart.

"The very first time, they came at 10:30 at night. I had a hang-up phone call just before they knocked," she says.

A few minutes later, there were two detectives at her door. As soon as she saw them, she knew why they were there. Her immediate reaction: "Oh my God. Thank you. Thank you." It was all she could say.

They told her they needed to come in.

"You don't," she told them, but they insisted. "In those days, they were mandated to put a notice in the newspaper once they had a positive I.D. You got a number and the medical examiner's retrieval information. I was stunned. What arrangements do you make for a small piece of tibia bone?"

Margie buried Joel's leg fragment in a small box. Two years later, the medical examiners identified a knucklebone fragment. It was buried in a container. Almost a decade later, three more fragments of Joel Miller's body were found after another excavation uncovered 1,800 pieces of human remains. She is planning her husband's third and hopefully, his final funeral.

When people ask, as they often do, "Aren't you over it by now?" Margie understands that they just don't get it.

"It's not something that ends at the cemetery," she says.

With empathy, she recognizes there is no point in making them suffer. She shrugs, "When I bury the last three fragments, I'll let you know."

A Badge of Honor

"Getting up and putting on your shoes after a disaster is a badge of honor," says Dr. Demaria, the founder of the World Trade Center Family Center on Long Island. "True healing is when you somehow transform the nature of how you perceive what you have gone through."

> "Getting up and putting on your shoes after a disaster is a badge of honor. ... True healing is when you somehow transform the nature of how you perceive what you have gone through."

Like Chicago Mayor Rahm Emmanuel who said, "It's a pity to waste a good crisis," Dr. Demaria believes that a catastrophic event like September 11th "helps you sort out what is really important."

Any critical incident can serve as "a cleansing even though it's a hard time," he says.

While some people apparently seem to "magically go through life without having to face a death or a job loss, it's important to face adversity and face into anxiety to rise above it," he says, adding, "Like it or not, we grow through pain."

Running for Her Life

Nora Quinn had just made the turn onto Boylston Street and was heading for the finish line.

"It was jam packed with people. A young man screamed, 'You're almost there. You're almost there.' With that, I heard the first bomb go off," says Nora, a runner in the 2013 Boston Marathon, where three people were killed and 260 wounded by two homemade bombs.

Quinn recalls that there was so much noise, no one reacted to the sound. She thought it was a celebratory cannon.

When the second bomb exploded, Quinn saw smoke.

"Everyone slowed up or stopped to look at that area," she says.

When runners started asking each other where to go, she told them not to run past the large glass convention center because the windows could blow out.

"When you finish a marathon, you get very cold. I sat down and started shaking," she recalls. Someone lent her a phone to call her husband. When he didn't answer, she left a voicemail message, saying she was okay.

A tall man with white hair and a runner's bib told her he would lead her to the spot near the finish line where the runners kept their bags.

"We started running, but we weren't allowed to go near the finish line," she says. "We were trying to get back to our buses. Then I saw a foot with a sneaker in the street. I said, 'Oh my God!'"

She pushed through her shock and kept running to the bus where a volunteer was there to give Nora her belongings.

"My body was shaking. I was crying. I couldn't open my bag. Someone had to open it for me," she says.

When she looked for the man with white hair to thank him, he was nowhere to be found.

Nora says, "I think he was an angel who came to guide me to safety."

Back home on Long Island the next day, Nora felt calm enough to go for a walk. "Wednesday, it really hit me. I could not stop crying. People were sending me flowers," she says. "It sent me over the edge."

When she could not shake off the intrusive, recurring images of that severed foot, Nora called me. It wasn't difficult for her to describe the chronology, but when she got to the point in her narrative where she encountered that severed foot in its sneaker, her voice broke. I reassured her that her reactions were normal and appropriate, given the situation.

Information is the most powerful remedy for acute stress reactions and it helped her calm down. Nora's breathing slowed and deepened. Breathing is our primary nonverbal language. Sharp, uneven breaths convey a message of stress, even though someone might insist she is perfectly all right. When she was telling her story, Nora's breathing had been shallow and tight. I was relieved to observe the change.

Nora experienced a flood of relief after exploring a few of the emotional first aid tools. She especially liked color breathing and rubbing her feet on the ground (See Keys to Emotional First Aid, page 63). I showed her how to anchor a sense of safety by linking a gesture, in this case a clenched fist, with a positive memory of being in a safe place. When a wave of anxiety hit, Nora would inhale, clench her fist, and smile as a cascade of calm and well-being flowed through her body. Years later, she continues using these tools to lower her stress levels.

Soon, she was running again. Four years later, she finished the Boston Marathon.

"I think 2013 made me more determined to become a better runner," she says. "And it has definitely made me more empathetic."

Even though she was thousands of miles away, when a truck bomber drove through a crowd in Nice, France, in July 2016, killing 86 people, Nora was personally affected.

"I knew the panic they must have been experiencing and what they were going through," she says.

Some Will, Some Won't

Not everyone recovers, however. In working more than 200 disasters, from the 1998 terrorist bombing of Pan Am 103 in Lockerbie, Scotland, to the 2012 Newtown, Connecticut, school shootings, Dr. Demaria has found that about one-third of a post-disaster population faces recovery difficulties. They are most likely to develop chronic post-traumatic stress disorder, leading to severe anxiety, chronic depression, and a greater tendency towards substance abuse. They are at higher risk for suicide.

Of the other two-thirds, one-third will recover to some extent while remaining vulnerable to triggers, such as anniversaries, gunshot sounds, or news footage. They are more likely to experience spontaneous flashbacks years later, in which they feel they are reliving sights, sounds, tastes, sensations, smells, and emotions of the original horror.

The remaining third are those who transform the event into a major catalyst for positive change. With post-traumatic growth, they can say that while they wished they had never gone through it and would never wish it on anyone else, it opened a way for them to receive the fifth gift.

POST-TRAUMATIC STRESS EFFECTS
IN DIFFERENT POPULATIONS

When it comes to healing after a catastrophic loss, we don't get there overnight—far from it. As we begin to understand that nobody heals on a schedule and the path is often one step forward, two steps back, humility and patience become the gifts we cannot leave home without.

Humility opens the way for us to accept how deeply we hurt.

Everyone's timeline is different and there is no schedule for healing.

More than fifteen years after the 9/11 attacks, they remain stuck in the initial stages of shock and anger. "Some people are 'glass half empty' people," says Margie. "Patience helps us relinquish the idea that we should be over it already."

Her resolve to find meaning in her loss and to live "*with* the grief, not *in* the grief" gave her strength to reframe the loss as an opportunity to grow. She also believes that losing her home and possessions in a fire five years before September 11, 2001, helped to season her and give her endurance to keep going.

"As much as you don't want to cope and you want to just lie in bed, what we do and how we learn to cope is how we teach our children to deal with bumps in the road," she says.

After six years as a peer counselor at the WTC Family Center, Margie remains humble and empathetic within the community of 9/11 families and is generous with her support.

"I'm just one of you," she tells them. "Maybe I'm one step ahead today, but I may be one step behind tomorrow."

KEYS TO LIVING
WITH TRAUMATIC LOSS

- TAKE CARE OF YOUR HEALTH. Stay hydrated and eat well.
  Rest whenever you can. Same goes for exercise. Get professional
  help if you continue to experience acute stress reactions for more
  than three months.

- GIVE YOURSELF AS MUCH TIME AS YOU NEED TO GRIEVE.
  The heart does not follow a timetable, nor is healing a straight
  line. To develop tolerance for confusing and ambiguous situations,
  remember: There are good days and bad days, and today is one
  of them.

- KEEP YOUR HEART AND MIND OPEN TO THOSE AROUND
  YOU. You may not be able to help right away, but knowing you are
  concerned may be more helpful than you realize.

- TURN OFF THE SCREENS. Obsessively watching the news can
  trigger anxiety and exacerbate depression. You might try taking a
  24-hour break from the news. If you feel calmer, try giving yourself
  a 24-hour newsbreak once a week until you get stronger.

- PRACTICE ACCEPTING YOURSELF FULLY AND COMPLETELY.
  Wishing you were further along in your healing journey is just
  another way of blaming yourself for being hurt. Now is a good time
  to get acquainted with the first two gifts: humility and patience.
  Humility opens the way for us to accept ourselves fully and
  completely, right here, right now. Patience can alleviate
  our resentment about how long it takes to start feeling
  better. You *will* smile again. Maybe not today or tomorrow,
  but you will.

PART TWO

Self-Care in Troubling Times

This life is not for
the chickens.

–Pepi Palmer

3

Aftermath:
Survival and Self-Rescue

*F*irst responders go to work knowing that by shift's end, they will probably have gone *mano a mano* with life and death. Trained as professionals to rush into danger, and seasoned by years of experience to stay clear headed during a call, does not prevent them from feeling shocked and disturbed by what they see, hear, feel, smell, and taste at the scene. As civilians living in unstable times, we have opportunities now to learn from these masters of stress how to rescue ourselves so that we can get back on our feet.

Unless you personally know someone who trusts you sufficiently to reveal emotions in the aftermath of a disaster, it's natural to default to a stereotype of someone who can function at a high level under extreme stress without becoming temporarily ungrounded.

Such events, called "critical incidents" by police, fire, and rescue personnel, are acknowledged as packing an intense emotional punch. The International Critical Incident Stress Foundation (ICISF), founded in 1989 by doctors George Everly and Jeffrey Mitchell, gives first responders a suite of pragmatic and cognitive tools to cope with the emotional impact of a dangerous event in which there is usually loss of life and a threat to the safety of others.

"Critical incident stress management is a toolbox to help you develop a coherent way of thinking after an event," explains Dr. Everly, who is considered one of the fathers of disaster mental health. Although the first critical incident stress management workshop drew only two attendees, there are now 1,800 CISM teams and more than 7,500 members around the world.

CISM sessions are confidential and closed to outsiders. The peer support model provides first responders with nonjudgmental support, acceptance, and the emotional safety needed to open up. A crisis management information briefing spells out the signs of acute stress and gives tools for self-care: healthy nutrition, sleep, physical exercise, and hydration for physical health; coping skills to lower stress levels; and communicating with peers, family, and friends instead of withdrawing into isolation.

Practice in the art of swiping away whatever we don't want to face leaves us ill prepared to face tragic events in our own lives.

Although the instinct to go into a cave and hibernate may feel like the only thing to do after a traumatic event, pulling away from others can become habitual. In isolation, the mind tends to wander into the Land of "Could'a, Should'a, Would'a," prompting guilt and depression, which, in turn, can lead to addiction and ruined relationships. Emotional well-being after a critical incident requires social support, much as the body needs water to regenerate and thrive.

To be clear, critical incident stress management is not psychotherapy nor can sessions be considered group therapy. It is psychological first aid that can stop the emotional bleeding and mitigate the disturbing and painful aftermath of a tragic event.

The system and structure of CISM sessions help people put life in perspective after a critical incident. Paul Schweinler, CISM clinical director for Broward County, Florida, worked with airport personnel after the Fort Lauderdale airport shooting. On Friday, January 6, 2017, Esteban Santiago-Ruiz opened fire at Terminal Two's baggage claim area, killing five and wounding six. Thirty-one additional people were injured when the crowd panicked after false reports of a second shooter.

"There was no direction. It was chaos," Schweinler says. "People found themselves on the edge of the airport on the railroad tracks. They were more exposed than had they stayed in the airport." Food service workers who were closest to the scene locked themselves in the kitchen. Travelers and other airport employees tried to hide behind food counters. "They thought that was the safest place to be. It's a good example of how something as banal as air travel can suddenly go . . . ." With a sad shake of his head, Schweinler's voice trails off. His face shows concern for the safety of those who got caught in the wrong place at the wrong time.

Schweinler notes that the October 1, 2017, Las Vegas shooting brought up issues of survivor guilt for many who were working at the venue. "As the event unfolded before their eyes, having planned and developed this series of concerts to be a wonderful and fun experience, they felt that their life's work was now ruined."

"There is a profound significance in watching the affect on people's faces as they are getting to the end of a CISM process," says Schweinler. "They are catching their emotional breath and thankful they got through it safely. They leave, aware it could happen at any time . . . and with the strength that they are now more prepared."

An Empathic Movement

ICISF co-founder Dr. Jeffrey Mitchell is a former paramedic and firefighter. After witnessing an auto accident in which a passenger died, he recognized that he was not alone in having problems processing what he had seen and experienced. Other firemen, police, and rescue workers struggled with reactions similar to his, which inspired him to bring about positive change.

"I felt we had to do something to help our people so they wouldn't be holding on to these images," he says. "I was a volunteer firefighter, and I was not on duty when there was an auto accident in front of my vehicle."

Reaching into the passenger side to feel for a woman's pulse, he saw that the car had crashed into a low truck carrying pipes.

"One of the pipes went through the vehicle and through her chest. That was why she was dead," he says. "That stuck with me for a long time. It was a very gruesome image."

He told himself, "There has to be a better way."

When he asked himself who he would talk to about a similar incident, he realized that the most natural person would be someone in a similar line of work.

Because the groups are confidential and homogeneous, run by peers instead of mental health professionals, the critical incident stress incident model destigmatizes potential fears about appearing vulnerable.

"It's reassuring to know that others are going through the same thing," he says. "You hear someone else say something similar to what you yourself are thinking, and then you can tell yourself, 'I must not be crazy because others are saying the same thing.' "

Brooklyn Girl Meets Georgia SWAT Team

During critical incident stress management training on suicide prevention and aftermath, I was assigned to a breakout group with some special weapons and tactics (SWAT) team members from a town in Georgia. For this Brooklyn girl, it was a once-in-a-lifetime experience. With exaggerated eye rolls at each other when I spoke, it didn't take much to figure out that they considered me a Yankee civilian with nothing to offer. But, to their credit, they let me speak before ignoring my ideas, which, come to think of it, were probably not as useful as theirs because yes, I am a civilian.

Not only did members of that group look like they worked closely together, there was a sincere concern for those they knew who were struggling with suicidal depression. They had designed an ingenious one-page handout to help their colleagues cope with extreme emotions after a difficult call. (I have adapted the SWAT team handout to make it relevant, helpful, and easy to use. See Dr. Laurie's Pocket Guide to Self-Care for Acute Stress in the Appendix, page 247).

A Guide to Regaining Your Balance

While the CISM model was not designed for a general population, following the sequence of thoughts and questions here will help you reach a calmer state of mind. The first and last points show you how to take better care of yourself in acute stress conditions.

Information: Acute stress affects most people who are directly or indirectly exposed to a sudden, violent event. Become aware of the signs and symptoms so that you can take better care of yourself and help those around you, as well. ICISF co-founder Dr. Everly says, "Most people do not want you to cure them. They want information."

Facts: This element works well in a dialogue format with another person. You can keep notes in a journal as well. Focus on two questions: "What was your exposure during the event?" and "What happened from your point of view?"

Thoughts: "What were your first thoughts as the event began?" and "What were the most important thoughts that stayed with you during the event?"

Reactions: "From where you are now, what stands out as the worst part of the event?"

Symptoms: Physically, mentally, and emotionally, what did you feel *during* and *after* the event? Immediately after the event? Within the first 48 hours? After a week?

Self-Care: Although you probably do not feel normal, it cannot be overemphasized that acute stress reactions are normal in the wake of an abnormal event. This is a good time to read or review the information about self-care in this chapter and the appendices.

Find Support: Reach out to someone in a similar situation to yours. Texting is great but there is nothing like the comfort of hearing someone's voice. Research into communications shows that 93 percent of our messages are nonverbal; 55 percent of what we mean gets expressed through our facial expression, posture, breathing, and other physiological indicators; 38 percent is communicated through tone of voice, and only 7 percent of our message comes through verbally. With this in mind, my preference is voicemail over text when reaching out to offer or receive support.

Fear + Ignorance = Greater Pain

In his memoir *FBI and an Ordinary Guy: The Private Price of Public Service,* Mark Johnston writes that failing to address your own reactions in the wake of a critical incident can make them worse. He did not know this early in his career when he and his partner responded to an eviction in which agents used tear gas to subdue a homeowner who had started firing his gun. After several hours of bar hopping, they got home drunk at 1 AM.

"That's what we thought 'critical incident stress management' was forty years ago," he writes.

Johnson defines a critical incident as "any sudden event outside the usual realm of human experience that . . . evokes intense fear, helplessness, horror or dread," and states, "such events have the power to overwhelm an individual's or a group's coping abilities."

He called trauma "the actual hurt/harm or injury to the *mind and body*."[8]

Eventually, Johnston moved from being an agent in the field to the FBI's Northeastern Employee (EAP) manager, offering support and stress management tools to agents in the field. "Experience demonstrates that often the worst part of a critical incident is not the incident itself, but what happens afterwards," he writes, as he cautions: "Fear and/or ignorance about critical incidents and their aftermath can also contribute to the pain."[9]

He wrote his memoir to educate us about the emotional price of exposure to traumatic events and what we can do to recognize the symptoms and take care of ourselves.

Reframing Loss

In my interviews with first responders and CISM debriefers, I have seen and heard how their firsthand encounters with tragedy have strengthened their motivation to serve others. They are able to reframe their loss into motivation so that over time, exposure to multiple traumas serves to nurture a continuum of concern for people's needs.

An EMT/paramedic with the Miami-Dade Fire Department for thirty-two years, Vern Oster is dedicating his retirement to campaigning for safer medications in rescue vehicles.

"I have been dealing with mental trauma because of what I have been through," he says.

The gift of empathy drives him to continue fighting to replace the drug Versed (midazolam), a controversial medication used for sedation before a tube is inserted to aid the patient's breathing. Working helicopter rescue, Oster found that due to the medication's side effects, he was unable to properly intubate patients with head injuries, which he believes resulted in deaths.

"If you are sick or weak," he says, "you have a 94 percent chance it will make you worse or take your life."

Oster's worldview was irreparably altered by continual exposure to deaths that he was unable to prevent. One in particular continues to haunt him.

"It started off early at a wedding. The maid of honor collapsed as they were marching down the aisle," he says. "We were coming from another territory. Took us about seven minutes to get there. When we arrived, three physicians were standing over this twenty-one-year-old woman. Her color was off. She wasn't breathing. As soon as I looked at her, I knew she was in cardiac arrest. We yanked her out to the truck and worked and worked and worked her, but she was dead. The autopsy report showed that stress had caused an arrhythmia, which caused her heart to go into fibrillation and finally stop."

In another call toward the end of the same shift, Oster responded to a case involving another twenty-one-year-old woman.

"This girl's parents bought her a brand-new Corvette and she got into a drag race on Biscayne Boulevard, hitting a concrete pole going 100 miles an hour," he says, shaking his head, and inhaling deeply. "We didn't have to pry her out of the car, but this accident split her right open and she was conscious."

Recalling how he held her hand as the ambulance rushed her to the hospital, he can still hear her voice: "I'm going to die, I'm going to die." In response, he kept telling her to hold on. In the end, despite the ER doctors doing everything they could for her, Oster's patient bled to death on the surgical table.

Here's the takeaway: Even the most experienced responders are emotionally wounded in the aftermath of certain incidents in which circumstances rendered them helpless. In time, the depth of pain over those losses can serve as a focal point for even greater empathy in the future.

You Are Not Going Crazy

Sometimes, the initial stages of acute stress—shock, numbness, difficulty concentrating, and fear—resolve on their own. When they persist, they can lead to impaired decision-making, anxiety, intrusive flashbacks in which you relive the most horrifying moments, difficulty eating or sleeping, and flashes of irritability. Let's not forget hypervigilance—being flooded with dread—and feeling like your body is hotwired, making you want to jump out of your skin.

These are all normal reactions to an abnormal situation.

Since the early 1990s, when I started working with people dealing with acute stress and post-traumatic issues, the most frequently asked question

I hear is, "Hey, Doc, am I crazy?" In reassuring someone that his or her responses are appropriate for having survived or witnessed an accident, shooting, or disaster, I am often asked, "How do you know for sure?" This may sound facetious, but in my clinical experience I have found it to be true: Crazy people never ask this question. They tend to believe that their model of the world is accurate and that they are only disturbed because another person or the rest of the world has done something "wrong." There is no formal research to back this up. It is an anecdotal observation based on nearly three decades of clinical work with hundreds of individuals.

The stigma of appearing crazy or vulnerable scares people from being honest about their reactions. It cannot be overemphasized that acute stress reactions are not indicators of mental illness. In developing the critical incident stress management protocols, Drs. Everly and Mitchell opened the way for the first responder community to recognize the need to talk about these issues in a safe setting.

Destigmatization is a work in progress on both sides of the pond.

In London, the British Fire Brigades' Union (FBU) has been encouraging its 33,000 active firefighters to open up about mental health issues connected to their jobs. When Sean Starbuck, public information officer for the FBU, started his twenty-one-year career as a firefighter, such issues were not discussed.

"It's always been firefighters are tough guys and don't suffer from mental health issues, but they do. It's a taboo subject, but over the past ten years, people realized we have to talk about these things," he says.

A recent survey of FBU members showed that 36 percent of firefighters reported that they would not speak up about their own issues because, Starbuck says, "They thought they would get undue negative attention."

The FBU offers training courses for management and union members.

"We have gone to management. We want to work on this together," says Starbuck. "We want to be proactive. We don't want a situation where people develop PTSD."

After Sky TV reported in 2016 that 41,000 firefighters' shifts were lost that year due to mental health issues, Starbuck said, "If there were 41,000 firefighters off with a broken leg, you would address it and you would be putting it right."

Acute Stress Disorder

When acute stress persists for more than three months it is called acute stress disorder (ASD).

In "After Hurricane, Signs Point to a Mental Health Crisis in Puerto Rico," *New York Times'* reporter Caitlin Dickerson wrote, "There are warning signs of a full-fledged mental health crisis on the island, public health officials say, with much of the population showing symptoms of post-traumatic stress."

Hurricane Maria struck Puerto Rico on September 20th, 2017. The *Times* published Dickerson's article on November 13, 2017, too soon for a diagnosis of post-traumatic stress disorder, which is now part of our everyday vocabulary.

It is easy to confuse the two, but one key difference between PTSD and acute stress disorder is that PTSD tends to be chronic, with symptoms that can surface spontaneously years later. For example, a recent study of the psychological impact of flooding in the United Kingdom during the 2013–14 season showed that 36 percent of people whose homes flooded reported symptoms of PTSD; 28.3 percent with different anxiety symptoms; and 20 percent with depression. Among those in flood zones whose homes were spared, 15 percent reported PTSD symptoms and 10 percent had depression. In comparison, only eight percent of people who were outside the high water areas reported PTSD and six percent with depression.[10]

ACUTE STRESS DISORDER BY THE NUMBERS

As reported in Medscape.com, both within and outside the United States, ASD tends to occur at the following rates:

✓ 20–50 percent of cases follow interpersonal traumatic events (e.g., assault, rape, and witnessing a mass shooting)

✓ 13–21 percent of motor vehicle accidents

✓ 14 percent of mild traumatic brain injuries

✓ 19 percent of assaults

✓ 10 percent of severe burns

✓ 6–12 percent of industrial accidents[11]

Information Is the Best Defense

The best defense against ASD is information. When you know what you've got, you can take better care of yourself. Sometimes, a critical incident can be a wake-up call for us to start doing that. On a daily basis, first responders and emergency medical personnel put their patients' needs first. From time to time, it takes a critical incident to make them aware that they need to manage their acute stress so that they can continue to excel at what they do.

Expecting the Unexpected

"Everyone is going to face at least one traumatic event," says Paul Schweinler, clinical director of CISM in Broward County, Florida, who won a Lifetime Achievement Award for CISM. "I've lost count of how many."

His first accident, at the age of three, happened when he fell out of a three-story window. He has also been hit twice by cars.

"This has helped me to understand and describe how the body shuts down and why we often don't remember," he says.

Fewer than five percent of people remember the moment when the airbag deploys.

"The brain says, 'You don't need to remember,'" says Schweinler, who emphasizes the importance of this cognitive distortion during his critical incident briefings. Whether you are directly or indirectly affected, you and those around you will present with memory loss, confusion, and disorientation.

Whether you are trying to help someone in need, or you yourself are in shock, the gift of patience will prove invaluable. While we cannot know specifics ahead of time, understanding how we are likely to be impacted at some point in the future will lessen the shock. In the immediate aftermath, we can expect changes in sleep patterns, appetite, and breathing. There may be dizziness, headaches, muscle tension, digestive issues, and rapid heartbeat. Internal emotional responses may range from a "deer in the headlights" paralysis to numbness, shock, fear, depression, and guilt. We may feel sorrowful, lonely, vulnerable, frustrated, or angry.

Or all of the above.

Our behaviors—how feelings get expressed—can range from crying, outbursts of anger, irritability, substance abuse, loss of self-worth, a sense of hopelessness, and withdrawal from others. These patterns are usually short-lived and resolve naturally.

(See Keys to Emotional First Aid on page 63.) Please note: If Emotional First Aid, social support, and stress management tools are insufficient and these patterns persist, it is important to seek professional help.

Stress Inoculations

Knowing how to deal with probable reactions ahead of time can help you conserve your energy, although none of us can predict exactly how we are going to feel in the moment. Schweinler advocates thinking ahead of the curve about unplanned special events.

"What's important is to anticipate what could happen. Let's say a plane crashes in your neighborhood at night. What are you going to do? If you aren't dead, you need to get out of there, like now. But since the area could become a crime scene, you might not get home for a long time."

A plane crash in your neighborhood is highly unlikely, but think of it as a metaphor for catastrophe in general.

One month after writing this, a woman who escaped from the World Trade Center on September 11, 2001, witnessed American Airlines flight 587 crash into the bay near her home in Rockaway, New York, just four weeks after 9/11. "Will planes please stop crashing near me?" she joked during our initial phone call. Her contacting me as I was working on this chapter reminded me once again that life is by its very nature unpredictable and terrifying.

"Parallel things could happen. You will do better if you are prepared," says Schweinler.

Questioning Answers

What would you do if you had to leave home in a hurry? Where would you go? What would you do if you had to stay indoors for weeks at a time? What supplies would you need? What would you do if electricity and communications were knocked out for more than a few days? Who could you count on for a ride? A place to stay? Basic first aid? Most important, who can you trust to understand and support you during and after the event?

While you might be tempted to think this line of thinking is "negative," in this case, negative equals a dangerous level of denial. Make a task list and switch each item on the list into a question that cannot be answered as yes or no.

⚶⚶⚶⚶ Stress Inoculation Questions ⚶⚶⚶⚶

INSTEAD OF: "Can I live without electricity?"

ASK: "How long can I hold out without electricity?"

INSTEAD OF: "Does climate impact my emergency plans?"

ASK: "How does climate impact my emergency plans?"

INSTEAD OF: "Do I need to store fuel?"

ASK: "How would I store fuel if needed?"

INSTEAD OF: "What if I can't sleep?"

ASK: "How many hours of sleep do I need to function?"

Open-ended questions, known as the Socratic Method, strengthen critical thinking skills, which can help you zero in on missing pieces of information or potential solutions. The practice of questioning answers stands alone as a "stress inoculation" to prepare you for situations in which you will need to make effective decisions quickly.

From Denial to Hope

Disaster scenarios help prepare us for huge events that are outside our control, but it would be unrealistic to expect a fool-proof strategy for not losing it when the world around you becomes chaotic. You are not alone. Even seasoned professionals suffer distress because of a heartbreaking loss while trying to save someone.

With regard to becoming proactive in mapping out potential responses to dangerous situations, we have much to learn from ICISF's groundbreaking work with the first responder community. They have opened the way for us to develop informed responses to critical incidents so that we can take care of ourselves and those we love.

"Denial costs lives," says ICISF co-founder Dr. Mitchell. "Every year, hundreds and even thousands of people die in misadventures because they spent time denying it could happen in their backyards. It is natural and normal for us to deny that bad things are going to happen, but if you want to be prepared, you need to work against your own natural denial."

Rescuers are often forgotten heroes. So are those survivors and witnesses who emerged from destruction saying, "Although we have had significant losses, we did not lose our most important things: our health, our children, and those we love."

ICISF co-founder Dr. Everly observes: "This can turn a lot of negatives around and give us a lot to live for. It goes a long way to helping people recover."

STAYING SAFE

If you ever bear witness to a shooting or some other mass attack, first responders recommend the following[12]:

✓ Escape.

✓ Hide.

✓ Fight back if you are capable of doing so.

✓ Advanced Law Enforcement Rapid Response Training Center security experts have their own catch phrase: "Avoid. Deny. Defend." They suggest the following:

- Always be aware of emergency exits whenever you enter a public space.
- Avoid getting into the middle of a crowd.
- Barricade entrances whenever possible to deny entrance to the shooter.
- If you are trained in martial arts or carrying a weapon, fight back.

KEYS TO FINDING SAFETY

Critical incident specialist Paul Schweinler recommends asking these five questions after a dangerous event:

- ARE WE SAFE?
- IF THE ANSWER IS "YES," GIVE THANKS. If "no," ask: "Where can we go to be safe?
- WHAT IS YOUR MOST PRESSING NEED?
- WHAT IS IN YOUR CONTROL? What is not in your control?
- CAN I HELP SOMEONE ELSE?

Paul Schweinler's Guide to Emotional First Aid

- Go to places that feel safe, comfortable, and familiar.
- Seek out people who will listen without judgment.
- Set boundaries with those who are not helpful.
- Communicate clearly. If you feel uncomfortable with someone, say so.
- Be patient with yourself.
- Focus on tasks that are concrete, reasonable, and relatively easy to accomplish. Even tasks like going to the post office or paying household bills can seem overwhelming. If so, limit yourself to one or two tasks a day.
- Do not compare your reactions to anyone else's. You are entitled to your emotions.
- Don't allow anyone to try to make you feel guilty.
- Keep writing or drawing your thoughts, feelings, and reactions. Getting them out of your body onto the paper is healing all by itself.
- Above all, never ask someone who has gone through extreme loss, "How are you feeling?" "How do you *think* they feel?" Schweinler asks. Speak from the heart: "I am so sorry. What do you need? Have you eaten? Do you need water? Is there anything I can get for you?"

4

Gas Masks
and Dom Perignon

J started prepping in first grade. It was 1954, and if you are among the 76 million baby boomers, you remember how we lived in fear of the Russians dropping an atom bomb on New York City. At Public School 193 in Brooklyn, New York, Mrs. Bardy had us kneel under our scarred wooden desks while she closed the tall windows with a long wooden pole crowned with a menacing hook. It was our job to cover our heads with our hands and wait until the siren stopped wailing and Mrs. Bardy said it was safe to come out. As we faced away from the window, it never occurred to us that we would be covered in shards if a bomb fell from the sky.

Since we expected to be killed, my best friend Abby Ferrante baptized me with our family's green rubber garden hose so that she and I could be together in heaven and I wouldn't have to go to Limbo with the other Jewish kids. I still remember the cold water splashing over my forehead as she intoned the emergency ritual designed to save my soul. I knew it was sacrilegious—so sacrilegious that I have never told my family. But the prospect of getting stranded in Limbo for all eternity was even more terrifying. Abby was very clear on the consequences, and I can still remember the relief I felt when the cold water hit my head—just in case—because, after all, we were six years old.

The air raid drills continued through sixth grade. We were encouraged to practice at home, instructions I diligently followed. In second grade, I took to crouching under the piano at home a few times a week, covering my head with my hands. One Sunday, when my dad came home from playing golf, he found me under the piano.

"What the hell are you doing?" he demanded.

Calmly, I explained how I was "practicing, like Miss Dalton said."

Miss Dalton was our second-grade teacher, a dragon lady whose orders were never disobeyed.

"Practicing for what?" he asked.

"For when the Russians drop an atom bomb on New York City," I said, still kneeling under the piano.

But instead of the praise I expected for being a good girl, no sooner had I finished than my dad burst out laughing.

"I can't believe they are teaching something that stupid at PS 193! If the Russians drop an atom bomb, you'll be dead before you know it."

As I remember, I was more upset by his reaction than the prospect of being vaporized. You see, after the bomb, I was going to be in heaven with Abby Ferrante. Little did we know that more than half a century later, the threat of nuclear attack would manifest again in all its ugliness. As two guys with bad hair, infantile rage, and nuclear arsenals tweet ballistic insults at each other, 76 million alumni of those "duck and cover" drills are saying, "Here we go again."

The headline splashed across the home screen of ChelseaPatch.com's April 17, 2017, issue says, "HEY, NYC: HERE'S WHAT TO DO IF WE GET NUKED." It says that if you survive the blast and see "sandy particles falling from the sky or already on the ground, go indoors immediately."[13]

Indoors, you will want a book like *How to Survive a Nuclear Emergency* by British nuclear physicist Dr. Keith Pearce. His wording might be considered old-fashioned but his advice cuts straight to the point:

"So in summary," he says, "if there is a nuclear accident near you your priorities are to stay safe and protect your family, friends and neighbors. You do not want to have an accident of your own so try to stay calm and behave sensibly. Listen to the advice from the police and local authority which will be on the local radio channel and on TV."[14]

While I worked on this chapter, CNN reported that the Centers for Disease Control were issuing new guidelines about what to do in the unlikely event of a nuclear blast. "For instance, most people don't realize that sheltering in place for at least twenty-four hours is crucial to saving lives and reducing exposure to radiation," according to a CDC press release.[15] In 2017, first responders, the Federal Emergency Management Agency (FEMA), Homeland Security, and military personnel participated in Operation Gotham Shield to prepare for a nuclear emergency in the New York metropolitan region. While no one wants to believe it could happen to them, we have historical examples of terror's aftermath.

Just in case: What's your plan?

Baby Boomers: A Generation of Preppers?

Six months after the September 11th attacks, at a Jungian seminar on "Trauma, Dreams and Nightmares: Psychic Images Before, During and After September 11," I learned that in the year or so prior to the attack, hundreds of people had reported dreams to therapists, which included images of planes flying into buildings, birds crashing into towers, The Tower card in the Tarot, which depicts people jumping from a burning tower, and people flying through flames.

Swiss psychiatrist Carl Jung wrote, "Sometimes a dream is of such importance that its message reaches consciousness, no matter how uncomfortable or shocking it may be."

Whether you prefer to call this coincidence or synchronicity—a term Carl Jung described as a "meaningful coincidence," according to Katherine

Olivetti, a Jungian analyst who presented the seminar, "September 11th was not a total surprise to the unconscious mind." She pointed out that even if you did not have such a dream, you have probably seen movies in which airplanes crash into buildings. Although feature films are not reality, their images implant subliminal possibilities, which, in this case, manifested in real time. In other words, on a subliminal level, we knew it could happen. On a conscious collective level, it was unthinkable.

If, like Abby and me, you practiced those "duck and cover" drills in elementary school, witnessing the planes on September 11th may well have triggered one or two seconds of déjà vu.

Like me, you probably shut it down right a way. Cognitive dissonance would have overridden the subliminal factor with the only logical interpretation being that we were bearing witness to an illogical, unreal, and impossible event.

Since then, several dozen people reported experiencing a weird sense of calm, flashbacks to those childhood drills, and a surreal sense of having seen it somewhere before.

"I saw this scary air raid alarm thing on black-and-white TV," says Ron Haugen, who participated in the drills during second grade at Saint Adalbert Elementary School in Queens. "I can still see those grainy black-and-white images of prop planes and mushroom clouds."

Another contemporary writes, "I consider myself a caring person. I sometimes wonder why I did not have more of an emotional reaction to that day's events."

My office stood across the street from St. Vincent's Hospital, about one and a half miles north of Ground Zero. In addition to my private practice, I wrote several articles about the psychological impact of 9/11 for the *New York Times* Long Island section, volunteered at holistic health fairs, and ran the adolescent program at South Nassau Communities' Hospital's WTC Family Center. In working with eyewitnesses, it was not unusual to hear similar responses from eyewitnesses who had grown up during the 1950s:

a mixture of shock, nausea, and an eerie calm, because on some level, they weren't surprised. Prepped as children, the subconscious mind stored the images. When the real-time attack occurred, it seemed somehow familiar.

The Anthrax Scare

One week after September 11th, letters containing anthrax spores were mailed to several media offices in New York City and Boca Raton, Florida. Three weeks later, another set of letters was sent to Senators Tom Daschle (D-South Dakota) and Patrick Leahy (D-Vermont). Anthrax is a disease contracted by cattle and sheep, which can be transmitted to humans. It can cause skin infections or a deadly respiratory illness. The anthrax letters killed five people and sickened twenty-two, one of whom was a colleague in Dan Rather's office at CBS News.[16] CNN.com reported "an assistant to NBC News anchor Tom Brokaw and a baby of an ABC News producer have also been diagnosed with skin anthrax."[17] Seven years later, the FBI identified Dr. Bruce Ivins, an Army microbiologist, as the perpetrator. Ivins committed suicide on July 29, 2008.[18]

Coming on the heels of the September 11th trifecta—planes crashing into the World Trade Center, into the ground at Shanksville, Pennsylvania, and into the Pentagon—the anthrax attacks fed a media frenzy that understandably left us feeling vulnerable and helpless—because we were.

Writing in *Journalism and Mass Communication Quarterly*, Kristen Alley Swain identified "833 stories in 272 newspapers, AP, NPR, and four television networks (ABC News, CBS News, CNN, and NBC News)."[19]

The anthrax story was characterized by "conflicting reports, speculation, use of unnamed sources, and coverage of vague advice and hoaxes/false alarms."[20] The author observes that reportage using scientific explanations with statistics helped to ameliorate panicked reactions about a generalized, nonspecific threat.

Which isn't to say I wasn't scared. But when a young mother brought her nine-year-old son to see me because he had suddenly developed a germ phobia, it reinforced my awareness that exposure to frightening news can induce vicarious trauma. (We sat together, off and on, through his adolescence. He went on to become a paramedic.)

A Conversation with the Gas Mask Man

"Death can cause people to become fearful and feel overwhelmed. It can have a similar impact to going through a disaster," says Dr. Demaria. "We need to find the humility to admit that we are indeed powerless and helpless so we can take the first steps in finding ways to heal."

It can also be humbling to seek out ways to improve our odds of survival, which is why I stood riveted in front of four mannequins in a Greenwich Village shop window in early October 2001: Amerithrax season. (Amerithrax is the FBI's nickname for the anthrax attacks.)[21]

Although one khaki-clad mannequin looked like it was about to fall over, staring at her gas mask was strangely reassuring. Maybe one of the statues was wearing the gas mask that would help us stay alive in the event of an attack.

Inside, at a glass counter, the storeowner looked like Andre the Giant in camouflage. Yes, he was a veteran and yes, he would explain the differences between the battle-tested Israeli model 4a1, the Canadian C4, the Korean K1 Evolution 5000, and the British Avon 510 with drinking straw.[22]

"Remember, you have thirty seconds to put it on and maybe two minutes to clear the room," he said.

"What if I trip on my own feet?" I said. "I have klutzy DNA."

"That's a problem," he agreed. "You gotta practice."

I attempted to visualize a scenario where the room would be filling up with gas. I could see myself doubled over, coughing.

Confession time: "I have asthma."

"No worries!"

He flashed an Andre the Giant smile and I swore there was light bouncing off his teeth.

"Asthma? No worries," he chuckled. "You'll be dead in seconds."

"So I don't have to buy one of these things?"

"You'll be dead before you put it on."

Before I could ask the price of the Israeli battle tested 4a1—clearly the most reliable choice—I was skipping down 8th Street, heading west into the sun, wondering if the late afternoon sky was especially blue or whether I was just happy, because like my father's words many years before, my conversation with the gas mask man had freed me from yet another worry.

The Soup Nazi, Repurposed

My friend Abby from PS 193 did get her very own gas mask. She had joined the Foreign Service and was returning from an overseas posting in 2002.

"The whole world had changed. Everyone was sort of in shock," she says.

At the State Department, everyone was required to attend a movie before being issued a gas mask.

"Prior to that, we were told to bring three days of food and water in the event of an emergency," she told me.

"You mean the government isn't going to give you lunch if you're in lockdown?" I asked.

That seemed unfair. Not that Congress has ever asked how we would like our taxes to be allocated, but if it did, I would definitely vote for funds to feed Federal workers in lockdown due to a terrorist attack. It seems like the least we can do for them.

The movie illustrated how to assemble and put on a gas mask.

"It showed a guy in a hazmat suit who showed us parts of the gas mask and how to make sure it was working," Abby said. "As long as you can hold your breath is as long as you have to put on your gas mask. I kept shooting my hand up to ask if we were going to get the gloves and the hazmat suit. From my understanding of chemical warfare, your skin is going to be falling off your bones, so how are you supposed to arm the gas mask unless you are issued a hazmat suit and gloves?"

"No hazmat suit for you," she was told. "And no gloves."

The Soup Nazi, repurposed. Who knew?

Ever resourceful, Abby asked about bringing her own gloves.

"The guy doing the briefing after the movie said not to bring your own gloves," she recalled. "They would melt."

The prognosis was not encouraging.

"I was like a deer in the headlights," she told me. "What would happen if I was in the ladies room when the attack started? How would I get my gas mask?"

The question went unanswered. She was told to try hers on.

"It was like a Darth Vader hood, so dark and claustrophobic you could hardly breathe. I was resigned to death." Hyperventilating, she wondered, "Is this the last scene on earth I am going to be witnessing?"

Instead of giving in to dread, Abby went for the gold.

"I bought a bottle of Dom Perignon, caviar, and crackers. If anything happens, I'm going out in style."

Imminent Danger

Not only had Abby served where colleagues were murdered and rockets were fired at the U.S. Embassy, her portfolio included reading intelligence briefings.

"Working on terrorism issues was terrifying," she says. "Every day you are reading about credible, validated threats. You cannot underestimate the efforts to dismantle those threats, which were made daily against different United States targets around the world. There was absolute imminent danger at any time. I did not enjoy that portfolio. But it was better than being assigned to a post where I was told that, as a woman, 'it's less likely you will be beheaded.' I lived. I left. I retired. I survived."

After drinking her Dom Perignon and savoring her caviar, Abby sold the gas masks she had bought for her mother and aunt (just in case).

"I had to feel I was doing something," she said. "I didn't want to come home to a house full of dead people thinking I knew better and hadn't done something to save them."

I consider Abby a model of preparedness, not because she stores water and batteries (just in case), but because she maintains a positive yet realistic mindset.

"You have to go out and enjoy your life," she says. "We don't want the terrorists to win, and if they paralyze you, they win."

Tips for Prepping

Websites like *www.ready.gov* provide information about preparing a go-kit with emergency supplies and important documents. They emphasize taking time to think about the things you would need and where you can keep them so that you can grab them and go when the time comes.

Having seen homeowners who were flooded showing up at our local bank in tears because their financial documents had been destroyed by seawater and slime, I cannot emphasize how important it is to scan or copy your important documents and keep them in a waterproof, fireproof box on a high shelf. You can store digital files in the cloud, on a flash drive, or in your phone, but it is not uncommon to lose cell phone service and electricity after a disaster. That's why God invented paper.

PREPPING 101

✓ **Know your hazard zone.**
Are you living/working in a region prone to fires, earthquakes, mudslides, blizzards, droughts, floods, tornadoes, or hurricanes? Pick up information at your local fire department or police station, or go to *www.ready.gov*.

✓ **Make two emergency plans**—one for backup, just in case.
Plan A: Ask yourself, "Where will I go in an emergency? Who can I call on to help? How long can I expect to stay put after the event? Where am I likely to find shelter after emergency shelters close down?"
Plan B: Ask yourself, "What will I/we do if Plan A turns out to be impossible?"
Keep two lists with you at all times: emergency contacts and any medications you need.

✓ **Trust but verify.**
Factual information is your rational source of information before and after an event. Be aware of the media flow. Pay attention to facts and opinions. Be careful and selective about what you decide to believe.

✓ **Recognize that traumatic events are painful.**
They are part of life—including yours. Look for lifelines. They can keep you from despair.

Healthy Pessimism

So many people have suggested that thinking about these subjects is "negative," perhaps because of a shared assumption that the pursuit of happiness equals always having fun. Anything unpleasant is considered "negative."

Holding that thought can be hazardous to your health. A leading disaster psychologist, Dr. Demaria, says, "One thing I've learned about resiliency is

that it is not about not facing trouble. It's about going
through it and coming out
stronger."

"One thing I've learned about resiliency is that it is not about not facing trouble. It's about going through it and coming out stronger."

Nelly Yefet grew up in the Swiss Alps, where her family was snowed in for three months every winter. It taught her the importance of self-sufficiency and storing three months of basic supplies.

"People are in denial that they need to be ready. People think it's negative thinking and you don't want to go there," she says. "But you have to have things on hand for an emergency: candles, matches, canned food, flour, sugar, and salt. What happens if there is a riot outside and you can't go out?"

To Yefet, denial and weakness go hand in hand.

A resident of south Florida for more than thirty years, she lived through the worst hurricane in Florida's history: Andrew, a Category 5 storm. Andrew's 165-mile-per-hour winds destroyed 25,000 homes and left another 100,000 severely damaged. More than a million people had no electricity for weeks.[23]

In a *New York Times* article that appeared on August 25, 1992, Larry Richter wrote, "Throughout today hundreds of thousands of people ignored warnings to stay off the streets. Instead they roamed metropolitan Miami in cars or on foot to search for ice, canned foods, gasoline, batteries and charcoal for barbecue grills, the only method of cooking that many people have."[24]

Teresa Baker, a psychotherapist who lived an hour north of Miami, recalls that her therapist "rode it out in his closet with a mattress as buffer while his townhouse collapsed around him." Not only was the experience life-altering for him, it altered their therapeutic relationship.

"He and I were never the same after that," she says.

Nelly remains stunned by a neighbor's response to the disaster.

"She came in crying, because she couldn't charge her electric toothbrush," she says, shaking her head. "We were brought up to use our heads to solve problems and we grew up thinking on our own. Here, we are not taught how to think and analyze."

There are two types of problems: the ones we pay attention to so that we can come up with solutions, and those from which we run away.

"People think, 'If I don't see it, it doesn't exist,'" Nelly said. "But what will you do when supermarkets and restaurants close?"

Staying Positive

Ron Haugen and I were at dinner the other night. Ron was the boy who practiced "duck and cover" drills and still remembers grainy black-and-white TV footage from back in the day. After dinner, we went to the supermarket next door. I picked up some fruit salad and Ron bought a year's supply of rice. This made him extremely happy. (Unlike those of us who live in small places, he has someplace to store it.) I couldn't help but wonder what it was about buying a year's supply of rice that made him so cheerful.

"We live on the edge of uncertainty," Ron says. "At the same time, it's human nature to say, 'I can't deal with the future.' What stops me from dwelling on the uncertain future thing is doing something small—no matter what it might be." This might mean remembering to pick up a couple of gallons of water or a few packs of AA and C batteries the next time you're in the supermarket. Look around and see if there is anything that speaks to you, as in, "It wouldn't hurt to have that—just in case."

It goes even further. For Ron, the prospect of things going wrong is inherently mind-expanding.

"With disaster, you have to step outside your normal bounds of operation to extraordinary and different ways of perceiving things."

"With disaster, you have to step outside your normal bounds of operation to extraordinary and different ways of perceiving things," he says. "People want things to stay like they are and normal. You have to move beyond your previous mode of operation. You have to be ready for whatever it could be."

KEYS TO EMOTIONAL
FIRST AID (EFA)

When preparing an emergency go-kit, I strongly recommend that you have one or more tools to help defuse panic so you can keep your head clear before, during, and immediately after impact. But first, take a picture of the following five EFA tools. Store it on your phone. You can also print it and keep it in your wallet or go-kit.

The following tools meet **SEQ** standards: **S**afe, **E**ffective, and **Q**uick.

- **EFA Tool #1**: Look up!

    When you feel frightened or overwhelmed, looking up quickly shifts your focus of attention from your feelings to your visual thinking. (This is a great tool to help kids calm down. Point to the sky and say, "Look up!") Looking up works like swiping the screen so that your brain refocuses on what it sees instead of disturbing physical sensations or emotions.

- **EFA Tool #2**: Extend both arms as far as they can go.

    Looking at a scene of destruction can literally cause nausea. As you extend both arms, check out the tips of your fingers in the corner of your peripheral vision. (In the past, driving tests used this to ascertain the driver's peripheral functionality.) Engaging your peripheral vision helps to neutralize harsh reactions. In effect, it creates a safety shield between you and the ugliness of the scene.

- **EFA Tool #3:** Visualize a two-way mirror.

    Picture or imagine that you are looking through a two-way mirror. You can see out, but nobody can see in. This, too, creates a safety shield that can help you navigate and make decisions.

- **EFA Tool #4:** Color breathing.

    As you inhale, notice where in your body you are holding tension or stress. Focusing on the discomfort, ask, "What color will help me to feel calm?" You do not have to ask out loud. Within a couple of seconds, you will see, sense, or hear the name of the color.

Breathe it in and allow the soothing color to find its way anywhere in your body that would like to feel relaxed and calm. When you exhale, release any unwanted sensation by breathing out a different color.

- **EFA Tool #5:** Focus on your feet.

  When you are feeling anxious or overwhelmed, imagine that you are swiping a cursor from your head to the soles of your feet. Rub your feet on the floor. Do not think of anything except what your feet feel like as they rub against the floor. This easy piece disconnects the anxiety "app." Instantly calming. Your feet cannot "do" anxiety.

5

After the Cameras Leave— The Story Is Not Over

*J*ournalists provide an important service: They focus our attention on the survivors' critical needs. Until the cameras leave, that is. Then, the world seems to forget about you. Friends and coworkers stop listening. People whom you thought you could count on say, "Get over it, already."

"There's a honeymoon period when everyone wants to help. Survivors feel that people really care about them. But then the news cycle changes and the survivor feels abandoned," says trauma specialist Dr. Demaria. While the importance of psychological first aid cannot be over emphasized, it is not a magic wand. Nor is it a shortcut for deeper healing.

"Psychological first aid does primarily focus on loss, which takes several years to fully process," says Dr. Demaria. "There is no protocol for this that can quickly bring closure to this type of loss."

As one critical incident stress management (CISM) trainer puts it, "Americans have a robust ability to respond to crisis. We maintain no level of preparedness for after the event. We suck."

How Do You Feel?

In the aftermath of tragedy, the ubiquitous "How do you feel?" must be among life's most loathed FAQ's. As Paul Schweinler observed in Chapter Three, "How do you *think* I feel?" may be the most fitting response.

The presence of media at the scene who persist in asking that very question can be disturbing, especially to children, teens, and young adults.

"I hated going to church with my mom after 9/11. The cameras were creepy," says a young man whose father was killed in the World Trade Center attacks.

Although his reaction reflects how many people feel about reporters in the wake of tragedy, journalists are doing a job under pressure to get their stories out on tight deadlines. They have to push, pull, and verbally probe for sound bites and quotes they can use. After the interviews, they have to write and/or produce their assigned story, file it with their producers and editors, and post to social media. Even professionals say that sensitivity can take a hit on their list of priorities.

Facing the Camera: It's Your Choice

Getting comfortable in the presence of journalists can take practice. Those of us who are naturally extroverted and love attention will enjoy the experience, while those who tend to be quiet and private are more likely to find it distressing.

Whether you find yourself facing a camera or overwhelmed by well-wishers when your house is in ruins, you can just say no. You are not obligated to answer questions. It is your choice. Although many survivors, mourners, and eyewitnesses say that giving an interview about their disaster experience brought them relief, others find it unbearably stressful. You do not need extra stress at this time. But, it may be cathartic to let it all out. Your story of survival and endurance may touch a broken soul who takes heart from your honesty.

If you choose to face the camera, take a breath and collect your thoughts. This can help to relieve performance anxiety. You can ask the reporter or producer to please slow down or give you a minute if you need to calm yourself.

If It's Not on Our Screens, It No Longer Exists

TV news stories run between 30 and 90 seconds. A 90-second piece is considered long. It could be an obituary of a world leader, a military situation report, or a background report on a breakthrough in cancer research.

In the edit booth, producers and in-house editors choose sequences of footage. When I started in the industry, we worked in sixteen-millimeter black-and-white film. The editors who showed me the ropes were twenty-year veterans of newsreels and documentaries who believed that any scene or sequence shorter than three seconds is too fast for the mind to absorb.

But that was B.D. (Before Digital). Now, from the time we turn on our devices, we are exposed to digital streaming of flash frames intercut with shots that are less than two seconds long. In the 1980s, we were told the audience's attention span was about three minutes long. In 2015, a Microsoft Corporation study found the average American adult's attention span was eight seconds. Our growing deficit in attention, focus, and concentration skills is attributed to the effects of what *Time* magazine called "an increasingly digitalized lifestyle."

Continual exposure to rapid-moving images of destruction combined with a shorter attention span takes a toll on our short-term memory. It seems to be getting harder to focus on anything that is not flickering on a screen right in front of us—such as other pedestrians, fellow passengers, and groups of friends who are more likely to be staring at their phones and texting, rather than making eye contact with each other.

If it's not on our screen, it no longer exists.

But in real life, once a disaster moves off the screen and away from the headlines, it's all too easy to forget about the people who have to get up again tomorrow to deal with the wreckage of their lives. Soon, images of a new tragedy will play nonstop, throughout yet another news cycle. Seriously, who can remember what happened last week?

"The public consciousness wants everything to be fine. But destabilizing events throw people off," says Dr. Demaria. "We become emotionally numb and frozen, like we are in a trance and can't figure it out. People are still processing what 9/11 meant. When we don't have any way to organize the experience in our consciousness, we remain fearful and can become more dissociated."

Vicarious Traumatization (VT): A Civilian Epidemic?

Glued to our phones, tablets, TVs, and other devices for most of our waking hours, we spend as much time—or more—looking at screaming images of pain as do many media professionals. It is my belief that millions of us are probably traumatized to a certain degree because of so much indirect exposure to trauma.

Exposure to violent images is not considered a diagnostic criterion for post-traumatic stress disorder (PTSD), according to the American Psychiatric Association's *Diagnostic and Statistical Manual (DSM V)*. There is an exception for professionals whose daily work requires hours of exposure to pictures of traumatized people.

Vicarious traumatization (VT) presents with similar symptoms: avoidance of triggers, anxiety, arousal, and hypervigilance, plus flashbacks in which the body gets to feel what it's like to go through a traumatic event again.

A Newsroom Insomnia Club

In 1982, the Israeli military bombed refugee camps in Lebanon. Several newsroom colleagues reported nightmares about screaming children and adult victims were persistently interrupting their sleep. While I had not yet decided to go back to graduate school to study psychology, I felt at the time that since most of our shift was spent screening pictures of gruesome deaths and injuries, the emotional impact of so much pain might be affecting our sleep. When I brought that up, no one laughed. I took it as agreement. I had no way of knowing that years later, I would be studying the impact of dreams in connection to September 11th and Hurricane Sandy.

PTSD: An Overview

If acute stress reactions do not resolve within six months, they can become post-traumatic stress disorder (PTSD). They are similar but not interchangeable. PTSDUnited.org, a not-for-profit organization that provides information and resources about post-traumatic stress disorder offers the following facts:

- An estimated eight percent of Americans—24.4 million people—have PTSD at any given time. This equals the total population of Texas.
- Seventy percent of the US adult population has experienced at least one traumatic event. That equates to roughly 223.4 million people. Up to 20 percent of these people—approximately 44.7 million— go on to develop PTSD.
- PTSD and other anxiety disorders cost the United States economy more than $42.3 billion annually. The condition is often misdiagnosed and under treated.[25]

Acute Stress or PTSD?

PTSD is not a bad hair day although it comes up a lot in conversations. Trauma refers to a life-threatening event. According to the Veterans Administration, the following symptoms of post-traumatic stress disorder present six months or longer after exposure. They must last for at least one month to qualify for a clinical diagnosis. As we previously discovered, many of these criteria are identical to acute stress disorder, which presents immediately after a traumatic event and resolves within a few months. Sources of PTSD include: direct exposure; witnessing the trauma; learning that a relative or close friend was exposed to a trauma; and indirect exposure to aversive details of the trauma, usually in the course of professional duties (e.g., first responders, the media, and medics).

THE THREE THRESHOLDS OF PTSD

1. **Re-experiencing the event**
   - ✓ Intrusive thoughts
   - ✓ Nightmares
   - ✓ Flashbacks
   - ✓ Emotional distress after exposure to traumatic reminders
   - ✓ Physical reactivity after exposure to traumatic reminders

2. **Avoidance of triggers**
   - ✓ Inability to recall key features of the trauma
   - ✓ Overly negative thoughts and assumptions about oneself or the world
   - ✓ Exaggerated blame of self or others for causing the trauma
   - ✓ Negative affect and changes in mood and behavior
   - ✓ Decreased interest in activities
   - ✓ Feeling isolated
   - ✓ Difficulty experiencing positive affect
   - ✓ Irritability or aggression
   - ✓ Risky or destructive behavior

3. **Hypervigilance**
   - ✓ Exaggerated startle response
   - ✓ Difficulty concentrating
   - ✓ Difficulty sleeping
   - ✓ Dissociation, the feeling of being out of body, numbing out (loss of feeling), and depersonalization, in which nothing feels real[26]

Reformatting Flashbacks

My cousin Jay invented a method of cleaning out air ducts that was so successful it earned him numerous industry accolades and awards. His reputation attracted the attention of a national business magazine whose editors decided to make him their cover story. It was big news in our family, and we could not have been more excited for him.

A few months after the shoot, his mom called me, crying.

"You have to go see him. He's a wreck," she sobbed.

When I asked what happened, she whispered, "He'll have to tell you."

Jay and I have been very close our whole lives. An only child, twelve years my junior, he looked at me as his older sister. On the Staten Island Ferry after school, we were fascinated by the parade of tankers and ocean liners coming into New York harbor. Naturally extroverted, he grew into a young man whose exuberance was nothing short of contagious.

That Jay was gone when I got to his home. The man sitting in the June sun wrapped in a blanket reminded me of Michael Corleone at the end of *Godfather III*, where he keels over, dead in his chair. Beads of sweat gathered on Jay's forehead, but his face was pale and his pupils dilated. His voice was so low I had to lean in to hear him.

The morning of the shoot, everyone in his crew and the photographer suited up in full hazmat gear for a walking tour of the site. Jay planned to point out where the environmental damage was and explain how it would be mitigated. After telling the photographer to stay close to the group's leader, they started their tour on the roof. Apparently, the photographer wanted a different angle so he stepped away from the group.

Suddenly, Jay heard glass shatter. He rushed over, only to see the photographer had stepped onto a skylight and had fallen to his death.

It was ruled an accidental death, but lawsuits were pending, and Jay was unable to eat or sleep. He had stopped going to the office.

"I keep seeing his body. It won't go away. It just comes back, whether I'm falling asleep or wide-awake. I can't work, and I don't know how I'm going to go to court."

Flashbacks are usually spontaneously recurring movies of the mind that you cannot stop watching. They are visceral in intensity and impossible to ignore. A strong flashback can feel a kick in the solar plexus, taking away your breath. After days or weeks of them, you can start to question your own sanity.

These images are nothing like those that we construct in creative visualization or daydreaming.

In fact, there is nothing about a flashback that you would consciously want. I believe they are a mechanism that the unconscious mind uses to metabolize the unthinkable. However, the repetitive nature of the flashback means that feelings and sensations get worse with each replay.

Flashbacks usually present as associated three-dimensional, life-size images, meaning that we see what happened in the present tense because we are *in* the movie, looking out through our own eyes as the scene unfolds around us. This perceptual perspective is so compelling that we are back there, reliving every horrifying second in real-time.

Through the science of neurolinguistic programming (NLP), a flashback can be neutralized by shifting our perspective from a three-dimensional association to a two-dimensional, dissociated frame. Based on principles of cognitive psychology, hypnotherapy, and anthropology, NLP use protocols that work quickly at the unconscious level to release unwanted, unhealthy beliefs, values, and emotions and replace them with new images, thoughts, and behaviors. To alleviate painful flashbacks, NLP exercises tap into your brain's unique patterns of storing and accessing memories in visual, auditory, and kinesthetic systems.

Since a flashback tends to be a visual image, which we see in our mind's eye as if it were happening around us, visualizing the traumatic event in 2-D lets us observe ourselves on a screen as we went through that event at an earlier point in time. Seeing what happened to ourselves then, knowing that now we are safe in real time, usually brings relief from the repetitive pain caused by flashbacks.

As Jay held an imaginary remote control in his hands, he gained mental control over his mind movie. Following a protocol from neurolinguistic programming (NLP), he switched the movie from color to black and white, froze the action at the end of the scene, and whited it out. In addition to gaining a sense of control over the battlefield that his mind had become, Jay was immensely relieved that the flashbacks stopped.

It can be debilitating to find ourselves flooded again and again with the neurochemicals of dread. Understanding the structure of a flashback gives us the keys to resolve it. Once we recognize that our flashback is a mind movie, we can mentally project it onto a wall so it can be screened from a neutral position. Once we can detach, we are on the way home.

Dreams and Nightmares

Rachelle Quiyara was in school when she heard "three really loud bangs." She had no idea what they were.

"I don't think it registered that it was something bad, but I knew it was something out of the ordinary," she says. "Then I saw my teacher. Her body language told me something horrible was going on."

Rachelle, then fifteen, was among a group of some twenty students who were rushed into a classroom that could be locked.

"Let me be honest with you," her teacher said. "Those were definitely gunshots. But you are safe."

Then a SWAT team knocked on the door and hustled the students downstairs to a waiting bus that brought them to the middle school where they were united with their parents. No one was killed but two teachers were shot. Rachelle learned later that the shooter was a boy from her homeroom who brought a rifle to school because he was upset with his girlfriend. Luckily, he did not find her.

A few nights later, the nightmares and insomnia began. They would haunt her for years to come.

"Although I hadn't seen him at the time, in my nightmares I saw him and the rifle. I had trouble with that for years and I was very jumpy," she says.

When she got to college, the nightmares were replaced by hypervigilance. In April 2007, during Rachelle's freshman year on a New York City campus, a lone shooter on the Virginia Tech campus in Blacksburg killed thirty-two people and injured eighteen more.

"Even though I was in New York, I was always scanning, waiting for the next explosion," she says. "That feeling of anxiety whenever there is a shooting, I don't know if it ever stopped." Several years later, her PTSD nightmares increased when she survived a gang shooting on a New York City bus.

When Nightmares Are Good News

No one wants nightmares but they serve a purpose.

"Recurring dreams after a traumatic event are good news," says Kathleen Olivetti, who taught the seminar *Trauma, Dreams, and Nightmares* after September 11th. "They show us that the psyche is working on it. If the dreams continue for months or years afterwards, the message is, you haven't processed this yet."

The process of metabolizing a traumatic life event has an organic rhythm that cannot be hurried.

As we move out of shock and survival towards the six-month anniversary, disturbing dreams and nightmares frequently surface, making people wonder why they feel worse. Visceral dreams stir up feelings of vulnerability and sorrow, which are too deep for words. Six months to the day after Hurricane Sandy, I was standing in my home, watching the water gush in through the seals on my greenhouse window. Standing on the terracotta tile floor, my feet felt the icy water swirl around my ankles. My own screams woke me up.

As I described in the Introduction, I am one of those people who gets calm in a crisis. The night that the water came in, I felt no fear. But it didn't take long before my waking life was a tangled mess of contractors' bills, lawyers' documents, and to-do lists, which had to be tackled one at a time, day to day. I had no idea that I was harboring residual emotions until that six-month marker dream woke me up. It was far from pleasant, but it made me aware there were unsettling emotional themes I would need to explore.

Catastrophe Serves a Higher Purpose

Disaster strips us of our masks. We face each other emotionally naked, unable to be anything other than honest. It may not be elegant but it's true: There is no place for BS in a disaster zone.

"Disaster impels us from our fantasy world and our fanciful self-image, to which most of us are attached. The reality of who we are and what our lives have been can be such a shocking contrast," says Dr. Anne Redelfs, author of *The Awakening Storm* and a retired psychiatrist, who evacuated from New Orleans one day before Hurricane Katrina.

Although more than a decade has passed, when she returns to New Orleans where she resided for twenty-six years, people still need to talk about what happened to them as a result of the storm. "Most have not dealt with all the layers of this trauma—the physical, emotional, mental, and spiritual—so there is more to resolve. Secondly, the Katrina disaster may symbolize some major unconscious threat, such as the fear of God or of their own mortality," she says. "They need to talk about it in an indirect, less-threatening fashion; thus, the need to talk about 'Katrina.'"

As we sift through the wreckage of life as we knew it, disaster brings us closer together with people we might not have known before. Sometimes, we lose friendships because those we thought we could count on are unavailable. In her own life, Dr. Redelfs has found that "disaster taught me to engage with people with a new regard for our mutual humanity and human need."

She and I both believe that catastrophic events serve a higher purpose.

"Disasters can move us to become more fully alive. The

Catastrophic events serve a higher purpose. "Disasters make us aware that the life force within us needs tending daily. This is why we are here."

suffering—as individuals and communities—expands our minds and welcomes our spirits," she says. "Disasters make us aware that the life force within us needs tending daily. This is why we are here."

KEYS TO STAYING
BALANCED UNDER PRESSURE

- CONFUSED? FOCUS ON YOUR BREATH. Slow your breath down to two counts. Inhale for one, two seconds. Exhale for one, two seconds. Repeat. Slow down the count. Repeat.

- SPEAK YOUR PIECE. Say what's on your mind. This is not a time to worry about how someone else will react. Emotional survival means doing what's best for you and your family. No one else can do this for you.

- CLOSE YOUR EYES. TAKE FOUR 5-MINUTE MINI-BREAKS THROUGHOUT THE DAY. To keep stress levels in balance, Harvard researchers find that we need 20 minutes a day of mental and physical relaxation. When you are recovering from a catastrophe you don't have 20 minutes, but here's the great news: Four mini-breaks of 5 minutes each provide the same health benefits as one 20-minute session. Close your eyes, listen to soothing music, or remember a place and time when you felt completely relaxed and safe. Let yourself drift into that time and place as if you were there. Enjoy!

- KEEP A LOG OF CONVERSATIONS AND PHONE CALLS. Keep a list: Name of person/organization. Date. Time of call. This is a good place to jot down key words and questions that have come up. Keep it simple.

- KEEP ALL RECEIPTS IN ONE PLACE. As the months go on, receipts pile up. Take a few minutes every night to put the day's bills and receipts in one place: a folder, a drawer, or a zip lock bag. It will save you time and aggravation down the road.

6

My Life with PTSD

*J*t was the robocall that got me. Thursday, October 1, 2015. 3:30 PM. Nassau County executive, Ed Mangano, was on the phone:

"Hurricane Joaquin could reach Long Island by Tuesday morning. Now is the time to get your emergency Friends and Family plans in place. And prep those go-kits."

His voice releases a nasty kaleidoscope of images, sounds, and sensations.

Flash back to October 29, 2012: cold water, gushing through the walls. Jump cut: squished in the attic's cramped crawl space watching water inch up the aluminum stairs. Natural sound in background, with 110-mile-an-hour winds banging the silver spruce against the roof.

(If the tree crashes into the roof, I'm dead.)

"You don't have to watch this now," I remind myself, while breathing in a wave of soothing indigo. As I exhale the color grey, the images fade and I start to relax into the present. (Color breathing is one of the keys to Emotional First Aid, page 63.) The coastal weather forecast says that Joaquin will soon head out to sea. No landfall this time, at least not here. *(Whew!)* Packing 155-mile-an-hour winds as it whips through the Caribbean and up the South Carolina coast, Joaquin will end up taking thirty-four lives and causing $200 million in damages. In the meantime, no harm in being careful, right?

My go-kit is parked in the front closet. For two and a half years after Hurricane Sandy, I checked that bag twice a week. I know it's ridiculous. No one else ever touched it. In fact, no one even knew it was there. My ritual of taking everything out, counting supplies, and putting them back, is a sheer waste of time and effort. Each time I unzip it, I cannot help laughing at myself. Like Mickey Mouse in *The Sorcerer's Apprentice*, I have no way to turn off this compulsion. I must complete the entire ritual until the go-kit is repacked and safely parked in the closet.

Good news: The robocall makes me aware that I haven't checked my go-kit in at least six months. Coming up to the third anniversary, it's a sign I'm getting better.

I cannot suppress a smile or two when I reacquaint myself with all the wonderful goodies that are going to save me in the event of another disaster. I know it's absurd to feel happy about rubber gloves and a dust mask, but what really lifts my spirit is the RESTOP. Boy, am I glad I now have RESTOP#1 and #2.

This may be too much information, but after creeping upstairs to the crawl space, dripping wet, the sound of rushing water made it impossible not to feel the need to pee. My prepping had brought in thirteen gallons of water, a year's supply of plumbers' candles and matches, six flashlights with batteries, and two emergency radios with LED lights, one of which could be powered by a solar panel, batteries, electric power, and/or a hand-crank. Plus blankets, pillows, and lots of towels. But when that call of nature came—and given the suggestive power of rushing water, you can imagine that sooner or later it had to happen—I wished I had remembered the RESTOP portable toilet I had given my daughter prior to her trip to Thailand.

"I've never been to Thailand," I'd told her. "But I'm thinking that the toilet facilities are probably not what you're used to." Who'd a thunk that Mom should have kept a RESTOP or two for herself?

Artfully arranged on the tile floor are my rubber gloves, dust mask, dry cat food (for Bogart in case you're wondering), wet wipes, water purifying tablets, mouthwash strips, first aid kits, and assorted emergency toiletries in a Red Cross bag. Not to mention a smorgasbord of Meals Ready to Eat (MREs), including beef stroganoff with noodles (contains wheat gluten, hydrolyzed corn gluten, sugar, and "flavoring,") chili mac with beef (contains potassium chloride, maltodextrin, disodium inosinate, and disodium guanylate), sweet and sour pork (contains maltodextrin, hydrolyzed corn gluten, and "natural flavors"), and scrambled eggs with bacon. Don't ask.

No peanut M&Ms? Hmm. What was I thinking?

After reading the labels, there is no way I'm gonna pop open one of those aluminum pouches. MRE could stand for More Retching Expected.

What if I swapped them for boxes of peanut M&Ms? There's nothing like a handful of peanut M&Ms. Sweet, salty, and crunchy, they have to taste a lot better than those MREs. I can probably use them to barter for items like batteries and toilet paper. With peanut M&Ms in my go-kit, I'll be the most popular girl in the shelter.

A Hypervigilant State

As defined by *www.brainworks.com*, hypervigilance is:

"A heightened state of awareness is part of the fight / flight response, resulting in a state of chronic hypervigilance . . . brain resources are on constant alert, causing inappropriate or even aggressive reactions in everyday situations."[27]

Two words: *coastal flooding*.

That's all it takes, and I'm running to the closet to make sure everything is there. I keep a local tide table app on my phone so I can stay alert during high tide. Not that I can do anything about it except watch, knowing I am helpless. I would force myself to stay awake through the early hours, unable to go to sleep until the tide started to ebb. Trapped in cognitive dissonance, I understand that choosing a behavior that leads to helplessness is counterproductive. But PTSD has its own logic. The hypervigilant state feeds my illusion that if I do (x), then I will be safe.

After a few years, it tends to subside, although friends report that they will sit up through the night, watching for water gushing down the street whenever there is a "coastal flooding" weather alert.

This leads to an obvious question: Why continue to live near the water? It's a question I ask myself every hurricane season. People come to the sea to relax and to let go of worry, grief, and sorrow. The ocean can absorb those feelings, replacing them with calm and hope. At the same time, loving the ocean is like being in a relationship with someone who has extreme mood swings. Maybe it's insane, and sure, it's calmer in the hills, but I get claustrophobic when I'm stuck more than thirty minutes from the coast.

Most of my friends and neighbors feel similarly. A neighbor who rebuilt her home after Sandy described her life as "living in a house of fear." Asked why she didn't move, she told us, "I need to be close to the ocean."

Flashbacks and STUGs

Now I can laugh at myself when hypervigilance is driving the personality. But there is nothing humorous about a flashback. In less than a heartbeat, you find yourself back in the experience you wish you had never had. PTSD behaves like a retro virus. Dormant for years, it can come back unexpectedly years later, triggered by a few bars of music, a smell, or the touch of a breeze against your skin.

Sensory based, a flashback feels a lot like its cousin STUG: a Sudden Temporary Upsurge of Grief. You're driving, and suddenly Judy Garland is singing *Over the Rainbow,* and you can hear your dad crooning along, only he's dead. He's been dead a long time, but *Over the Rainbow* whacks you in the heart, and then you're crying as if it had just happened.

Your body remembers. Your limbic system stores the molecules of emotion going back to birth. A few bars of music, the delicious smell of turkey roasting on the holidays, or the sensation of an ocean breeze against your cheek—any sensory trigger can release a cascade of powerful memories.

For Marcel Proust, the gentle scent of a madeleine cookie on a late afternoon released a flood of recollection that became his seven-volume masterpiece *À la recherché du temps perdu (Remembrance of Things Past).* Literary references notwithstanding, flashbacks are like Post-it's stuck inside you for the sole purpose of reminding you never to forget. It's a life lesson I first learned after working as a reporter in Chile.

"It Can't Happen Here"

Six months after a military junta seized power and assassinated the country's democratically elected president, Chile was in a state of siege. American and British journalists who had been there prior to the coup had been expelled after reports about mass executions and disappearances. Soldiers were raiding homes and seizing books, which were burned in giant bonfires. Suspicious of ideas they did not understand, the militias even burned *Revolution in the Arts* and a book on Cubism, believing it referred to Fidel Castro's regime.

As a young, bilingual journalist with an unquenchable thirst for adventure, I had arrived in Santiago, Chile, after days of traveling overland through the desert in the hope of avoiding any unpleasant questions about my portable Olivetti typewriter and the letter of introduction to the Santiago bureau chief of United Press International.

A few minutes after reading the letter, he put me to work. During the next few months, I covered a search team from Chicago that was looking for information about the death of twenty-four-year-old Frank Teruggi, an American student who had been killed in the first few days after the coup. Teruggi and filmmaker Charles Horman were last seen in the Chilean national soccer stadium, where some 20,000 people had been rounded up— forty-one had been shot in public, including Victor Jara, a folk singer who had been ordered by soldiers to play the guitar. When he sang *Venceremos*, the Latin American version of *We Shall Overcome*, the soldiers shot his hands until they were bloody stumps. Jara continued to sing until he was executed. Charles Horman, who was also killed in the national stadium, became the subject of the movie *Missing* (1982), directed by Costa-Gavras and starring Sissy Spacek and Jack Lemmon. Teruggi's story remains untold.

Nothing prepared me for seeing troops with machine guns stationed behind sandbags at everyday intersections. You couldn't get to a grocery store without passing a checkpoint.

Chileans coped with dark humor. As dinner would end, someone always joked, "We'd better get home before we're corpses in the street," a reference to a 10 PM curfew.

If you were not indoors by then, you could be shot on sight. After midnight, it was not uncommon to be woken up by lions in the zoo across the street, who roared every time there was a burst of machine-gun fire.

Even more unsettling were the reports of concentration camps and torture centers. The family of one of President Allende's ministers took me under their wing. Letters from the concentration camp arrived heavily censored, but we learned that in Dawson Island, near Antarctica, former cabinet members were forced to do heavy manual labor outdoors without gloves or winter clothes.

The family of former Defense Minister Jose Toha, who stood at six foot seven inches, was told he had committed suicide by hanging—in a room with a four-foot ceiling. Later, they learned he had been taken from Dawson Island to the military hospital in Santiago, where he was interrogated, tortured, and ultimately killed. The Chileans' nickname for Dawson Island was "Disneyland South," and "Disneyland North" was somewhere in the desert that I had somehow managed to cross without attracting attention.

"We always thought it could never happen here," people used to tell me.

Considered the Switzerland of South America, Chile had been a stable democracy since 1932 with a constitution and three branches of government modeled after the United States. Sitting in the living room of my friend's mock Tudor home, surrounded by pine trees and roses, I couldn't help but think it looked a lot like Scarsdale. Like Alice in Wonderland, maybe I had slid down a rabbit hole to some weird, distorted version of life at home. But, of course, it could never happen here. That's what I kept telling myself, just like everyone else around me. I couldn't help hoping that if I repeated it enough, it would turn out to be true.

Without going into the complicated back story of how President Nixon, his Secretary of State Henry Kissinger, and the CIA supported Chile's military junta, suffice it to say that it wasn't until 1988, some fifteen years later, that democracy was reinstated in Chile.

According to a 2011 Valtech Human Rights Commission report, 2,279 people were killed and more than 40,000 were detained, held without charge, and tortured as political prisoners during that reign of terror. My friend's husband, Orlando Letelier, was eventually freed and granted asylum in the United States. He was assassinated by a car bomb in Washington, DC, on September 21, 1976. His murder was a contract hit ordered by the Chilean secret police to be carried out on US soil. I was privileged to have gotten to know this intelligent, charismatic man before his death.[28]

The Rule of Three

I don't know what was more unsettling—the mask of normalcy during the daylight hours or the dark nocturnal silences, punctuated by random gunfire. You could walk through a fragrant park, admiring the majestic snow-capped *cordillera* to the west of the city, but when you sat down to lunch, the conversation inevitably turned to people being arrested by secret police in unmarked cars. Reports of torture included beatings, rape, waterboarding, and excruciating electric shock.

A detention center in the middle of the city, Palace Grimaldi, was nicknamed "The Palace of Laughter."

A few weeks after I received an assignment from *Newsweek* to work on a six-month anniversary background report, I was awakened around 1 AM by the sound of an engine idling. It was a Mercedes bus with blackened windows, an ominous presence in the middle of the night. As I watched, a neighbor in the apartment building across the street was hustled onto the bus, in handcuffs. I never knew who he was, but I knew as sure as I was standing at the window that it could have been me.

With that unsettling knowledge, I continued interviewing sources for the *Newsweek* piece. The bureau chief who had given me the assignment wanted me to find out the number of *desaparecidos*—those who had disappeared—since the military coup on September 11, 1973.

A close friend had called in a favor to get me an interview with a prominent lawyer. He would know, I was told. But when I presented myself his first words were "I just want you to know that I hate Americans. I hate journalists. And I especially hate American journalists."

Then he asked what I wanted.

"I'm looking for the number of *desaparecidos*," I said, making eye contact.

"*Desaparecidos?* I can find out for you," he sneered, picking up the phone and calling the office of General Agosto Leigh, one of the three members of the military junta. Word on the street was that the air force intelligence officials were the most vicious during interrogations. The palms of my hands broke out in sweat and I seriously considered jumping out the window.

But I was in luck. It was a Friday afternoon in February, which is mid-summer in the southern hemisphere, so General Leigh had choppered to his villa on the coast. At least that's what my source told me the general's secretary had said, adding that I was to present myself in General Leigh's office on Monday at 9 AM so he could answer my question.

Right.

"You have to go into hiding."

My boss, my friends, and the family who had taken me under their wing were unanimous. To this day, I have no idea where they brought me. I remember scrunching down in the back seat of a sedan and someone holding a coat over my head while I scurried indoors. There were no flights back to Lima until Wednesday. From Lima, I had an open ticket to New York. From what I remember, I vomited several times, then wrapped myself in a blanket, huddled in a fetal position on a cot, while friends trickled in to comfort me and bring me food.

About twelve people came to say goodbye the night before I was to leave. We were joking about the Rule of Three, a draconian order that said no more than three people were allowed to assemble at any given time. In the wisdom of the junta, four people would be enough to hatch a plot to overthrow the military. Citizens were encouraged to inform on their neighbors, and had anyone been watching, they could have had us arrested for violating the Rule of Three.

Around 9 PM, there was a loud knock on the door. A chilly, clammy sweat broke out at the back of my neck, and I can still feel the sensation of one cold wet drop of perspiration slithering along my spine. I noticed that the young man across the table was staring blankly ahead, his pupils swollen and dark, in contrast to his complexion, which had suddenly transitioned to a waxy glaze.

"They're looking for you," my boss said. "You never showed up for your appointment on Monday."

"They'll never find her," said someone else.

Of that, I was not sure.

Then someone joked, "Maybe we'll get to visit Orlando in Disneyland South."

"It's going to be the Palace of Laughter," another friend said.

I realized that it didn't matter, in the end. There were more than three of us and we were about to disappear.

By that time, everyone had stopped speaking, and I think we were all holding our breath. I know I was. Someone answered the door and shrieked. I slid off my chair, hoping I could hide under the table. But it turned out to be a shriek of unexpected happiness. My friend's father had driven past several checkpoints to hug me goodbye.

The next morning, with my notes taped to my body, I went through three checkpoints and watched calmly as soldiers emptied out my suitcase and carry-on bag. They were suspicious of the poor Olivetti.

"Why do you have that?" two of them asked.

I smiled as sweetly as I could and lied.

"My fiancé is in Vietnam and I write letters to him every night."

They let me on the flight.

Jorge Chavez International Airport, named after a Peruvian pilot who crashed his plane into the Alps, had never looked as good. There were no incidents and I got home in one piece—sort of.

Lima, Peru, used to remind me of the Bronx with palm trees. Even though it was grittier than Santiago, after my experience there Lima seemed like an apex of civilization. I was welcomed back with dinners and nightmares and lots of cigarettes and wine. Due to severe censorship in next-door Chile, neither my bureau chief nor my friends in Peru had a clue as to how bad things were there.

Six months later, back in New York, I was working as a reporter for the United Nations news service. My apartment, across the street from the UN, overlooked a pocket park. It was about as peaceful a setting you could find in midtown Manhattan, except in the middle of the night when sanitation trucks rolled up for their nightly collection. When a truck drove over a manhole cover, releasing a loud crackling sound, I rolled out of bed onto the floor and rolled myself under the bed, hyperventilating. I spent the rest of the night there, waiting for a knock on the door.

If it only happened once I would have written it off, but it soon became a pattern. There was not a lot of information about post-traumatic stress disorder in 1975 B.I. (Before Internet). Working in newsrooms in New York and London in the early 1970s, I had produced several stories about Vietnam veterans having similar reactions in public places.

That couldn't be happening to me.

I was never in the military and did not think I had been through anything comparable to Vietnam. But when the pattern persisted, I went for psychiatric help and was relieved to find out that yes, escaping with my life counted, and yes, I had a classic case of PTSD.

"Let Us Dare to Be Tender"

My first resolution after being diagnosed was to volunteer with human rights organizations: Amnesty International and the National Council of

Churches human rights division.

Nobody wanted to know. Concentration camps? Those ended with Hitler, I was told. Torture in Chile? Isn't that the country that Henry Kissinger called "a dagger pointed at the heart of Antarctica?"

It was an uphill shlog. My UN colleague, Lelai Lelaulu, and I started a human rights committee at the Overseas Press Club in 1976 and in 1980, I suggested to Michael Massing of the *Columbia Journalism Review* that there was a need for an independent organization dedicated to helping journalists in other countries who were often targeted for indefinite detention without charge simply for doing their jobs. That suggestion led to the formation of the Committee to Protect Journalists, which continues to fight for journalists' rights around the world.[29]

Ten years later, after I got sick due to burnout while covering the Iran-Contra hearings at CBS News, I changed careers. After completing a doctorate in cognitive psychology, I started my practice specializing in helping people through acute stress and traumatic situations.

The most important work to grow out of my experience as a young reporter in Chile is the commitment to be present with those who have gone through life-shattering events and to offer information and support so that they do not have to go through it alone.

In addition to years of clinical study, specialty certifications, and work in the field, I believe that my biggest strength is living with PTSD. Time and again, I get feedback that because I know what someone is seeing, hearing, and feeling—because I have been through it myself—it has helped someone to accept that it is normal to be wounded and it is okay to feel hurt. With humility and patience come the acceptance that opens the way to a path of healing and growth. After our descent into the heart of darkness, we can now begin moving towards the light.

In the words of Belguim's King Philippe, on the first anniversary of a terrorist attack that killed thirty-two people and injured some 320, "Let's learn to listen to each other again, to respect each other's weaknesses. Above all, let us dare to be tender."

KEYS FOR
LIVING WITH PTSD

Ask yourself:

- ARE YOU EXPERIENCING FLASHBACKS, AROUSAL, AND AVOIDANCE OF PEOPLE OR PLACES THAT REMIND YOU OF THE DISASTER A YEAR OR MORE SINCE THE EVENT? Do these symptoms interfere with your ability to think clearly and make decisions? If so, please seek professional help. (See Online Resources, page 253)

- ARE YOU SURPRISED WHEN YOU START CRYING DUE TO A SUDDEN UPSURGE OF GRIEF (STUG), FEAR, OR SOMETHING YOU CANNOT NAME? STUG reactions surface unexpectedly, sometimes years later. Understand that they are a natural part of the grieving process and give yourself permission to feel whatever comes up.

- DO YOU HAVE DISTURBING DREAMS ABOUT THE EVENT? Upsetting though they are, dreams are the psyche's way of metabolizing—literally digesting—elements of the experience that you have not yet processed. They are a positive sign of healing.

- ARE YOU HAVING TROUBLE SOCIALIZING WITH PEOPLE WHO HAVE NOT SHARED YOUR EXPERIENCE OR SOMETHING SIMILAR? PTSD can make it difficult to reintegrate socially. Don't push yourself into unnecessary venues where you do not yet feel safe. Be gentle and go slowly when it comes to attending parties and big social events. It can take several years before you are truly ready.

- WHAT STIMULI TRIGGER YOUR FLASHBACKS? What steps can you take to avoid those triggers?

PART THREE

Regrouping

The silence of the night
Is broken by the bird's first cry.
A new awakening is upon us.

—Wolfgang Christoph

7

The First Anniversary: There Are Good Days and Bad Days, and Today Is One of Them

*H*eading into any one-year anniversary, our emotional climate shifts. We enter a new season of the heart. Instead of waking up shocked, depressed, or terrified, we can sense that our emotional baseline is evening out. It's not that we feel "better." It's more that living through a nightmare has seasoned us. Bruised and confused, but managing, we have become wounded survivors putting one foot in front of the other.

THE FIRST GIFT—*humility*
—*helps us appreciate that after all
we've been through, we are still alive.*

Be it newsworthy or deeply personal, the first anniversary honors those we have lost and those family members, friends, and neighbors who have been there to help us. Pausing, with gravitas, we can take a deep breath and review what we have learned. Whether we set aside personal time to reflect or attend a public ceremony, the anniversary of the year that everything changed has now become time stamped in our psyche.

Don't be surprised by a sudden, unexpected wave of sadness the morning after. The recognition that our losses are permanent can trigger new surges of anger as well, and this new season of the heart may be stormy and unpredictable.

When Grieving Begins

Just when we thought we were getting over it, we find ourselves vulnerable to recurring STUGS: Sudden Temporary Upheavals of Grief.

THE SECOND GIFT—*patience*
—*helps us deal with not knowing how long
this is going to last.*

For example, after Hurricane Katrina, "Some people didn't begin to grieve until after the first year," says Dr. Redelfs, who remembers that New Orleans residents "were pretty much in shock at first, taking care of mundane things, such as insurance, FEMA applications, and loans, as well as finding family members and friends. We focused on the day-to-day tasks at hand. It was only when things started falling into place during the second year after Katrina that many people became aware that they were grief-stricken, furious, or bewildered. Some suddenly didn't know what to do with their lives."

The one-year anniversary reminds us that the damage has penetrated more deeply than we realized. It starts to sink in that our "before" way of life is not coming back. Even if we are back in our homes, we do not yet feel comfortable about being there.

Speaking on NPR's *Here and Now* on the first anniversary of Hurricane Sandy, a Long Beach resident put it this way: "First, it's that initial shock, and now it's the realization that we're a year later—this isn't the neighborhood that I bought into; it's not the community that I bought into. A lot of my neighbors are not coming back, the stores are not coming back, my little local library didn't come back. So we talk about it, like we are fighting so hard to come back, and what are we coming back to?"[30]

Insensitivity Hurts

THE THIRD GIFT—*empathy*
—*is the antidote to insensitivity.*

Loss is not a popular topic of conversation. Most of us fear it and will do anything to avoid it.

"People normally try to avoid facing hardships," says Dr. Demaria. "A lot of people then don't have the capacity to practice those skills to get past future challenges in their lives and subsequently need to be reminded that they have the capacity to cope."

Now more than ever, people need support. Many who first sought counseling four years after Sandy were struggling to make sense of where they found themselves.

"I just moved back to my house but nothing is the same," several clients reported. "I'm fortunate that I was able to rebuild but something is missing."

Helping individuals figure out what that is and guiding them through the confusion has become an integral aspect of my post-disaster work. Dr. Demaria's work at the WTC Family Center created a long-term model for healing from disaster. Those who lost someone on September 11th developed lifelong friendships based on patient understanding for whatever each one was experiencing.

No one was judged for not "getting over it" a year after the terrorist attack.

"We were at a picnic in a state park where a woman we didn't know asked what group we belonged to. 'You look so happy to be together. Is this a club?'" recalls Margie Miller. "We laughed. 'Yeah, in a way, you could call us a club.' But it's not the kind of club anyone wants to join.'"

Whether we recognize the need for it or not, empathy connects us to another person's experience without judgment. It never fails to surprise me how difficult it can be to find it. Even people who we trusted to be supportive can hurl javelins of insensitivity when we least expect it.

One widow who lost her husband in the World Trade Center attack was told that she wasn't smiling enough and needed to go on Match.com to feel better. A woman who lost everything she owned in Hurricane Sandy was attending a relative's bridal shower in Connecticut a few months after the December 4, 2012, Sandy Hook school shooting, in which twenty-seven people were killed, including Adam Lanza, the shooter, and his mother.

The woman who survived Hurricane Sandy says, "I hadn't said anything about my own situation. A relative told someone that I was a Sandy survivor. That person attacked me, saying, 'There are plenty of parents in Newtown, Connecticut, who wished they could have those problems instead.'"

Insensitive remarks like these are not uncommon. People who are recovering from disasters are often told not to feel upset because, after all, what they are going through isn't Auschwitz. Such verbal abuse is offensive and unacceptable. It adds a layer of trauma that no one needs.

Holocaust survivor Dr. Viktor Frankl, author of the classic *Man's Search for Meaning*, spoke out against this bizarre type of shaming. He said, "Never compare suffering. Everyone has their own Auschwitz."[31]

It happens more frequently than we would expect.

"It is pretty common among people who believe their emotional pain is not really justified to blame others who express that they are feeling hurt," says Dr. Demaria. "If you are angry at people who have been victimized like you, it just means that you haven't sorted out your own baggage or addressed your open wounds."

THE FOURTH GIFT—*forgiveness*
—*helps us release anger towards
those who hurt us.*

Those who blame the victim have not worked through their own issues from earlier trauma, according to Dr. Redelfs. "When people have received insensitivity from others, this is what they pass on instead of considering what each person needs and how can I help him or her?"

She tells survivors that "We need to understand that these people who are so insensitive have their own PTSD. They are passing onto others what was passed on to them. They have evacuated from that part of themselves that is compassionate because of what they've been through themselves."

The Myth of Closure

After listening to people say, "Aren't you over it yet?" another layer of meaning starts to sink in: Complex traumatic grief is socially uncool.

"People have a hard time with open wounds," says Dr. Demaria.

Or perhaps we remind others that what happened to us could happen to them. Just as we were helpless to prevent what happened, others recognize they could be rendered similarly helpless by a critical event. No one enjoys feeling helpless, but without awareness, shifting blame can be a reflexive response. Sandwiched between needing to express what we are feeling and fear of being judged, we tend to pull back, shut down, and isolate to protect ourselves from being stigmatized for not being "over it" quickly enough to please someone else.

As for "closure," it's a myth. Paradoxically, we need to stay open to what our hearts are telling us if we are going to work through the pain.

"Losing my dad on 9/11 made me grow up immediately. Then I saw that the world changed for everybody, but I ignored my grief and it made me a very angry person," says Ian Grady, who was nineteen at the time of the attacks. "It was ruining my relationships and my friendships. It's important to use your grief as motivation, but also confront it. If you won't deal with it, it will resurface."

The Art of Grieving

Getting angry at ourselves for "not getting over it by now" amounts to shaming ourselves for feeling hurt. Like a Chinese finger puzzle made of woven straw, finding relief requires us to relax rather than pull in order to gain release. It may not make sense at first, but this paradoxical practice can lead us to a place where we are no longer fighting with ourselves about our true feelings.

"We all have trauma at one time or another," says Dr. Redelfs. "By encouraging feelings and listening to the deeper soul messages in each communication, we can help wounded people work through their intense emotions. Everyone's healing timeline is different. No matter how long after the event grief surfaces, it should be encouraged. People repeatedly need support to talk about all their feelings instead of retreating from them."

It's equally important to understand that the signature stages of grief—denial, anger, bargaining, depression, and acceptance—are not sequential. Before her death, grief pioneer Elizabeth Kübler-Ross confessed to a colleague that she regretted identifying these stages without explaining that the process is not linear. We can become flooded when several of these emotional states occur simultaneously.

As difficult as it is to stay present and let these feeling wash through us, by focusing on the gifts of humility and patience, our pain will eventually peak and subside. The best antidotes are taking breaks throughout the day to nap, walk, exercise, or spend time in nature. There is nothing we can do to force the process, and we need to be gentle with ourselves when we hurt. Retreating into drugs or alcohol puts our mental, emotional, and physical health at risk.

No "New Normal"

In our search for stability in the strange new terrain in which we wander, it's not uncommon to reach for a label like "the new normal." It's easy to grab onto, and on the surface, it seems to fill in a few blanks. But there is no "new normal" because becoming habituated to severe pain is neither "normal" nor healthy.

The "old normal" was an illusion that catastrophe shattered. No matter how attached we were to the belief that our lives were predictable and under our control, any sudden, violent event provides us with an incontrovertible counterexample.

We can plan our work and work our plan; however, being organized and methodical will not protect us from the unexpected.

Moving Forward

THE FIFTH GIFT—*growth*—
*lets us release harsh emotions
we no longer need.*

When life, our greatest teacher, brings change of the unexpected type, holding on to beliefs that life "should" go back to what it used to be only makes it harder to get through each day. Moving forward requires us to reframe our basic assumptions about life.

But moving forward does not mean that we heal in a linear, sequential way. Just as recovering from a physical illness can mean one step forward, two steps back (and three sideward), getting stronger after a devastating loss can be an uneven process.

"Think of it like an emotional bowel movement," says Dr. Redelfs. "Just as we do physiologically, emotional toxicity is best released daily. We have to regularly release old feelings and disturbing thoughts that are holding us back."

A Psychological Roadmap

Understanding that there are cycles of hardship and healing can serve as a psychological roadmap to help us find our way through the landscape of loss—at our own individual pace.

I wish I could say that nearly three decades of work and study in this field had led me to a perfect shortcut, a magic wand that I can wave to accelerate the process. Numerous therapeutic modalities can help release flashbacks and fears. In my office, I combine hypnotherapy, eye movement integration, meditation, and Emotional Freedom Technique (acupressure), all of which are safe, effective, and quick (SEQ) in an appropriate setting. Conventional and homeopathic medications, including supplements and herbs, can help lower stress and anxiety levels, but there is not a universal protocol or a uniform schedule to fit everyone. (See Appendix Homeopathic Remedies for Acute Stress, page 249.)

Coming to Terms with Loss and Change

Coming to terms with helplessness may be our greatest long-term challenge. As a member of a critical incident stress management team, I am learning how important it is to balance professional competence with the reality that some tragedies are beyond anyone's control and that they are difficult, or even impossible, to understand. It takes humility to admit that sometimes even expertise and experience cannot protect us from events that are larger than life.

But we can transition to a more productive viewpoint. Traumatic loss gives us an opportunity to reassess values and beliefs.

"If I am organized and logical, my life will always be safe" is one example of a belief that a tragic event can instantly render obsolete. Loss makes us question what I call the Four Assumptions of Western Civilization: More is better. Bigger is better. Faster is better. Newer is better. In fact, whenever I have asked someone who has been living without clean water or electricity for a month, "How are those assumptions working for you now?" I never hear back, "Great."

Building a Proactive Mindset

Perhaps it's time to take a new look at beliefs that no longer work. Many of us believe that "positive thinking" always attracts what we want. Sadly, a tragic event can show us that what we called "positive thinking" may have been *wishful* thinking. Coming to terms with that can be uncomfortable until we choose to explore how a proactive mindset can give us the thinking skills needed to integrate these new harsh truths.

This is not "negative thinking." Many believe that anything that is not "fun" or "happy" in the moment is "negative." Facing in to some of our new realities requires that we re-examine that assumption. When life becomes radically different from the belief that anything not fun is "negative," it's time to clear out ideas that don't work in order to make way for pragmatic ways of thinking that address life as it *is* in order to take better care of your needs.

I am not negating the value of positive thinking, but if you believe that it means believing that you are entitled to get whatever you think you want, it's time to redefine it. Thinking positively can point us towards solutions, even when the way appears to be blocked. But it is not a "Get Out of Jail Free" card to avoid dealing with painful emotions.

Finding Silver Linings

No one says, "Wow! I can't wait to lose what I loved most in the world so I can find a silver lining."

Silver linings rarely show up right away. They take time and require patience before we can see them.

Silver linings rarely show up right away. They take time and require patience before we can see them.

"Who are we to be outraged that we suffer things? It's part of life every-where," says Dr. Laura Haigh, a psychologist in London. "There is always a silver lining from this type of crisis. You will emerge a different person and it's hard to see when you are in the thick of it."

After Sarah Mahoney's ninety-six-year-old beach cottage was destroyed by Hurricane Sandy, she never received the funds she had been promised and was unable to rebuild. Eventually, she lost her home and her marriage, which deteriorated due to financial trauma spanning several years.

"It showed me what really matters, who I could count on, and who I couldn't. People are always surprised by this when something huge happens," she says. "Sandy made me start over. She cleaned out all the crap and showed me that God never closes a door without opening a window. But we have to look for it."

During shifts at the WTC Family Center, we would spend hours on the phone with people who had lost someone in the September 11th attacks. What was most important to me was being able to validate and accept the other person's experience. Some conversations were more productive than others. It's not easy work, but when I needed to push through, I would pause to read a sign on the wall:

"There is no change without loss; no loss without change."

Duality in Action

Like the north and south poles, or two sides of a coin, loss and change represent the duality of our human experience. No one likes to hear this, but it can take a few years until we get how we are different because of whom or what we have lost. We start coming to terms with the truth—that life itself is impermanent, and the future, uncertain.

"No one feels and grieves the same. Everyone handles it differently. Know that you are going through whatever it is that God handed to you at this time. You can do it, if you just look inside yourself. You are powerful enough to handle it."

Loss jump-starts change, and the process of changing helps us come to terms with our loss.

"No one feels and grieves the same. Everyone handles it differently," says Ian Grady's mom, Judy, whose husband was killed in the World Trade Center attacks on 9/11. "Know that you are going through whatever it is that God handed to you at this time. You can do it, if you just look inside yourself. You are powerful enough to handle it."

"I am much more of a fighter than I thought I was," says Rachelle Quiyara, the young woman who survived two random shootings. "The important thing I learned is about pushing yourself to come back and not letting yourself completely dissolve and letting whatever has happened to you win. The first time I took the subway again I knew that I am never going to be where I am not feeling the discomfort. But at least I got to the part where I could do it. I'm not a prisoner anymore."

KEYS FOR GETTING
THROUGH THE FIRST
ANNIVERSARY ... AND MORE

- AS THE ANNIVERSARY OF YOUR LOSS DRAWS CLOSER,
  if you find that video and photographs of that event bring on
  anxiety, tears, or anger, turn off the television and restrict your time
  online to necessary activities. Do not watch the news until you feel
  more centered.

- DO NOT FEEL OBLIGATED TO ANSWER EVERY PHONE CALL,
  TEXT, OR EMAIL offering condolences or support. When feeling
  overwhelmed or concerned about becoming emotionally drained,
  remember the Power Question: "If I do (x), will it A) Give me energy;
  B) Help me conserve my energy; or C) Drain my energy."
  Be ruthlessly truthful with yourself.

- IF YOUR ANSWER IS C, PUT THAT ITEM ON YOUR
  "*NOT-TO-DO*" LIST and reward yourself by doing something
  nice for yourself, or someone you love, with the time you saved
  by not doing C. Only you can protect, maintain, and conserve
  your own energy.

- WHETHER OR NOT YOU CAN FIND A SILVER LINING,
  right now is an optimal time to take stock of where you were at
  the time of the event and where you are today. Think of it as
  checking in with your emotional barometer. Ask yourself:
  What is different about your life? What have you learned?
  How have you grown? What would you like to change when
  you are ready?

- IS THERE SOMETHING THAT MAKES YOU SMILE?
  Remind yourself to do it more often.

8

The Second and Third Waves: Financial Trauma and Institutional Betrayal

*T*he smell of your own sweat wakes you out of a restless sleep. Wherever you look, unpaid bills have spilled over chairs, tables, and counters onto your floor. Maybe your mortgage is due today or maybe it was last week, or last month. Ditto your phone, internet, and utility bills, not to mention the kids' tuition and your credit cards, which are close to maxed out.

Never one to be late on payments, you cannot shake off a sense of failure and foreboding. You try fighting it off and fall back asleep instead of getting out of bed and forcing yourself into financial triage mode. Which bills do you defer or negotiate a partial payment? From which account can you scrounge just enough to cover the minimum? Your credit is hanging on by a thread and most of your investments and savings have been tapped.

The dawn brings deeper shame and confusion than you felt yesterday. Are you ever going to get through it? What happens if you can't? You used to be so organized and took pride in never missing a payment. Now, the thought of opening your inbox or mailbox triggers a flood of nausea. That knot in your stomach that never goes away pushes up toward your throat, making it hard to swallow. The phone calls are already starting: persistent, hostile, and threatening. If only you didn't have to get up.

Unmanageable debt is the leading cause of financial stress, according to a 2016 survey by GoBankingRates.com. The elephant in the room that never gets addressed is the shame that accompanies financial failure.

The Second Wave: Financial Trauma

When it follows a catastrophe, the second wave of trauma often supersedes the original event. But financial trauma qualifies as a disaster in its own right. Rarely if ever talked about, the primary emotional wound of catastrophe can be superseded by a new deluge of stress hormones triggered by a state of financial emergency that can dominate your life for years. Personal disasters can include the devastating costs of such events as catastrophic illnesses, divorce, and job loss. A mass disaster inflicts financial damage on families and communities as well as individuals. Although most misfortunes in my life have turned out to be blessings in disguise, the pain of losing everything for which you have worked can do serious damage to your sense of self-worth.

Lynn Robinson, author of *Real Prosperity: Using the Power of Intuition to Create Financial and Spiritual Abundance* says, "Financial trauma is very scary, partly because it's such a taboo subject. If you talk about it, you may feel you have a big L on your forehead for 'loser!'" As an intuitive advisor, she's seen financial anxiety occurring with greater frequency over the past several years. "It's awful to look at your bills and believe that you have no way of paying them. It makes you feel very helpless, anxious, and worried. Fighting for respect when dealing with institutions doesn't help when you're consumed with fear," she says. "But if you can find peace of mind for the day, that's powerful."

In her own life, Lynn has used visualization as a tool when she's been anxious about finances. She imagines a golden bowl or tray in front of her.

She says, "God, I am worried about money and about my husband and my home. I am going to put this worry in this golden bowl and give it up to you. Please bring it back to me filled with answers, peace, and guidance." She imagines receiving it back into her heart.

"You might not get the next $100,000 you need, but the answer will come back in the form of a peaceful feeling. Or you might be guided to an article, a podcast, or a conversation that has just the right phrase to bring you peace or give you an idea to bring more prosperity into your life. Sometimes someone will call and offer to help," she says. "What is important is remembering that we are here on this planet to surrender, have patience, and allow ourselves to love and be loved. Crises help us to learn these things."

"What is important is remembering that we are here on this planet to surrender, have patience, and allow ourselves to love and be loved."

Financial Issues After the Las Vegas Shooting

We don't immediately think of the financial impact of a mass shooting, but after gunman Stephen Paddock killed 58 people and wounded 500 others in Las Vegas on October 1, 2017, those who survived—and the loved ones of those who didn't make it—discovered complicated and costly legal issues. The financial fallout from a shooting can affect the safety and well-being of a victim's children, spouse, and immediate family members.

Only 44 percent of Americans have a will, according to a Gallup poll conducted in May 2016, two weeks after Prince's untimely death on April 21, 2016. The lack of a will, trust, or estate plan puts a legal and financial burden on those family members and friends who are responsible for sorting out someone's affairs upon his or her death.

This and other issues are concerns for Christine Miller, a community outreach director at the Legal Aid Center of Southern Nevada. She told Bloomberg News, "Loved ones of those killed will find themselves navigating complex legal territory when they attempt to settle the affairs of murdered wives, husbands, and children. It will just be a matter of the dust settling."[32]

Miller anticipated that once people started coming out of shock they would need to deal with estate, immigration, and child custody issues in addition to health care paperwork and negotiating family leave with employers. Those who need time off may need legal assistance with debt issues, as well.

Thinking proactively, the State Bar of Nevada offered pro bono legal assistance to shooting victims. A Nevada-based attorney did pro bono work for victims of the Emanuel African Methodist Church massacre in Charleston, South Carolina, where nine worshippers were killed by a white supremacist on June 17, 2015. In addition to forty-five lawyers on staff, Miller's Legal Aid Center of Southern Nevada has more than 1,000 local attorneys who do pro bono work for the Center.

You Could Not Have Known

Since any financial disaster affects your key survival needs, post-traumatic aftershock can resurface long after the initial event. Years after the 2008 recession, several people began sessions for post-traumatic stress flashbacks, hypervigilance, and severe anxiety due to their financial losses at the time.

"Even though everything is solid now, I can't stop worrying about what will happen if there's another recession," a vice president of a bank told me at our first session.

Working with the Five Gifts helped him recognize that these inner resources would help him stay balanced through any future financial storm. The most important gift, to him, was forgiveness.

He says, "When I understood that I was still blaming myself for those financial losses, the gift of forgiveness stopped me from ruminating about past decisions."

Eileen and Denis Kelly have worked with more than 500 clients who were financially traumatized after Hurricane Sandy. Denis is an attorney in Long Beach, New York. He says, "People sit here and say, '. . . and I should have . . .' and I tell them, 'Your sins are completely forgiven. You could not have known. You bear no responsibility for this. Even though I am the lawyer you are coming to for help, I never saw it coming. We had no idea how this was going to play out.'"

Looking at the Numbers

Statistics in the news show the big picture but they fail to illustrate the harm suffered by millions of people in the impact zone. In the three years following a hurricane, states that suffered a direct hit show a 50 percent increase in filings for bankruptcy. During the same period, adjoining states report a 20 percent increase in bankruptcies.[33]

A representative of FEMA explained that due to the population density along the northeastern coast where Hurricane Sandy did the greatest damage, the government agency projected staying in the area for the coming decade. More than one million people, including me, took direct hits.

Hurricane Sandy killed 159 people and caused as much as $75 billion in damages along a thousand-mile length of coastline, according to the National Oceanic and Atmospheric Association (NOAA). More than 650,000 homes, 250,000 vehicles, and 300,000 businesses were flooded. FEMA statistics show that 8.5 million people went without power for a month. For several months after the storm, abandoned vehicles randomly burst into flame whenever salt water leaked into batteries, causing the cars' alarms to go off.

In "Triage in a Trolley," published in *Lifenet*, the journal of the International Critical Incident Stress Foundation, a volunteer EMT with the Long Beach, New York, fire department described the scene:[34]

"As we drove through the streets, we came across a traffic light floating in the street: a traffic light, pieces of the boardwalk, and a sewing machine.

Tons of debris. Cars were all over the street, up on the sidewalk. It was problematic trying to get to the emergency or fire scenes. Contaminated seawater put more than half of the fire department's fleet out of commission for more than a month. Sanitation soon became a major concern."

The financial wreckage from Superstorm Sandy is dwarfed by the long-term damage from Hurricanes Harvey and Katrina. It is too soon to add up the bill for Harvey, which outranks Katrina as the most expensive storm in U.S. history, with initial damage estimates running from $150 to $180 billion.

Not only did Katrina claim 2,000 lives in five states, the storm caused $108 billion in damages. But numbers mask human suffering and the financial hurt endured by flooded communities and businesses.

Here's what an article in the *American Bankruptcy Institute Law Review* published in 2007 said:

"Survivors will have to rebuild their lives and recover from their debilitating losses. However, Hurricane Katrina and Hurricane Rita did not completely wash away all the remnants of their past lives. Mortgages, credit card bills, and other debts still remained. Survivors still had to contend with the costs of escaping the hurricane, as well as credit card bills and new mortgages to replace the items and homes they used to have."[35]

In *Communities and Banking*, Massachusetts Senator Elizabeth Warren writes:

"When there is a series of major disruptions like the 2005 hurricane season, hundreds of thousands of middle-class families may deplete their savings and turn to credit cards to supplement the aid they receive from charities and the government. Additionally, victims of natural disasters often return home to find they have lost substantial assets. Insurance may cover some of the damage but . . . every aspect of a family's financial circumstances is exposed to the effects of a natural disaster."[36]

A Crash Course in Surviving Financial Trauma

The three cycles of loss—control, safety, and freedom—help to explain the emotional impact of financial trauma. When you are unable to generate income or obtain the loans and funding needed for basic living expenses, you lose a sense of control. If you are displaced from your home by a disaster, you might not be able to return until you have raised sufficient funding to rebuild and satisfy current building codes. As a homeowner, you would normally get to choose when, how, and if you are going to replace siding or windows.

In an interview with the *New York Times*, I said that that one million people did not wake up the morning of October 30, 2012, saying, "Let's redecorate our houses."[37]

Once a disaster has damaged your home, your choices must comply with regulations and stipulations from the bank holding your mortgage, your insurance company, and multiple government agencies. It's not uncommon for regulations to change in ways that stall the process. For example, after Hurricane Sandy, residents of several Long Island towns were told they could make repairs without needing costly building permits. Two months later, building permits were suddenly required. For thousands who had already started rebuilding, the added stress of filing permits, paying several thousand dollars in permit fees, and stopping work for several months until the permits were granted pushed people to the breaking point.

At our support group meetings in the Long Beach city hall courtroom, people came to share information, resources, and their frustrations. While there were no immediate solutions, in realizing that losing control over their home situations added yet another layer of trauma to their lives, attendees reported they felt better for having their experiences validated.

As Denis Kelly says, "You don't have control. The bank has got control. You wouldn't have had the money to buy your house if you hadn't given them control. The government has control because you wouldn't even have insurance if it wasn't for the US taxpayer."

As days turn into weeks, then months and years, you lose your sense of safety. Before a disaster, very few of us consider what it's like to struggle for food, clothing, and shelter. We take for granted that clean water will automatically flow from a faucet. We take our faucets for granted, too. When we are cold, we turn up the heat. And when we are hungry, we can open the fridge because we assume our basic survival needs will be met.

Catastrophic events disrupt that expectation. If the disruption is short-term, we soon forget what it was like to stand in line for a bottle of water and a sandwich at the American Red Cross tent.

"I will never forget what it was like to have no clothes, no contact lenses, and trying to find milk for my kids," says Andrea Michaelson, an attorney who lost her home to Hurricane Sandy.

When that disruption continues after the Red Cross and other organizations leave, our sense of safety begins to crumble. In a literal sense, home is shelter. It is supposed to be our place of safety, which originates in the reptilian brain, according to the late Dr. Paul MacLean, who discovered the triune (three-in-one) brain at the National Institutes of Mental Health. Also known as the primal brain, this is our center of automatic patterns, habits, routines, and territory. It does not like sudden change, and when our territory is threatened, the reptilian brain gets agitated. Tempers flare and stress levels go through the roof.

"It can be property damage, zoning, or permits; when it's home, that adds another level of anger to it," says Eileen Kelly, who manages her husband Denis Kelly's law practice in Long Beach. "If it's medical malpractice, if a doctor hurt them or they were in an accident or fell off a ladder, they don't have the same need to protect as they do when it's about home."

Coming Home to an Unstable Environment

Our environment is an extension of home. Whether we live near a forest that is vulnerable to wildfires, in an earthquake zone, or close to the sea, living through a catastrophe sensitizes us to how vulnerable we are to our environment. Fear, anxiety, nightmares, and phobias often develop in response to our perceived loss of safety.

Rebuilding emotional safety while remaining physically present in an environment that once proved destructive and continues to be potentially dangerous is a complex process that takes time—and the second gift of patience.

Remember: There is no predictable timetable and each of us moves through our losses in our own unique way.

Five years after Hurricane Sandy demolished her house, Andrea Michaelson was still fighting her way through a morass of bureaucratic obstacles to obtain the funding she needed to rebuild. Untouched since it was condemned by FEMA after the storm, her house was rotting. Gutters, window frames, siding, and pieces of the roof were peeling away from the hundred-year-old structure. Although five years of wrangling had familiarized her with the process, Andrea was shocked to find that she had regressed.

"When I had to call my insurance carrier, the bank that holds my mortgage and the organization that distributes government grants, someone slammed a door nearby and I jumped out of my skin. The noise hurt my ears," she says. "I tell myself, 'You're an attorney. What's wrong with you?' I do paperwork for a living."

If you have never experienced financial trauma, Andrea's reaction may seem extreme or over the top. But what happened to her could happen to you, or me, or anyone. Understanding that each of us would be as helpless as Andrea, we try instinctively to protect ourselves by shutting down, numbing out, turning off our emotions, or suggesting she is being "too sensitive." It might make us a bit more comfortable to label Andrea's case an anomaly. But given that mass catastrophes affect hundreds of thousands or even millions of lives, I would confidently estimate that at least 50 percent of those who sustained a direct hit would find themselves dealing with these themes years after the event.

"I get a kick out of people who talk like it only happened to them," says lawyer Denis Kelly. "I wonder, 'Didn't you notice that everybody else is going through it?'"

A Tsunami of Shame

Financial crises cut deep into the psyche. The lack of financial stability and the loss of ability to generate sufficient funds to take care of whatever is needed can have a negative impact on our core sense of ourselves as productive, competent human beings. It's not uncommon for people who are worn down after years of struggling to get back on their feet only to doubt their value and question their identity. As feelings of failure build into a tsunami of shame, coping with small tasks like telephone calls or writing checks can become overwhelming.

"I'm frustrated that financially I haven't recovered and I am still in this holding pattern after five years," says Andrea. "I lost the abilities that I once had. I used to live by my datebook but I can't keep one now. There are days I can't look at my phone because I get so overwhelmed I can't deal." She copes by coaching herself to keep going, adding that, "I feel like if I stop, everything is going to fall apart."

Barbara Kaplan, an employee of Merrill Lynch, who escaped from 2 World Financial Center across the street from the World Trade Center on 9/11, has been struggling financially since being laid off from her job there.

"The World Trade Center was my world," she says. "I never recovered professionally." A string of lower-paid jobs ensued. "I was working at the fragrance counter of a department store but I could not focus or remember any details. It was so hard to pay attention that I started breaking down and crying."

After leaving that job, the continual stress took a toll on Barbara's marriage, which ended in divorce in 2007. She moved to an oceanfront apartment, where on the night of October 29, 2012, she witnessed the destruction of everything she owned and watched her car get swept out to sea. Five years later, she says, "The financial trauma is still haunting me. I worry about ending up a bag lady."

The Bag Lady Archetype

Barbara is not alone. Some 49 percent of women are afraid of ending up as bag ladies, and 57 percent report that particular fear keeps them up at night, according to a 2013 study on women, money, and power, conducted by Allianz Life Insurance Company of North America.[38]

Surprisingly, one-third of women who earn more than $200,000 share those fears. The Allianz study surveyed 1,416 women between the ages of twenty-five and seventy-five with incomes of $30,000 or higher. While there is no corresponding study of men's fears about ending up broke and homeless, the third annual Chapman University Survey of American Fears, published in 2016, shows that 39 percent of men and women surveyed have a fear of not having enough money for their future. Nearly 38 percent are afraid of another economic crash. The Chapman University Survey of American Fears questioned 1,511 people about terrorism, crime, death, and government-related concerns. Financial fears ranked third after government corruption and terrorist attacks.[39]

Full Disclosure

The financial fallout after a catastrophic event makes those fears real. Chellie Campbell teaches people how to confront and challenge fears about money. The author of *A Woman's Guide to Financial Success without the Stress: From Worry to Wealthy*, her Financial Stress Reduction program has helped hundreds of people take charge of their emotions, beliefs, and talents so they can rebuild their financial foundations.

Chellie's knowledge is hard-won. She herself filed for bankruptcy in the 1990s after her bookkeeping business failed because her biggest client left. After maxing out her credit cards, she found herself living hand to mouth and unable to pay her mortgage.

"Bankruptcy was the only way out but I was humiliated," she says. "After all, I was teaching financial stress reduction workshops and was president of the National Association of Women Business Owners."

She was too ashamed to tell anyone until six months later, when two students in her financial stress reduction class challenged her by asking, "How would you know about our problems? You've never been through anything like this." In that moment, she says, "I knew I had to tell the truth and explain that I had to file for bankruptcy six months earlier."

That full disclosure set her free.

"As I spoke, I relaxed and started to heal because I admitted it. People came up after the class to thank me," she says, adding that now she teaches from a perspective of having gone through it. "There is always something else you can do. You won't lose your mind and you won't lose your talent. No one can take that away from you."

When speaking to someone who is experiencing financial trauma, Chellie says, "You don't have the skill or the talent to be a homeless person."

Rather than focus on fear, she recommends making a list of things you can do right now to generate income. Ask yourself, "What do you love doing even though you don't get paid for it?" Whether it's looking after children, baking, taking care of pets, painting, or organizing clutter, it's possible to launch a small business on a shoestring budget. Focusing on what you can do, even in small increments, is one of the best antidotes to the sense of helplessness and loss of identity that accompany financial trauma.

"I tell people that they have the ability to create an income no matter what. That is something you cannot lose," she says. "You can figure something out. If you get the heebie jeebies in the middle of the night, get up and read your list of things you can do to make money. It will reinforce that you are going to be fine. Life might not look so fine at the moment, but in time, everything changes."

In *The Wealthy Spirit: Daily Affirmations for Financial Stress Reduction,* Chellie emphasizes the importance of patience, the second gift, which she sees as a strengthening tool for coping with the frustration of waiting for money to come in. Patience allows you to shift attention in a positive way.

"Focus on what you have instead of what you don't have," she says. "It's a gorgeous day. I live in the United States of America. I have freedom. I can go to work. Nothing lasts and this, too, will pass."

Institutional Betrayal: The Third Wave

The term "institutional betrayal" generally refers to cases of sexual assault where the victim gets blamed by the authorities instead of receiving support. Although it is rarely mentioned in the context of post-disaster trauma, survivors in need of assistance are frequently subjected to verbal hostility, blame, and bureaucratic abuse. In this context, institutional betrayal constitutes what I call "the third wave" of traumatization that occurs after the catastrophic event.

"Betrayal trauma occurs when the people or institutions on which a person depends for survival significantly violate that person's trust or well-being."[40]

Sarah Mahoney's experience with institutional betrayal lasted for three years after Hurricane Sandy destroyed her home.

"In Kentucky, it would cost $27,000 to fix this little house," Sarah was told by the insurance adjuster, who showed up soon after the flood. She replied, "Maybe in Kentucky there are no building codes and you can get away with duct tape, but in this part of the world $27,000 will get you a new heating system ($10,000), a new electrical system ($11,000) and some Sheetrock. You won't be able to replace the bathroom, kitchen, or flooring." After months of attempting to negotiate, Sarah filed a lawsuit against the insurance company but it was dismissed because, as the CBS News

Magazine *60 Minutes* reported, her insurance company was among those indicted for filing false engineering reports.

Moving on, she filed an application with New York Rising, a state fund that was administering $33 billion in federal funds allocated to New York State. They "lost" her paperwork six times. After being told in the spring of 2014 that she would finally be getting a check to help pay to lift her house, Sarah was waiting for the check when an engineer from New York Rising called to schedule an inspection of her new construction.

"What new construction?" she asked. "My house has not been touched since Hurricane Sandy."

She called New York Rising to find out what was going on but no one had any record of her having applied. She and her son went to the office, only to be told that her application was not in the system. Understandably frustrated, she raised her voice. That's when an armed security guard positioned himself in front of her, with his hand on his holster.

"Mom, it's not worth getting shot over," her son cautioned, as he pulled her out of the office. I couldn't help but wonder what kind of society we are becoming when a fifty-year-old woman who lost her home to a natural catastrophe has to endure being threatened by a rent-a-cop carrying a gun.

After three years of paying for an unlivable house—mortgage, taxes, insurance, and water/sewer fees—plus their rental apartment, financial and emotional stress took its toll on her marriage. She and her husband of twenty-five years separated. Eventually, she could not afford to keep paying for both residences.

She says, "One day I got a letter from the mortgage company telling me that I had abandoned the property and it was going to auction."

Andrea Michaelson reports similar issues:

"New York Rising lost my paperwork for the rebuilding program no less than four times. When I applied to the buyback program, a bureaucrat with extremely long nails sat there licking her fingers. She put three-quarters of the papers into one pile and said, 'We have to reject these papers because they are not in blue ink.'"

To give her a hand, Andrea's father, a Vietnam veteran who served in the US Navy, brought in a new round of documents. He, too, reported being harassed by a security guard, who threatened to pull his gun on him.

"I thought you were exaggerating," he told his daughter.

To Andrea, her dad's experience validated her own.

"Every time I had to go there I came back emotionally devastated. All I want is information and they treat you like a criminal. You shouldn't have to go through hostile, damaging, disrespectful hazing when you try to claim what is rightfully yours," she says. "My dad is now walking in those shoes. He says, 'I thought you were crazy but something really horrible is happening.'"

DARVO

DARVO refers to how institutional abusers react when challenged about their behavior. A relatively new term, it has been introduced into the conversation about sexual trauma by Jennifer Freyd, who has published landmark research on betrayal trauma theory.

Until recently when women in media and politics began speaking out about sexual predators in high places, when a woman was raped or sexually abused, her efforts to report what happened would be met with DARVO:

Deny: The abuser denies the victim's claim.
Attack: He or she attacks the victim.
Reverse: The abuser reverses
Victim: The victim's role so that the victim is perceived to be
Offender: The offender.

"The perpetrator or offender may Deny the behavior, Attack the individual doing the confronting, and Reverse the roles of Victim and Offender such that the perpetrator assumes the victim role and turns the true victim into an alleged offender."[41]

In a post-disaster environment, DARVO behavior consists of repeated demands for the same paperwork and remarks that amount to character assassination. DARVO means "Harass, Abuse, and Blame the Victim."

One of the most blatant examples of DARVO in action is blaming the island of Puerto Rico for having "poor infrastructure" after the island was devastated by Hurricane Irma.

DARVO: Post-Disaster Edition

Fighting for funds so that you can have a safe roof over your head may not at first seem like a First World issue, but displacement from your home is a survival issue, whether you live in the suburbs of Houston or the mountains of Puerto Rico. It's important not to get lost in comparing tragedies or believing that because someone else has it worse, your loss doesn't count.

Many assume that after a natural disaster, your insurance and the government will come through. But it doesn't take long before you find out that is not how the system works.

"The bank and the insurance company are not your friends," says lawyer Denis Kelly.

After a natural catastrophe, it can take years of fighting for a fair insurance settlement and to receive government assistance to which you are entitled. Some of the games played include the following:

1. Losing your documents multiple times and then accusing you of not having submitted them.
2. Refusing to look for the documents when you produce proof that they were delivered and signed for by someone at that institution.
3. Being accused of "having something suspicious about your income" because you are self-employed.
4. Being accused of lying by individuals who are lying.

These are all strategies to harass the client.

"Not uncommon," says Kelly, adding that "there are several special interests involved here: banks, insurance companies, lawyers, and the real estate industry. We don't realize until we have to deal with it. There are people making lots of money who are geared up and waiting for the next one."

Empathy and Forgiveness

Financial trauma and institutional betrayal cause emotional damage to millions of innocent people, whose only crime is that they suffered a catastrophic event. The primary loss forces them to make survival decisions at a time when they are in a vulnerable state due to acute stress from the event itself. As discussed earlier, acute stress impairs the ability to think clearly, focus, and make effective decisions.

At this critical time, the gifts of empathy and forgiveness can help to restore faith in ourselves. It may take years before we can forgive the perpetrators of DARVO.

"Sometimes it's difficult to identify the bad actor or actors. Why did this happen? Does it happen all the time?" asks Kelly. "Do you forgive a bank or do you forgive the woman on the phone who put you through hell?"

Spending hours on the phone each day absorbing insults and false accusations is debilitating. Since each person must endure that alone, connecting with others who are going through something similar goes a long way towards building hope, even when the outcome looks bleak. The gift of empathy opens us up when the tendency to shut down and turn away from the world is often at its greatest. By asking for support we give someone else the opportunity to be generous in giving empathy, a renewable resource that replenishes itself and grows stronger the more we give. Don't think of it as weakness.

Forgiveness takes time, which brings us back to the second gift—patience. One of the best tools for accessing patience is color breathing, which was first introduced as an emotional first aid technique (See page 63). Breathe in a comforting color and allow it to find its way anywhere in the body where there is tension or discomfort. Exhale the unwanted sensations by breathing out a different color. It takes just a minute for frustration to release, clearing the mind.

In all honesty, it is unlikely that anyone who is fighting DARVO with multiple institutions simultaneously is going to be in a forgiving mood—at least not now. More important when it comes to financial trauma, is learning to forgive ourselves and acknowledging the hurt and shame we feel *without* self-judgment.

How Good Can It Get?

Cynthia Sue Larsen, author of *High Energy Money,* suggests learning how to infuse your relationship with money with positive intentions. Instead of focusing on what is wrong, she recommends using a power question:

"How good can my relationship with money get?"

This one simple question can stop the negative spiral of self-blame and despair so that we can inch our way to a cautious new optimism.

Your current financial position may not be your own fault, but you will have to deal with hostile individuals whose job is to get you to give up and go away. If you can give yourself a twenty-four-hour hiatus once a week and use the time to unwind, you will have more energy for the next round. Be patient with yourself. When you feel overwhelmed, it's because the situation is overwhelming. Give yourself a break.

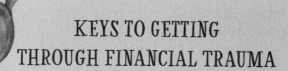

KEYS TO GETTING
THROUGH FINANCIAL TRAUMA

- STORE ALL OFFICIAL RECORDS (passport, birth, marriage and death certificates), financial records, bank accounts, will and living will, cash, and safe deposit keys in a waterproof, fireproof box.

- MAKE A LIST OF DOCUMENTS TO GRAB AND GO IF YOU NEED TO LEAVE IN AN EMERGENCY: Insurance policies for home, car, and business, state-issued identification, including pass-port and birth certificate (if available), bank account records and safe deposit keys, credit and debit cards, USB drive with passwords, and copies of important documents. Be sure to keep all papers in a watertight ziplock bag in your Go-Kit.

- REVIEW YOUR COVERAGE: Schedule time to review your current insurance policies and speak with your insurance brokers to make sure you have adequate coverage and that you understand terms of the policy and deductible amounts for which you are responsible.

- SPEND TIME ORGANIZING YOUR FINANCIAL PAPERS into clearly labeled folders, either on your phone/desktop or paper folders. You will thank yourself later on when you can easily find the papers you need.

- WHETHER OR NOT YOU BELIEVE IN GOD, ANGELS, OR A HIGHER BEING, try Lynn Robinson's Prosperity Prayer. You might not get the phone call informing you that your funds are coming through tomorrow, but if you read this prayer twice a day, you will start noticing a lowering of baseline anxiety about the financial trauma.

Prosperity Prayer

Since 2001, Lynn Robinson's Prosperity Prayer has helped thousands of people in financial crisis. Regardless of your spiritual beliefs or lack thereof, the Prosperity Prayer quiets anxiety about generating money.

Dear God (or Spirit/the Universe/Pachamama),

I surrender my financial affairs and concerns about money to your Divine care and love.

I ask that you remove my worries, anxieties, and fears about money and replace them with faith.

I know and trust that my debts will be paid and money will flow into my life.

I have only to look to nature to see proof of the abundance you provide.

I release all negative thoughts about money and know that prosperity is my true state.

I commit to being grateful for all that I now have in my life.

I learn to manage my finances wisely, seeking help where needed.

And finally, I ask you to help me understand my purpose in life and to act on that purpose with courage and strength. I know that prosperity will come, in part, by doing work I love.

Please help me use my skills and knowledge to be of service in the world.

Thank you, God.
Amen.

9

Soul Vitamins
for the Long Haul

*T*hank you for coming this far with me. It has been a tough read and I appreciate your time and attention. At this point, something has shifted internally. Perhaps you are less embattled or maybe you have grown accustomed to the daily struggle.

It may feel like you are living from the inside out, like your heart has been scraped raw, similar to when you skinned your knee learning to ride a bike. Your knee healed long ago but these soul abrasions may hurt all day. Yet you can function, just as you can with a low-grade fever. You might not be on top of your game, but somehow, things get done.

You probably continue to ruminate on how things were before that day, wishing you could time travel back to twenty-four hours *before* the event, as if time could have stood still for a precious moment. Knowing that you can't intensifies the recognition that your physical, financial, and emotional losses are now more complicated than you realized.

Spiritual PTSD

Working through grief gets exhausting and can lead to spiritual PTSD.

At a seminar on complex traumatic grief given by the New York Mental Health Association two years after the September 11th attacks, we were taught that sudden, unexpected death takes away more than a person, place, or things you loved. Those dreams about the future you were going to spend together were also killed, and just as suddenly. The loss of those dreams needs to be acknowledged, respected, and mourned—simultaneously and independently from the physical losses.

Spiritual PTSD is not a clinical term. Nick Arnett, a first responder who published *Stress Management and Crisis Response,* distinguishes it from acute stress and post-traumatic stress disorder. Symptoms of spiritual PTSD include the following:

- Core sense of emptiness; a void
- Absence of meaning
- Anger, blame, and lack of forgiveness
- Loss of one's beliefs or values
- Cynicism, apathy, and self-doubt
- A feeling that one's life is wasted[41]

Physical symptoms can include feeling like a part of you is missing, emptiness in the abdominal or solar plexus area, chronic nausea, and difficulty focusing.

When Travel Is Made to Be Easy

Living in a state of spiritual PTSD drains energy to the point of depletion. Life becomes so exhausting that you can barely move. Fatigued and demoralized, you exist in a netherworld of soul burnout.

You are like a baby bird that has fallen out of the nest, too weak and fragile to fly back. If you have ever found a baby bird in that state, you probably remember feeding it liquid vitamins through a glass dropper until it regained some strength. Now it's your turn to treat yourself like that baby bird. You need to learn how to feed yourself soul vitamins so that you can regain your energy and the will to live fully.

The eleventh-century Sufi mystic Rumi wrote, "When travel is made to be easy, its spiritual purpose is lost." Humility and patience,

As with severe illness, the process of healing zigzags from bursts of energy to moments of collapse. Patience gives you the grace to slow down and let your soul catch up in its own time and in its own way.

the first two gifts, can empower you to accept that exhaustion is your starting point, with the understanding that you cannot anticipate how long it will take to get your full strength back. As with severe illness, the process of healing zigzags from bursts of energy to moments of collapse. Getting angry because you cannot will yourself to push through it at your old pace will sabotage the pace of healing. Patience gives you the grace to slow down and let your soul catch up in its own time and in its own way. Now you can take a first step to an unknowable future.

Your Healing Intelligence

You have been through quite enough and the prospect of "exploring" probably makes you cringe. But this particular phase of the journey opens the way for you to reclaim and redefine what life means to you. The purpose of a soul wound is to wake you up so that new truths can become apparent. Just as there is no change without loss and no loss without change, it is equally true that healing and wounding reflect an inherent duality in nature. You need to be wounded in order to trust that your ability to heal is programmed into your biological operating system. Your conscious mind does not have to instruct it because your healing intelligence is an app that works perfectly on its own.

Examples of duality—light and dark, or north and south poles—occur all around you. Just as a coin has a head and a tail, the flip side of a soul wound is growth. The fifth gift frees you up to look toward the future instead of viewing your life through the filter of the past.

At this gentle turning point, you begin to understand that in taking away whom or what you love, loss can declutter the soul, making room for new beginnings.

"Self-reflection and self-growth are not something that should be on our bucket list at the end of life," says Alex Pattakos, PhD, coauthor of *Prisoners of Our Thoughts: Viktor Frankl's Principles for Discovering Meaning in Life and Work.*

A Holocaust survivor and author of the classic *Man's Search for Meaning*, Dr. Viktor Frankl believed that having a sense of purpose empowered him to survive four separate concentration camps. After the war, he developed logo therapy, a school of thought that focuses on finding purpose and creating a meaningful future rather than dwelling on events in the past.

"Logo therapy comes from the Greek word *logos*, which means, meaning, but it also means, spirit, so you are basically getting into the core of your human spirit," says Dr. Pattakos, who was mentored by Dr. Frankl. "When you go through crisis, other doors open up. There was a reason for that event to get you to where you are now. It makes you stronger and wiser."

Fear of Change

After a violent or unexpected event, nothing returns to where it was before. Like it or not, we are forced to change. Some of us don't like that very much—so much so that just thinking about it is frightening, although the fear of change is often more painful than the change itself. In less extraordinary times, it's easy to hold on to the illusion that we can control change. Sometimes we can, but there are such forces beyond our control, such as the weather, the economy, and random events. Nothing stays the same, no matter how much we try to cling to the status quo as we remember it. "You can change without growing, but you cannot grow without changing," says Dr. Pattakos. "A lot of people change locations, relationships, and jobs but twenty-five or thirty years later they haven't grown or learned. One of the problems we have is that we don't spend time going inward to gain insight into you as a human being."

A Conversation with Dr. Wayne Dyer

Dr. Wayne Dyer, a father of the New Thought movement and author of more than a dozen *New York Times* bestsellers, once told me that "When you are sitting at your table, so to speak, and you feel so comfortable, that's when God rips off the tablecloth. That's because He has something else for you to do."

When you are sitting at your table, so to speak, and you feel so comfortable, that's when God rips off the tablecloth. That's because He has something else for you to do.

I was interviewing Dr. Dyer for a column about his protégée, Immaculee Ilabagiza, who had survived the Rwandan genocide and gone on to write *Left to Tell: Discovering God in the Rwandan Holocaust.* Our interview took place a day after I had learned that the *New York Times* was closing its regional sections: Long Island, New Jersey, Connecticut, and Westchester. This meant that my column "Long Island at Worship" would die. Losing a monthly column for the *New York Times* was not a disaster but it was a milestone in my journalism career. I enjoyed my dual career in media and psychology; however, I found losing my column to be more upsetting than I would have expected. My colleagues felt much the same way but the decision was outside our control. Looking back, I can appreciate how Dr. Dyer's words that day helped prepare me for bigger unwanted changes down the road.

Katabasis: A Journey to Hell and Back

Stepping into a new way of understanding how life has changed you can be compared to traveling to a new place where some landmarks are familiar, yet the overall landscape is somehow different. In your day-to-day life, you wake up, go through your day, and return to where you started.

But when your perceptions shift, the internal process that helps you sort through and organize your experience changes the way you perceive even day-to-day routines.

As one of my clients describes this stage, "It's like being in a new place but not really."

The difference is that now you are stripping away old beliefs, values, and patterns that are no longer working and replacing them with new models of truth. The process of deep diving into yourself to uncover something you had not realized before is called *katabasis*.

Linda Lappin is the author of *Your Journey to Hell and Back: The Greek Concept of Katabasis Can Provide Analysis and Structure for Creating Strong Narratives*.

"This going down into, or *katabasis* in Greek, entails journeying into the deeps of the earth or into the depths of oneself," she writes. "It is a time of solitude and doubt, mourning and danger, anguish, fear, alienation, often estrangement from what we hold most dear: our sense of who we are."[42]

The journey begins with a wake-up call. Perhaps your old (pre-disaster) model of the world is not helping you navigate real-life situations. It's confusing, but that's a good sign. The conscious mind hates feeling confused, which motivates you to start doing research that goes way beyond Google. Since the goal is to acquire information that will resolve confusion and strengthen you for whatever comes next, don't be surprised when the sources of information come in surprising ways: a synchronistic meeting with someone who shares an insight that clarifies your confusion, or perhaps a weird coincidence, such as finding a book that opens to a

Don't be surprised when the sources of information come in surprising ways: a synchronistic meeting with someone who shares an insight that clarifies your confusion. Or you may have an "Aha!" moment, a flash of insight that suddenly and spontaneously repositions your understanding of the hell you have been through.

page where you find a paragraph that rewires your thinking. Or you may have an "Aha!" moment, a flash of insight that suddenly and spontaneously repositions your understanding of the hell you have been through.

"The first step is probably just becoming more aware of where you are at the moment, where you are in your personal life and in your work life so that you can start to see around you and start to observe and put in perspective where you are, relative to other people: your coworkers, your neighbors, your family, and so forth," says Dr. Pattakos, adding that "It's more important to be aware than to be smart in the traditional sense of the word."

POWER QUESTIONS

You have probably seen the Socratic method in courtroom dramas but you don't have to be a lawyer to use powerful questions to generate new ideas. Dr. Pattakos suggests starting with the last question on the list; however, there is no specific order. You may start with any one on this list or come up with your own.

10 Power Questions for Discovering Meaning

✓ What do I know about myself that I did not know before?

✓ Right now, what can I be learning?

✓ As a result of this situation, how am I going to grow?

✓ Who am I now compared to who I was before the event?

✓ Who do I need, want, and deserve to become?

✓ How has this event changed me—positively and negatively?

✓ What choices can I make to feel better?

✓ Who was I before that event? Who am I now?

✓ How can I help someone else who is having a hard time?

✓ What are the seeds of meaning in this particular situation?

Reframing Crisis

Power questions speak to the creative unconscious, the part of the mind that can synthesize data and ideas into new patterns of understanding. The creative unconscious deep-dives into paradox, seeking new perspectives

to help us find the light in painful

Learning to mind-shift determines whether you live in hell or are living through a crisis that has a beginning, a middle, and an end.

realities. Learning to mind-shift determines whether you live in hell or are living through a crisis that has a beginning, a middle, and an end.

After a disaster, life can become so overwhelming that you want to give up. "But let's not give up hope," says Dr. Pattakos. "If you can't change what you observe with your five senses because those are conditions out of your control, you can shift your own position as the observer. This is not to marginalize or minimize the value or the suffering you might be enduring. If we can get out of our mental prison, so to speak, we increase our likelihood that we might find a solution to our dilemma."

Author Deena Metzger shows us how in her brilliant reframe of sickness:

"A sacred illness is one that educates us and alters us from the inside out, providing experiences and therefore knowledge that we could not possibly achieve any other way."

The same principle can be applied towards the event—or injury, as it is sometimes called—that wounded you.

Empathy and Meaning

Viktor Frankl used to say, "The meaning of life is meaning."

"What that means is that it's a process, a journey of self-discovery," says

Dr. Pattakos. "It's not something

"Meaning can come in the form of moments of joy."

that basically has a destination to it. Meaning can come in the form of moments of joy."

When you find yourself facing a tragic event that is not of your own choosing, try to take a step back and ask yourself, "Where in this situation are the seeds of meaning?" This will show you a different path through the post-disaster landscape, one that will give you more wholeness, integrity, and a sense of purpose. Having learned something by shifting your perspective, you might be surprised to find that the third gift—empathy—naturally moves you to reach out and help other people find their way along *with* you. Whatever the circumstances, there are seeds of meaning in every moment, up to our very last breath.

Whatever the circumstances, there are seeds of meaning in every moment, up to our very last breath.

Soul Vitamins

Soul vitamins are moments when you feel that you are fully alive. You can experience them in survival situations, through vigorous exercise, or by shifting your attention from the outer world of people, activities, and things to your inner world of concepts and ideas—where you can reflect, regroup, and regenerate an optimistic mindset. Maybe the best you can hope for now is "cautiously optimistic," but that state of mind still works to inch you forward.

Just as you would not pressure a baby bird that fell out of its nest, this is not a time to pressure yourself with a major self-improvement program. Nor is it the time to stop smoking, lose weight, get married or divorced, change careers, or move—unless extreme circumstances demand it.

Soul vitamin time can be a few minutes where you consciously give yourself permission to relax fully. Some people like to go on mental vacations by listening to ocean sounds with their eyes closed. Sit in a garden, take a walk, ride a bike, or go for a drive.

Make a List of Positive Futures

You will recognize when your emotional baseline is calmer. Sleep becomes refreshing and insomnia diminishes. You wake up without abdominal spasms due to anxiety. You are able to push any underlying terror to the back of your mind.

Now is an opportune moment to start envisioning a positive future full of multiple potentials.

"I recommend listing ten positive things that could happen," says Dr. Pattakos.

One of his readers, who described himself as essentially negative, asked how could he become a positive thinker by listing ten positive things that could happen.

"I told this man he could go beyond the ten positive things," says Dr. Pattakos. "By doing that, you start to loosen up and see some of the silver lining, even in a catastrophic situation."

Two months later, the same man described how his wife had been diagnosed with cancer. The man said that it was the first time he had been able to apply the list of positive futures to his family situation. In his return email, Dr. Pattakos suggested that the man try to reduce his amount of stress so that he could at least be a better spouse, a father who takes care of the kids while his wife is going to treatment, and so forth, and that he could choose to have hope about his wife's prognosis.

His reader replied, "My wife and I came together more closely. We found out who our true friends and family members and loved ones were that came to our aid. My wife actually has a positive attitude herself, our children have been supportive, and I started to find positive things in my life."

None of this takes away the significance of his wife being diagnosed. To Dr. Pattakos, it was equally significant that this man was not only able to raise his energy level in a more positive way, but he became a little more enlightened about the significance and the miracle of life. He came to truly appreciate his life, his wife's life, his family, and his connections more intimately and authentically than before.

Journaling Tools

Although you might not consider yourself a writer, and, if asked, you might even say that it's not an activity you like, taking a few minutes a day to write down your thoughts and feelings offers another way to nurture yourself with drops of soul vitamins. The act of writing shifts attention from the world around you to the world within. Picking up a pencil or pen opens a circuit

The act of writing shifts attention from the world around you to the world within. Picking up a pencil or pen opens a circuit between the mind, the heart, and the hands.

between the mind, the heart, and the hands. Sitting in a quiet space releases words, images, feelings, sensations, and ideas that help you to retrieve experiences and impressions.

"Often the *hands* will solve a mystery that the intellect has struggled with in vain," wrote Carl Jung in his memoir *Memories, Dreams, Reflections.*

Writing with your hands instead of tapping on a screen is more effective. Something about the kinesthetic elements of watching words form and listening to the subtle sound made by touching pen to paper is more effective in reaching more deeply into the self.

Journaling requires very little: a pad or notebook, pencil or pen, and ten to fifteen minutes when you are not going to be disturbed. Even people who say they hate writing have reported that sitting quietly, pen or pencil in hand, can be comforting even if there isn't much to write that day. It is more important to sit with your pen and paper for five to ten minutes a day, whether or not you actually write.

There is a stage of the creative process called "incubation" in which the unconscious mind explores, aligns, and synthesizes what remains unspoken into a form that can emerge smoothly through the writing process. On days when nothing comes, let it go. Incubation takes time. When you plant seeds or bulbs in the soil, do you get angry at them if they do not bloom right on schedule? Or do you water your garden, watch the weather, and trust that new growth will appear all on its own, in the right time and the right place?

A "News and Goods" Journal

One of the simplest soulful writing activities is keeping a "news and goods" journal. I learned about the "news and goods" process through Harvard Medical School's Institute of Mind-Body Medicine, where I completed clinical training in mind-body medicine with *New York Times*' best-selling author, Dr. Herbert Benson. Since then, I have incorporated "news and goods" with groups dealing with the aftermath of the September 11th terrorist attacks, Hurricane Sandy, and a random shooting. Anyone who tries it for more than a week has reported it is a great way to focus on seeing things in a new light.

To keep a "news and goods" journal, you simply need to find one nice moment every day. Even when you are struggling with physical pain after an incident, flashbacks, anxiety, or nightmares, you will be surprised to find that when you look for it, there is always at least one moment of "niceness" in the course of even a hellish day. For example, someone you didn't know smiled at you, the sun came out, you took a nap, you joined a friend for coffee and enjoyed your time together, your kid drew a funny picture, or your mom cooked dinner.

Paying attention to such moments on a daily basis goes a long way toward relieving stress and anxiety while opening the way for optimism to begin flowing again.

A Couple's Journal

Paul Schweinler, the critical incident stress management team leader who gave us his self-care regimen in Chapter Three, suggests that keeping a couple's journal can relieve tension and reopen communications when partners are shut down. Its purpose is to create a safe way to communicate honestly.

Here are the steps to start and maintain a couple's journal:

1. Choose a notebook.
2. Put it in a safe place agreed upon by both partners.
3. One person writes first: anything he or she wants to get off his/her chest. Feelings. Concerns. Thoughts. Ideas for the future. Anything.
4. Return the notebook to its safe place.
5. Within 24 hours of the notebook's return, the other partner will take it and write.
6. Return the notebook to its safe place.
7. Within 24 hours of the notebook's return, the other partner will take it and write.
8. When it feels right, you will both be more comfortable talking about what you have written.

Celebrate Your Life

If baseball is a game of inches, life is a game of seconds. The short amount of time it takes to answer that phone call or respond to an email can make the difference between life and death.

If baseball is a game of inches, life is a game of seconds. The short amount of time it takes to answer that phone call or respond to an email can make the difference between life and death. Call it coincidence, call it synchronicity—a meaningful coincidence, according to Carl Jung—call it luck or God's will or divine timing, but it takes only a few seconds for the course of destiny to shift in such a way that your life is forever altered.

"Had I caught my usual train, I would have arrived at Windows on the World on top of the World Trade Center before the first plane hit," says Ed Gersh, a divorced investment banker who would have been killed the morning of September 11, 2001, if he hadn't been having sex with his girlfriend.

"It was an unexpected moment of intimacy," he says. "But it saved my life."

Gersh arrived at the World Trade Center concourse shortly after the second plane hit.

"I saw rubble in the street and about two dozen people falling through the air. I might have been one of them had I made it to that seminar," he says.

Gersh's colleague, who was already there, died in the attack.

"We used to joke that I was always early and he was always late," says Gersh. "It just happened that I was fooling around when I should have been on the train. I kept asking, 'Why me?' and I felt guilty. But I would not allow it to break me down."

A refugee from the Soviet Union, Gersh was fifteen when he and his parents came to this country.

"I was always grateful for my family but I was a workaholic, putting in one hundred hours a week," he says. Attributing his strong survival instinct to having grown up in a repressive communist regime, Gersh found himself shaken after witnessing the 9/11 attacks.

"It was a waking moment for me. I starting asking myself, 'Is this what you want?'"

Believing that "something in the universe wants me to do something greater," Gersh made a commitment to celebrate his life.

"September 11th gave me humility and grew my sense of empathy and connection to others," he says. "It gave me patience to cope with my daughter's health issues as well as my own. I realize that my life does not just belong to me. It belongs to those I love and care about. Every day I wake up and appreciate that life is not an entitlement."

Can you look around and find something in your life that deserves celebration, especially now, after all you have been through?

Find Your Music

In *The Roots of Buddhist Psychology*, Jack Kornfield talks about a man who used to play his cello in the main square of Sarajevo. It was the early 1990s, the height of the war in Bosnia.[43,44]

Every afternoon, as the bombs and sniper bullets flew around him, he would stand there playing his favorite pieces. When people told him he was crazy and asked why he chose to put himself in danger, he answered, "Because the world needs music more than anything."

Now is the time to find your music. It can be whatever nurtures your spirit and awakens your heart. Find a way to let it flow so that others can be moved.

Now is the time. We need you.

KEYS FOR THE LONG HAUL

- STOP "SHOULD'ING" YOURSELF. You should not be more humble, patient, empathetic, or forgiving than you are right now. Whatever you are experiencing is natural, understandable, and appropriate—as long as you treat yourself with respect.

- KEEP A "NEWS AND GOODS" JOURNAL. It can be a log you keep on your phone, but please take a few seconds to notice and log one nice thing a day. It may have nothing to do with the traumatic event. It could be a smile, a laugh, or a kiss, given or received. That's enough.

- CREATE A PLAYLIST OF MUSIC THAT RELAXES, SOOTHES, AND INSPIRES. Listen when driving, waiting in line, or running errands so that the music becomes part of your day.

- LAUGH. Whether you are watching a funny movie or your favorite comic, or just hanging out with a funny friend, laughter is the most powerful soul vitamin on the planet. In 2004, "Late Night with David Letterman" invited a group of young adults whose fathers were killed on September 11th to meet with Dave, Paul Shaffer, and Biff Henderson backstage. We presented Dave with "Seasons of Grief," a stunning poster of four trees that looked like the WTC towers in all four seasons. The flames at the top resembled autumn leaves for fall. In winter, the towers were covered in snow. Spring showed new plants sprouting at the buildings' base, and summer represented a fuller, new season of life. The images had been painted by a group of young children at the WTC Family Center the first months after 9/11. Deeply moved by the gift, Dave asked, "What have I done to deserve this?" "You made them laugh," I smiled. "For some, it's the first time since their fathers were murdered."

- ENJOY SOME COMFORT FOOD. This is not a good time to go on a diet, stop smoking, or make major lifestyle changes. Nor do you have to gorge to enjoy the pleasure of your favorite dish. Savoring a cup of hot chocolate or tea, a handful of peanut M&Ms, or whatever makes your tummy smile on a tough day is a wonderful vitamin for the soul.

10

New Strength from Ancient Wisdom

J was wondering what we would eat when the last jar of peanut butter was gone when Kathy stuck her head through the door to let me know her stove was working and offered to heat up a can of soup. "Our stove works, but we don't have any water," she said.

It was the morning after. Time had slowed to a breath-by-breath situation. Life as I'd known it was irretrievably broken, smeared with sludge and feces from our town's sewer system treatment plant, which had broken during the storm surge and contaminated our water supply. The nauseating stench seeped through the walls.

Every tiny movement required a decision. If you drink bottled water, where will you pee? If you move something, how many steps through slime will it take to reach that canister of antibacterial wipes? You can't carry them with you because there is no safe place to put them down.

A few months before the storm, my father and uncle came to me in three separate dreams, warning me that there would be an emergency and I should stock up on fresh, clean water. There were thirteen gallons upstairs and twenty-four bottles of drinking water on the kitchen counter. Since the house was becoming toxic with bacteria, we were going to leave the next day—if I could find someone nearby who would let Bogart and me stay for a couple of nights until I figured out where to go next.

All that was running through my head as I gave Kathy a gallon of water to take across the street to her own damaged home. She could come back if she needed more.

A bone-chilling cold settled in as the October afternoon light started to fade. Soon, it would be dark, and I did not look forward to a second night upstairs in that cramped crawl space.

Ten minutes later, Kathy returned, holding two cups of hot tea. I felt like crying. Her kindness left me feeling cared for and supported. It was the gift of empathy in action. We were in it together. We hugged, and in that moment of having lost everything, we were rich.

The Richest Man in the World

That stays in my mind like a Post-it, reminding me of a photojournalism assignment to shoot pictures of gold panners in the Madre de Dios jungle, a forgotten corner of the Peruvian rainforest. Our government-issued Ford pickup truck had gotten stuck behind a mudslide, which had buried the one-lane road under ten feet of muck. After an uncomfortable, cold night trying to sleep in the truck, the driver and our guide joined a crew of volunteers who were shoveling out. Looking at the mountain of mud and the pace at which the crew was working, the driver guesstimated it would take around five hours before the road was drivable.

For some reason that I don't understand, I had no fear about being alone there and went for a walk in the early morning cloud forest where cloudlets of dew clung to the trees. Pushing away branches and stepping carefully over slick, wet rocks, I entered a clearing where a skinny, bearded man with one tooth was living in a bamboo lean-to, covered with a blue tarp. We stared at each other—two creatures from different worlds. Maybe I was just an exotic animal from another, unfamiliar jungle. We nodded, exchanged "Buenos días," and then he pointed to a large rock next to the fire and motioned for me to sit.

Modeling his half-kneeling position, I watched him carefully pour water from his aluminum pot to a chipped white enamel cup. Foraging around in his lean-to, he retrieved a nearly empty can of powdered milk and measured two large spoonfuls into the cup. Maintaining eye contact, he stirred carefully until the powdered milk had dissolved. Then he gave me his cup and motioned for me to drink.

"Thank you but I cannot take this. It's your breakfast," I said.

He insisted, repeating the motion for drinking, pointing first at the cup, then at me. As I sipped the hot beverage, his weather-beaten face broke into the most radiant smile I had ever seen. This man, who possessed next to nothing, looked like my eating his breakfast was the greatest gift he could receive. I couldn't get over it. His happiness filled the space around the sputtering fire, expanding into the clearing and beyond, to the cloud forest itself. He kept thanking me for taking his breakfast. When I offered him money, he refused.

I had met the most generous and, clearly, the richest man in the world.

Fast-forward several decades to the morning after Sandy. I had no idea what to do next. Neither did anyone around me. Without phone service, there was no way to call for help. But help was already there. That cup of tea affirmed it while simultaneously bringing me back to that morning where I first encountered the gift of humility. Between then and now, I have started to understand the power of humility, which opens the way for us to embrace life as it is—like it or not—without regret for what we don't have. With humility, our sense of entitlement dissolves and we give thanks.

A Different Cultural Filter

In my travels to places where people lived without running water, electricity, phone service, or indoor plumbing, I noticed that despite their difficult circumstances, many of the people I met were able to endure long periods of hardship with relative equanimity. In dusty towns along the foothills of the cordillera, people loved, hated, fought, mourned, and danced on the edges of life and death.

They lived with earthquakes and avalanches, fuel and food shortages, violent strikes, guerrilla activity, poverty, and disease.

There were two key traits that seemed to give them strength and equanimity despite those difficulties: strong bonds with family, friends, and community and a deep respect for nature and their connection to the natural world. Here, you tell time by the sun and the cycles of the moon and the tides and seasons. So, too, after a disaster, your body rises and sleeps in rhythm with the coming and going of the sun, rather than obsessing over digital time. You are now living in rhythm with millions of people all over the globe who are sensitized to the natural cycles of time.

On a bright Tuesday morning in the Andes Mountains, a Quichua Indian mother and her teenage daughter walked patiently through the fields, carrying covered aluminum pots to a section where six men were working. Slowly, they unfolded a large blue cloth and laid it on the ground so everyone could sit. The mother ladled rice, corn, and a thick soup into shallow enamel plates, which the daughter passed out to her father, brothers, and each of the workers. They all sat together in a line, eating lunch under the noonday sun, as they did every day, and as their ancestors had done for hundreds of years before them. They did not have microwaves, but they took time every day to stay connected. In times of trouble, they would navigate crisis together. My friends and I wondered if perhaps they weren't better off than we were.

Indigenous Connections

It has been my privilege to sit with teachers from different spiritual traditions. The indigenous healers, who entrusted me with wisdom handed down from generation to generation by oral tradition, deeply influenced my worldview. Their reverence for the spiritual intelligence of nature and their belief that the physical and spiritual worlds coexist have strengthened me and given me hope in times of acute stress.

Although indigenous peoples make up less than five percent of the world's current population, there are, 5,400 indigenous languages of approximately 7,000 languages spoken according to Tiokasin Ghosthorse, host of "First Voices Radio" who prefers "original peoples" to "indigenous." Despite their differences in culture and language, the original peoples' message has been consistent across the board, transcending geographic boundaries and distances.

In *Stone Age Wisdom: The Healing Principles of Shamanism*, Tom Crockett writes, "When we are out of balance with the unseen world of spirit, energy and life force, we cannot be in balance in the physical and material world."

The indigenous healers I met in both hemispheres consistently reiterated that "You people from the north, your relationship with nature is out of balance." Whether or not you believe in the science of climate change, people who live close to nature believe that in refusing to accept that every one of us has a soul connection to nature, we show disrespect to the spirit of the earth, the sea, and the forest.

"Mother Earth is always giving, even if it's a lesson. She is always giving," says Ghosthorse. "Now that we are running out of food in the fridge

"Mother Earth is always giving, even if it's a lesson. She is always giving,"

and there is no water, we need to invite the indigenous peoples. We are the older brothers and sisters and parents to this land."

In his eyes, "The majority of Americans have never come out of their adolescent state. You see children in grown-up bodies running around reacting to everything. They are still looking for a nurse, for a mother that has more milk."

Our collective anxiety, doubt, guilt, inferiority, and confusion will continue to increase until we address our root spiritual crisis.

"We are stressed and suffer from PTSD, just as Mother Earth suffers from PTSD," he says. "Mother Earth needs to create a good catastrophe to wake us out of our zombie state."

At an interfaith retreat years ago at Auschwitz, Ghosthorse asked a Lakota elder whether the Lakota have a word for "domination." He was told, "If you have language that is in relationship with everything, there is no need to dominate. Therefore, there is no concept, and no word."

A Culture of Interconnection

When a Hopi cultivates plants, he believes he works in harmony with the sun and the rain, the wind, soil, insects, and birds. There is no separation. In the same vein, the Apache language has no "I," only "I am," as in the statement "I am connected to everything."

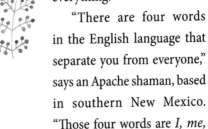

"There are four words in the English language that separate you from everyone," says an Apache shaman based in southern New Mexico. "Those four words are I, me, my, and mine. Try going four days without saying I, me, my, and mine."

"There are four words in the English language that separate you from everyone," says an Apache shaman, based in southern New Mexico. "Those four words are *I, me, my,* and *mine.* Try going four days without saying *I, me, my,* and *mine.* It will change your life."

Taking further the concept of interconnection, Ghosthorse explains that there is no separation between life and death. The Lakota have no word for death since life and death are seamlessly interwoven.

"We think that everyone thinks like us," he says. "But we see the whole. Our bodies are in the soul. The soul is not merely contained within the body. I can talk about the way people were before we got here and how we will live after we live here. It's a whole transition of one life."

Words like "empathy" and "compassion" hold deeper meaning for the original peoples. "We have to relate to that tree, to the air, to these other things that keep us alive as human beings. We relate to them because they have consciousness. They are able to cleanse and are able to produce air," says Ghosthorse. "Once we realize the tree has a relationship to whom we are, we see the tree inside ourselves."

In recognizing that the tree needs water, carbon dioxide, sun and wind, it is no longer so much a thing as it is a being "a tree-ing living being," he says.

The Science of Tree-ing

Since the 1990s, scientists in Vancouver have been studying how trees communicate through their roots. A network of "Mother Trees," made up of the oldest and tallest trees in the forest, form root hubs, which connect to younger, smaller trees around them. The root hubs function like a neural network to send and receive messages about what a specific tree might need to stay alive.

In one study, Dr. Suzanne Simard and her research team from the University of British Columbia found evidence of communication between paper birch and Douglas fir trees using fungi to carry necessary nutrients to each other as needed.

Not only do trees have closer bonds with others of the same botanical family, scientists say they share collective memories about prior emergencies. In Germany, forest ranger Peter Wohlleben came up with similar conclusions, which he published in the *New York Times'* bestseller, *The Hidden Life of Trees*.

Can trees know when one of them needs help? Can they respond with assistance? Do they experience fear? Do they remember?

These are some of the questions Dr. Julia Dordel asked Wohlleben and Simard in her documentary *Intelligent Trees*, available at Amazon Video on Demand.

In catching up with what the original peoples have known for centuries, science is showing us yet again that it is our responsibility as humans to live in balance with the natural world, even if we can do it five minutes at a time.

"Once you understand your relationship with the natural world, you understand compassion."

"Once you understand your relationship with the natural world, you understand compassion. The tree nation, the ant nation, the water nation, we view them as nations and beings as equal with us," says Ghosthorse.

Only when we put other beings in other nations on an equal footing with ourselves can we begin to understand empathy.

"You become the water. You become the tree," he says, adding that this cannot be explained in English because English—"the disconnecting language"—does not have the thought process to communicate with the nations of the natural world.

"Words distract you from really living," he says. "You don't know how to listen."

Spiritual Emergencies

In an indigenous model of the world, any sickness—physical, mental, emotional, or spiritual—is a call for cleansing.

"Sickness . . . is a cleansing process that washes away all that is bad, pitiful, and weak. It floods the individual like a raging river and cleanses it. The sickness becomes a gateway to life," writes Holger Kalweit in her essay, "When Insanity Is a Blessing: The Message of Shamanism."[45]

The term "spiritual emergency" refers to a soul-shattering experience that changes an individual's sense of self and her worldview.

In her essay, "Illness Heals the World," Deena Metzger describes a Navajo healing ceremony that was performed for her husband after he was diagnosed with multiple sclerosis, a debilitating and incurable neurological disease.

"As illness is understood to occur when the spirits, the community, or the natural world have been violated," she writes, "healing consists of reconstituting the world, gathering the community, entering into ceremony, reciting the prayers and telling the myths in perfect order. What has been disrupted is healed through the perfection of the sacred."

In the West African nation of Burkina Faso, collective grief is treated like an illness—a call to cleanse the soul.

In the words of Dagara elder Malidoma Some, "In indigenous Africa, one cannot conceive of a community that does not grieve. In my village, people cry every day. Until grief is restored in the West as the starting place where the modern man and woman might find peace, the culture will continue to abuse and ignore the power of water, and in turn will be fascinated by fire. Grief must be approached as a release of the tension created by separation and disconnection from someone or something that matters."

To the Dagara, as to the Navajo, connecting with others relieves individual suffering because you become connected to something greater than yourself.

In *The World Until Yesterday: What Can We Learn from Traditional Societies?* Jared Diamond writes, "Groups protect themselves by building a network of alliances with other groups, and individuals ally themselves with other individuals."[46]

Indigenous culture offers us a living model of empathy in action. Being part of a community of people who feel safe to share their experiences and feelings releases the burden of isolation so that empathy can flow and be received by every member of the group. Listening mindfully to those around us can give us the courage to speak up about our own loss. Sharing our stories can accelerate the healing process for everyone.

All of Nature Speaks

At some point during most of my conversations with people in the jungle, someone would stop to point at the forest.

"Señora, the trees talk to us."

At first, it struck me as one of those quaint beliefs like if you clap, Tinkerbell won't die. It took a while for me to appreciate their culture of intimate attunement, but one afternoon I became acutely sensitive to the breeze against my skin and the sound of each individual raindrop as it fell. Looking up at the canopy, I sensed the trees were comforting and protective. My hosts explained that I was connecting to Arutam, the Great Force of Life, a spiritual intelligence that communicates through the natural elements: plants, animals, water, fire, rocks, and sky.

It is a belief shared by original peoples around the world.

"Everything is alive. Everything has consciousness," says Ghosthorse. "What you see in creation: The air cares for you. The tree cares for you. They become 'ings.' Airing. Treeing. Caring. That is why we have to learn to care for everything around us. Because everything around us is caring for us."

When my daughter was ten, we went on a safe one-day jungle trip in Costa Rica. She was delighted by butterflies and monkeys playing in the trees.

Sitting on a riverbank before lunch with our boat crew and guide, I mentioned that the people whom I'd met in Ecuador believed that the trees talk. They nodded.

"Do you believe that?" I asked.

They looked at me with pity, as if I was mentally challenged.

"Señora," our guide spoke softly. "All of nature speaks. We just have to listen."

KEYS TO HEAR
HOW NATURE SPEAKS

- WAKE UP WITH THE SUN AND GO TO SLEEP WHEN IT GOES DOWN.

- IF YOU CAN GO OUTDOORS, FIND A SPOT where you can observe birds and native animals, such as squirrels, raccoons, and possums. You will be surprised by what you can pick up by paying attention.

- IF YOU ARE NEAR A STREAM, LAKE, RIVER, OR OCEAN, listen to the sound of water. If you are indoors, open a faucet gently and listen quietly for a few minutes before turning off the tap.

- LIGHT A CANDLE AND SPEND FIVE MINUTES WATCHING THE FLAME. Then spend another five minutes observing a plant (indoors or outdoors) or a tree.

- HANG OUT WITH YOUR FAVORITE ANIMAL COMPANION. Trust your senses. Listen with your heart.

11

Stronger in
the Broken Places

*D*o you ever feel like you're living in a science fiction movie? What narratives do you think of when you read the following headlines?

UNDERGROUND SHELTERS BACK IN VOGUE

CORPSES IN NEW YORK SUBWAYS

WHAT TO DO IF NORTH KOREA DROPS A NUCLEAR BOMB
(Don't hide under your desk!)

CANNIBALS ON THE NEW JERSEY TURNPIKE
(Okay, I made that one up.)

Weird news is not new but the new weirdness can't help but make us feel uncomfortable. Who thought we would be living under a genuine threat of nuclear conflict in our lifetime?

In Chapter Four, I reported with "hindsight humor" about the duck-and-cover drills we held in public school and what now looks like hyper-vigilance after the attacks of September 11, 2001.

With a foreign country threatening to send ballistic missiles with nuclear warheads headed our way, each of us can choose to hide from our own fear or find ways to stay steady—or relatively steady—with whatever comes.

"Only a Matter of Time"

There must be millions of American mothers like me who held our babies in our arms for the first time and never thought we would have a heart-to-heart talk with him or her about the pros and cons of iodine tablets for protection against radiation. Nor have I ever met a mother who pictured her newborn in a gas mask. It's a surreal, macabre image. But in a country like Israel, where the twin realities of terrorism and war are facts of life, a newborn—boy or girl—will become a soldier in the Israeli Defense Forces.

"Israel is a society that lives on its sword. We cannot survive unless we are skillful with it," says Dr. Omri Merose, an orthopedic surgeon in Tel Aviv.

Since its birth as a nation in 1948, the state of Israel has been involved in ten official wars and innumerable acts of armed conflict and encounters with terrorists.

"The next conflict is only a matter of time," Dr. Merose says. "Living with it in real time, all the time, and growing up with it, you have a different mindset. For us, living between conflicts and expecting the next conflict is clear."

It's a pragmatic mindset.

"We focus on what's good and keep optimistic on certain aspects of life," he says. "Because we are used to very intensive reality with a lot of unfortunate events happening all the time, we probably react with less panic."

Nor does he believe it is reasonable to expect people in the United States to think like Israelis. Considering how we Americans panic when our president tweets, I asked him what we will do when something real happens.

"There is no real threat to the existence of the United States of America," he said, "but we live with that threat all the time."

Even though the threat to survival is greater in Israel, the rate of PTSD among Israeli adults is slightly higher than nine percent, compared to eight percent of US adults suffering from PTSD.[47]

A significantly higher percentage of PTSD is reported in the Gaza Strip, where nearly 18 percent of adults surveyed reported lifetime PTSD. Chronic PTSD is prevalent among some 35 percent of Palestinian adolescents living on the West Bank and East Jerusalem.[48]

Living with the awareness that, at any moment, life can be shattered by a suicide bomber comes with a price.

"We are the first ones to know that aggression brings more aggression. Our society experiences fear and anxiety on a very high scale. Many people have PTSD," Dr. Merose says.

Emergency medical treatment after a terrorist attack includes psychological first aid. The surgeon attributes strong family bonds and shared commitment to the nation's survival as strong elements in the Israelis' resilience.

"When some kind of terrorism act happens, we mourn and express our sympathies to the families involved," he says. "On the other hand, we toughen up. We never want to get down to the point where we say, 'That's it. Let's lock the gate and go somewhere else.' People who emigrated out of pure Zionism left Israel during a time when buses were blowing up. They were so threatened and hysterical, so yeah, it's a big issue for us, but it doesn't define us as a people."

Dr. Merose believes the emotional climate is shifting as communication about these issues becomes socially acceptable.

"The importance of sharing and communicating has definitely become much more clear to everyone," he says. "Expressing your emotions is a much more legitimate thing now than in previous generations."

A Shared Memory

Like the Israelis, British people who were young during and just after the Second World War share a collective memory of enduring extreme hardship together. That, too, creates community.

"In my lifetime, people in Europe have a framework of 'life is bloody hard and tough; if we survive, well and good. If we don't, that's just hard luck,'" says Peter Jones, a retired investment banker and Commander of the British Empire.

Although the United States suffered through the Great Depression, he says, "You didn't have the impact of two world wars."

Noting that more than 40 million people were killed in each war and another five million were killed in ethnic fighting as boundaries and borders changed and people tried to grab territory, Mr. Jones says, "There was a long, long period of huge uncertainty, shortness of life, loss of life and injuring and maiming. That tends to color your view of the world."

In the United States, we are living in a long cycle of stability without a cycle of violence that consumed all of Europe. His position on historical realities includes the recognition that "a long cycle of hardship can happen to anyone at any time."

For Liz Turner, a lifelong resident of London, continual bomb threats from the Irish Republican Army seasoned her.

"We had years and years with four, five bomb scares a week. Pretty much, the feeling was 'fuck 'em.' I will not be made to feel intimidated in my city," she says. "One doesn't do things that are unnecessarily dangerous but you can't let these things ruin your life or everything would stop. There is no way you can institute enough security measures when you have millions of people coming into London every day. Of course, the possibility of a terrorist attack was troubling, but you still had to go on the Tube to go to work. You could not call your office to say, 'There was a bomb threat. I'm not coming into work.' That would have made as much sense as staying home because it was raining."

Jacqui Lait, a member of Parliament from 1992 to 2010, served as Shadow Minister of London on July 7, 2005, when 52 were killed and 700 injured after radical Islamic suicide bombers staged four separate attacks in Underground trains and a city bus. In the 1970s, Jacqui and I worked in a London newsroom together and shared a flat.

"The difference between Islamic terrorism and the I.R.A. is that the

I.R.A. always phoned and warned the police," she says. At the time, she and her husband, Peter Jones, lived close to one of the bomb sites.

"We heard it. The glass shook," she says. "We knew exactly what it was but there was nothing we could do except keep clear and let the medical experts get on with it."

She attributes her mindset of endurance to having grown up in the post-war era.

"Even more than after the First World War there were shortages of everything: heat, light, water, food, and clothes.

"You got your head down and got through it. You used ingenuity to solve problems," she says. "When there were insufficient food supplies to make a wedding cake, people got creative and made cardboard shaped cakes, which they decorated. Our grandchildren and the younger generation don't comprehend that level, but they do absorb the ethos of 'absorb the shock and keep going.'"

As she was working in the House of Commons during the suicide bombing attacks of 7/7/05, Ms. Lait was not directly affected.

"The first thing we heard was there had been a catastrophic power failure in the Underground. I don't know whether the House of Commons was isolated for security reasons or whether the authorities shut down all telecommunications, so there was enough space for what they needed to do," she recalls.

There was no cell phone service, just like during the 9/11 terrorist attacks on the World Trade Center. Unable to call her husband, she was able to email him so that he knew she was safe. From her window, she could see hundreds of people walking home across Westminster Bridge.

"There were no buses, no traffic, and no panic," she says.

"If it's got my number on it, it's got my number on it. And the chances of that are fairly low. You are more likely to get knocked down by a bus than blown up by any bomb. If one allows these attacks to affect you, the terrorists have won."

"If it's got my number on it, it's got my number on it. And the chances of that are fairly low. You are more likely to get knocked down by a bus than blown up by any bomb. If one allows these attacks to affect you, the terrorists have won."

London psychologist Dr. Laura Haigh says that anxiety has increased in the wake of the terrorist attack on pop singer Ariana Grande's concert in Manchester on May 22, 2017, when twenty-three people were killed and 250 people were wounded. That was followed by an incident on London Bridge on June 3, when terrorists used a van as a weapon of destruction and then ran into a nearby market, using knives to stab people—bringing a total body count of eight dead and forty-eight wounded. Not quite a month later, a massive fire engulfed the Grenfell Tower, a high-rise apartment building in London, causing more than eighty fatalities.

"When I spoke to the firefighters, they felt so helpless," says Shawn Starbuck, public information officer for the British Fire Brigades Union (FBU). "It was big. They were doing the best job they could with not enough resources. There were people we knew we couldn't get."

Dr. Haigh lost a friend of a friend in Grenfell Tower. Another friend was on London Bridge one month earlier when the van attack occurred.

"It makes you on edge. It makes you think about how easy it would be for someone to bomb the Tube," she says. "Statistically, you are more likely to get run over by a drunk driver or get a nasty illness. Something about the nature of being targeted to be killed by terrorists does something to your sense of safety."

Dr. Haigh draws upon Buddhist literature when counseling people who report anxiety due to an increase in violent news. Recognizing that it is more difficult for someone who lost a loved one in the attack and for anyone who witnessed one, she looks for balance between paradoxically distinctive modalities.

"I use mindfulness and meditation in my practice," she says. "Who are we to be outraged that we suffer things? It's a part of life everywhere."

Dr. Haigh also integrates what she calls Beirut/Tel Aviv mentality.

"You have to go out and do things and act like it's not going to happen," she says. "Go out and live your life."

Finding Freedom

Wolfgang Christoph grew up under a repressive East German regime.

"Although I was a kid, I knew something was inherently wrong. We could not criticize or even joke about people in charge. We could not listen to Western radio stations because if you did you got arrested," he says, recalling the hours spent waiting in line, hoping for a food truck delivery. "If you are the last in line, there is no food for the day. Then at night you have to go to the field in secret to look for vegetables. If you got caught you got arrested. Religion was outlawed and talking about God or philosophy could get you arrested and sent to a 're-education' camp."

Until the time he was ten years old, no physical border existed between East and West Germany but on August 13, 1961, the Berlin Wall was constructed, seemingly overnight.

"We visited my grandmother in West Berlin," Mr. Christoph says, recalling that he always slept over at his best friend's house when he went to his grandmother's. At sunrise on August 14, he woke up to the sight of soldiers, trucks, and construction equipment.

"People were jumping out of fifth-story windows," he says, "getting caught on barbed wire and getting shot. I was in East Berlin and my family was in West Berlin. It was traumatic."

Three weeks later, the ten-year-old jumped into the river that divides East and West Berlin and swam across while soldiers were shooting at him. Fortunately, he was reunited with his family that same day.

In 1977, at the age of twenty-six, Wolfgang Christoph immigrated to the United States and became one of the nation's first inspirational life coaches. He has given hundreds of motivational talks about his experience and recently published his first book *Sohni: The Human Will Against the Forces of Destiny.* Sohni is the nickname given to him by his grandfather.

Escaping to freedom transformed the boy's worldview.

"The point is that we never know what life brings. In an instant life can change. We can have a tsunami, earthquake, drive-by shooting, or slip in the shower and life is never the same," he says. "We have much more to be grateful for than we realize."

As a young adult, Mr. Christoph embarked on a worldwide journey for meaning. He lived with Eskimos, bush people in Ghana, desert tribes in the Sahara, and reindeer herders in the northern tundra. In Japan, he studied to become a Buddhist monk, but instead, he decided to return to southern California to become a life coach.

"When you're living with people in different places, they have the same hardships as we do and feel the same as we do. Yet they value their lives differently. Life has meaning. There is no thinking something else is better."

Acknowledging the positive power of the first gift—*humility*—Mr. Christoph believes equanimity under acute stress conditions comes down to the importance of accepting life instead of wanting things to be different.

"I was looking to find out who I am and to find the meaning of life. When I came back, I realized it was already within me," he said. "Once you realize that, it is an enormous awakening that will never leave you. In that split second, you already discovered your true self. Now you want to give it away to inspire others."

The heart of his message is "to find that spark in someone else and illuminate that to help that person find peace in himself."

He believes this principle is equally valid for anyone whose life has been disrupted by tragedy.

"Part of a catastrophe is looking at your values and expectations," he says. "Because this is not what you thought it would be, it is an opportunity to examine your thinking and ask, 'What wisdom is appearing before my eyes? What can I be learning?'"

In this new reality, we have no idea of what's coming next. We never have, although we believed so. As the pace and strength of disasters increases, so does uncertainty. If nothing else, uncertainty teaches that predictability is an illusion.

Dancing on the edge of uncertainty can be scary, exciting, or both. In any case, it can open your vision.

"When we are not in control, beauty appears," says Mr. Cristoph. In recalling his childhood, he now reflects that "there is beauty in that maybe there won't be a cabbage for me at the end of the day. And there is raw beauty when we focus in that moment because all our plans, goals, and spreadsheets are blown away."

"When we are not in control, beauty appears . . . there is beauty in that maybe there won't be a cabbage for me at the end of the day. And there is raw beauty when we focus in that moment because all our plans, goals, and spreadsheets are blown away."

KEYS TO BECOMING STRONGER IN THE BROKEN PLACES

- ASK YOUR PARENTS, GRANDPARENTS, OR OLDER RELATIVES ABOUT HARDSHIPS THEY WENT THROUGH AS CHILDREN. What did these tough times teach them about life?

- CONNECT WITH A FRIEND, COWORKER, OR RELATIVE WHO IMMIGRATED TO THIS COUNTRY. Find out what their daily life was like and how they coped. What values were they given as children to help them stay strong?

- IF YOU HAVE CHILDREN, SPEAK TO YOUR PARTNER ABOUT HOW TO TALK TO THEM ABOUT LIVING IN UNCERTAIN TIMES. How will you answer their questions about random acts of violence in which children are killed? What can you tell them so that they do not grow up afraid?

- FIND SUPPORT IN YOUR COMMUNITY. Talk to neighbors and community organizations about planning for emergencies. Find out if there is a shelter in your community. Ask your local police and fire departments their advice for sheltering in place during a disaster. Are there items they would recommend for your home and/or go-kit? If you have special medical needs for oxygen or other durable items that run on electricity, register at your local utility, fire department, and police department.

- DON'T LET YOURSELF GET STRANDED. Set up a phone tree, group text, or email chain in advance. In the event of an emergency, you will only need to make one phone call or send one text/email. The recipient will call, text, or email the next person in the chain. Tell those you care about to monitor your social media during a crisis as many people have used Facebook and Twitter to call out for help during disasters. Speak to family members, friends, and neighbors to set up a backup human to human communication chain in case there is no power or cell phone service.

PART FOUR

Renewal

Even the withered branch grows again
And the sunken moon returns.
Wise ones who ponder this
Are not troubled in adversity.

—Anonymous

Welcoming the Five Gifts

*L*ike you, I've been forced to change more times than I would have preferred. But I have come to appreciate what I have learned, even though at the time I haven't always enjoyed those "learning experiences."

This was brought home to me recently at a women's conference in New Jersey where I was the keynote speaker. A Fox News producer threw me a surprising question:

"What's your secret for getting through a disaster?"

I answered instinctively, without thinking.

"There must be another way."

This belief has kept me going— around, over, and through obstacles that would have caused me to give up if I didn't truly believe that there is always another way to approach a problem. Believing that is my default position whenever I'm up against an impasse. Without this mindset, I might not have taken the time needed, which led to my discovering the Five Gifts. Each gift offers another way to discover hope, healing, and strength when disaster strikes. Together, the Five Gifts strengthen our core. Think of them as "Pilates for the soul."

Meltdown

After the water receded, my initial euphoria was short-lived. One week later, a FEMA adjuster told me that my house was "fine" and I needed to rebuild in the same footprint. I felt that it needed to be demolished and replaced with a new, hurricane-safe, raised home. But FEMA insisted that I rebuild, thereby destroying my *Thelma and Louise* fantasy of collecting my insurance settlement and moving to a friend's house in the Midwest, where I would change my identity and start a cash business. (It turns out I lack the requisite *Thelma and Louise* DNA and that I'm really just a compliant, responsible, middle-class citizen.)

In terms of rebuilding, I fared better than most. The insurance settlement came quickly, thanks to my contractor, Sandy Denicker, who submitted the required forms in contractor-ese and negotiated a stronger settlement than I could have done myself. Before they could get started, a water mitigation company I had hired to clear out moldy Sheetrock, tile, and fixtures billed me more than twice the fee they had originally estimated. When I offered to settle, they threatened to put a lien on my house. As scared as I was, I knew that I was only one of about a million people who were going through something similar and hired Denis Kelly for legal protection. Not only did he resolve the lien situation; he secured a lower fee and a written apology from the company.

Simultaneously, I spent hours on the phone every day, trying to get the bank that held my mortgage to release the insurance settlement so that we could pay for supplies, labor, and building permits. Immediately after Sandy, the town had announced that building permits were not needed for repairs, but that changed suddenly. Construction stalled for a couple of months because the building department was swamped with permit applications.

The meltdown came when my insurance agency left a voicemail saying they were cancelling my homeowner's insurance because they received a letter from the bank that held my mortgage, stating that my house had been abandoned. Without homeowner's insurance, the bank would assign me to a high-risk pool, where my premiums would double or triple.

Listening to that message after a long day's work put me over the edge. How could they do that? Nobody I had spoken to had ever heard of anything like this happening, but as I found out, if a home is abandoned for 90 days and you do not inform your insurance company, you can lose your home-owner's insurance in New York State. But my house was *not* abandoned. It was *unlivable*, as I pointed out in the voicemail I left in response.

"My house has no floor, no electricity, no water, no toilet, no kitchen, and no heat. But you know that because your company gave me money to rebuild after Hurricane Sandy," I explained via voicemail.

It resolved the next morning with a voicemail promising not to cancel my insurance because "I checked my file and I see that you are a Hurricane Sandy house."

Wouldn't you think that person would have checked my file *before* deciding to cancel my policy? I couldn't help but wonder what would have happened if that voicemail had gotten lost.

A Forty-Eight-Hour Moratorium

The ongoing conflicts were taking their toll. My baseline state was agitated with surges of hypervigilance. Like my neighbors and those who were attending weekly group meetings in the courtroom, I bounced back and forth between feeling confused and embattled. Sleeping offered no relief because of the dreams that replayed the days' litany of frustrating phone calls. (Years later, those dreams resurfaced after watching hurricane coverage on TV.) After months of non-refreshing sleep, it was getting harder to stay focused and calm.

But that's what I was helping others learn—how to stay focused and calm while fighting for the money they needed to survive. The irony was impossible for me to ignore. It is never easy to live your own advice, but now that it was staring me in the face I had to ask: What would I tell myself if I was my own client?

First up was a forty-eight-hour moratorium on all things related to the disaster: no phone calls, no emails, and no conversations with friends and family. I took a walk along the ocean, went for a massage, took naps, and drank lots of water.

By the second day, I was ready to meditate, but if I stopped thinking about my "To-Do" list, I was sure it would open up a Pandora's box of fear and fury that would obliterate everything else. That level of vulnerability would release fears I needed to put aside in order to survive. On the other hand, I hated that my inner landscape had become a battleground. Like many of the disaster survivors I had counseled over the years, when I closed my eyes, streaming images showed a barren, burned-out terrain that symbolized the state of my inner world.

I started meditating and studying Buddhism in 1987 when I was bedridden and disabled with a chronic fatigue virus, which was probably caused by burnout from overwork during the Iran-Contra hearings. There were no conventional medicines for the disease, but new research into the health benefits of daily meditation looked promising. If I could only sit up for one hour a day, I could use that time productively to meditate. Even if it didn't boost my immune system, at least I was being proactive and felt like I was doing something to improve my health.

It was not easy at first. Working in newsrooms for nearly two decades, I had been so busy in the external world of people, activities, and things that I didn't even know I had an inner world! But two and a half years after I started my daily meditation practice, the word from several doctors was encouraging. My viral symptoms resolved in about half the usual time.

Daily meditation had become as integral to my daily routine as taking a shower. But since the storm, my mind was swimming in chaos soup and it was impossible to settle down. Increasingly frustrated with myself, I spoke with a Buddhist monk.

"That's why we call it practice," she said.

The forty-eight-hour reprieve took the edge off. Breathing to a count of ten floated me into a stillness that felt like home. My intention for the meditation was to "find another way" of paying attention to each crisis without agitation.

Seeing Around the Corner

Carl Jung once described intuition as "the ability to see around the corner," a trait that gets truncated with exposure to trauma. With a foreshortened sense of future, we cannot conceptualize a future that is different from the harsh aftereffects of a traumatic event.

When it comes to tragedy there is no competition, and while I would never compare my situation to Viktor Frankl's in Auschwitz, I took heart from his description of a turning point, when he saw his future self, talking to an audience about life in the camps. That vision of a meaningful future became the core of logo therapy, which he developed after World War II.

At that point, I was too worn out to believe in a different type of future. What if living in crisis was permanent? What if I didn't have a future self? Maybe she was dead—another casualty of the storm.

In my mind's eye, an image emerged. Watching it behind closed eyes reminded me of developing pictures in a darkroom. Immersed in the first bath of chemicals, a white sheet of paper would start to take on lines, shapes, and shades. Similarly, a future version of myself began to develop—standing in the sun and smiling, she looked pretty calm. Finding her there, in my own private mind space, was encouraging. From somewhere beneath awareness, five words floated into frame: *Humility. Patience. Empathy. Forgiveness. Growth.*

I repeated them. Then came a message:

"Write them down. These are the gifts you need for healing. Give them to those who need them."

As a former journalist, I'm always questioning the source. Where were these words coming from? Were they seeds of wisdom that had been incubating in the fertile soil of my unconscious? Or did they come from a spiritual reservoir of healing and creativity?

In the end, it didn't matter. When I said, "humility, patience, empathy, forgiveness, and growth" out loud, the tension released. Now I had a foundation for believing that things would improve.

The words themselves were a gift.

As I relaxed into this new truth, I didn't know how these gifts would impact my life, but I knew they would help me in my work with others who were fighting through similar obstacles. It never occurred to me to question the source. The origin of these gifts—Spirit, angel, or my own inner wisdom—was not as important as their meaning. I had been given a light that I could share with anyone who was struggling through his or her own katabasis.

Being intangible, they cost nothing. They weigh nothing but carry gravitas and hope. They have no monetary value but they are invaluable. We can bring them with us wherever we go or wherever we stay.

There is science behind them. A substantial body of research provides evidence that each of the five traits—humility, patience, empathy, forgiveness, and growth—can produce measurable, positive changes in belief, emotion, and behavior. In addition, these studies further our understanding of how science and spirituality are interconnected.

Some of you have asked if the Five Gifts are connected to the five stages of grief: denial, anger, bargaining, depression, and acceptance. The answer is, "Not directly." The Five Gifts coexist with those five stages of grieving. Those of you who have brought them into your heart after a loss have told me how each of these Five Gifts have helped you get through the worst days of your life.

FIVE MINUTES A DAY
TO THE FIVE GIFTS

At the end of each section, you will find "Five Minutes a Day to . . ."

When you make it a daily habit to practice self-care for five minutes a day, it takes about eight to ten days for your baseline emotional state to calm down. Many people report a 50 percent improvement after ten days of self-care practice.

12

Humility, the First Gift

*I*f you could choose between having a million followers on Twitter or humility, which one would you pick? I thought so.[49]

No one outside a religious order actually *wants* humility. Nor will you find patience, empathy, forgiveness, or growth high up on anyone's gift list for the holidays. These Five Gifts are like those poor animals in the shelter that keep getting passed over.

Humility, patience, empathy, forgiveness, and growth are unwanted because they break us open—again. Seriously, haven't we been through enough?

Here's the good news: We won't break in the same way, with depression and despair. Any one of the Five Gifts will release what we no longer need to be carrying. Speak them to yourself or out loud. Write them on Post-its and place them around your space at eye level so they can keep reminding you that they are yours now, to be used whenever you want.

The Paradox of Unbearable Gifts

Anything that threatens the ego's control over how we see the world can feel threatening, which is why I have come to think of these as "the five unbearable gifts." Some of you get the paradox, while some of you want to know why you should want these gifts if they are so unbearable.

Logically, and under ordinary circumstances, you would *never* be looking for them. But when disaster strikes, these Five Gifts will help you to heal more quickly.

Humility, Revalued as an Atypical Gift

Although it's undervalued and unappreciated in our ego-driven world, humility carries quite a few surprising benefits. In "Humility: A Consistent and Robust Predictor of Generosity," Julie Exline and Peter Hill's research finds that people with humility tend to be generous, grateful, and more authentic in their relationships. It may seem like an unlikely trait for leadership, but humility scores high as a leadership trait. Humble people tend to be more forgiving, too.[50]

In a fame-driven world, humility holds no value until life pulls the proverbial rug out from under our feet.

"Humility is not characteristic of our culture. It is just the opposite," says Dai-en Friedman, senior monk at the Ocean Zendo in Sag Harbor, New York.

Over the past two decades, I have had the privilege of being her student. Our conversation about the Five Gifts has continued off and on for the past few years, and I am deeply grateful for her perspective.

"We become humble when the world shakes us to our roots and we

"We become humble when the world shakes us to our roots and we begin to examine what's important in our life."

begin to examine what's important in our life," she says. "The only choice we have is to resist or work with what's coming up. That, in itself, causes humility."

Humility replaces the "Why me?" app with "Aaah!," the universal sound of release. When we step into the first gift, we stop judging ourselves or giving value to the judgments of others. We stand in awe of forces greater than we can comprehend—natural forces, as well as destructive archetypal forces, such as hatred and rage.

Humility: Antidote to an Epidemic of Violence

Known to spawn in rivers of hatred, intentional disasters have now reached epidemic levels. Our vulnerability to evil is real, and the world itself is in danger. Nobody likes reading that any more than I liked writing it. But as the frequency and intensity of disasters increase, the gift of humility can open the way to accept our vulnerability—as individuals, as communities, and as a species.

The late Nobel laureate Dr. Roger Sperry, who won the Nobel Prize in 1983 for discovering how the left and right brains work, granted me an interview a few years before his death in 1994. He was discouraged because we humans were the first species in the history of evolution who had designed and built the means to make ourselves extinct as a species, for no reason other than we were "smart enough" to figure out how to do it. As world leaders today compete by waving their nuclear penises, I wonder what Dr. Sperry would say. From a big picture perspective, our human arrogance now threatens our own survival on the planet.

Humility, Anyone?

"Conditions are urgent. This is a very historic time with the return of Nazism, anti-Semitism, and hatred for other people who are different. We face the threat of total annihilation of the human race at this time, in a way we have never experienced," says Dai-en, adding that "all situations are teachings. Everything that is happening around us is a teaching on impermanence."

Who among us was not humbled by that teaching on impermanence when two of the world's largest buildings dissolved on September 11, 2001?

Dai-en says, "Impermanence is one of the greatest sufferings in humanity. We hold onto whatever we can hold onto. We build a big warehouse to give ourselves security. But there is no security because of impermanence."

In the face of that, humility gives us inner strength in surprising ways when we step into letting go of what we think *should* happen.

"It Had to Happen to Someone"

Seeing this in action is striking. One of the first stories I wrote for CBS News was a profile of a legless man who wheeled himself around Rochester, New York, on a dolly while singing, laughing, and generally whooping it up. In his former life, it seems that Rocky was a professional gambler whose legs were shot off in a poker game.

When asked by a local reporter how he stayed so cheerful, Rocky said, "After it happened, I was very angry and I kept asking God, 'Why me? Why me?' But then I realized, "Hey, it had to happen to someone. And I guess that turned out to be me."

With newfound self-acceptance, Rocky discovered his purpose. Twice a week, he wheeled himself to the hospital where his legs had been amputated and made his way upstairs to the geriatric wing. There, he taught little old ladies how to play poker.

Rocky's humility makes him an unlikely hero.

The Christmas Tsunami

The Indian Ocean tsunami of December 26, 2004, sent tidal waves into fourteen coastal countries, killing more than a quarter of a million people, injuring half a million, and displacing more than a million and a half, according to the British charity, Oxfam.

Dr. Ronna Kabatznick, a psychologist and practicing Buddhist, was on retreat in Thailand when the tsunami struck. Thailand's famous beaches are popular rest and recreation destinations for tourists around the world, including Israeli soldiers on leave. When news of the tsunami broke world-wide, Israeli families were frantic to know what happened.

As an Orthodox Jew who has practiced Buddhism for decades, Dr. Kabatznick was so moved by the events of 9/11 that she and her husband, the poet Peter Scott Dale, decided to spend two years on retreat with the Dalai Lama in southern India and with two revered forest monks in Thailand. Their trip was wrapping up when she received a phone call from the chief rabbi of Bangkok, pleading for her to help an Israeli forensic team working to identify remains and help distraught families looking for loved ones.

It would not be her first exposure to death. Back in the States, Dr. Kabatznick belonged to a society that prepares Jewish bodies for burial.

"My purpose became quickly clear. I was to be a companion and support to survivors seized by overwhelming loss and what the Buddha described as the inevitable realities of life: sorrow, grief, pain, lamentation, and despair. I would receive their pain with compassion, and provide whatever comfort I could in the midst of this living nightmare."[51]

I first met Dr. Kabatznick in the late 1980s, when she became my PhD dissertation advisor. Although we have become friends, I always look up to her as a mentor, teacher, and spiritual advisor. In *Who By Water: Reflections of a Tsunami Psychologist*, she draws upon decades of Judaic and Buddhist study as a foundation for her experience confronting mass death and chaos in the wake of one of the most destructive natural disasters in recorded history.

She writes, "None of us knows when our time is up. We can take every conceivable precaution, but nothing negates the fact that death is a fact and can come at any time."[52]

Dr. Kabatznick also drew strength from a thousand-year-old prayer called *Un'taneh Tokef.* It is recited on Yom Kippur, the annual Day of Atonement as a "humbling recitation of the various ways we can exit this vale of tears."

Who by fire and who by water? Who by sword and who by beast? Who by hunger and who by thirst? Who by earthquake and who by drowning? Who by strangling and who by stoning . . ."[53]

Those words gave her something to hold onto when she came face-to-face with piles of decomposing corpses.

"Hundreds of body bags were lined up in neat rows on a grassy area of the beach," she writes. "Mourners were standing among them . . . the shock of grief needs both honor and time."[54]

The scene triggered flashbacks to photos of bodies piled high in concentration camps.

"The horror was here, now, hitting me harder and harder. The answer to 'Who by water?' lay at my feet."[55]

After two months working on-site as a tsunami psychologist, Dr. Kabatznick returned home to find that although the tsunami was a major news story that had been broadcast to billions of people around the world, none of her neighbors or friends wanted to hear about her experience. They told her it was "too depressing."

In writing about her disappointment, Dr. Kabatznick notes that this became a part of her tsunami experience.

"We are not agents of our predicament but we are not helpless either," she says. "We can act upon what is within our control by engaging in a wise response to whatever life brings. We can be agents of defeat or agents of transformation."

The first gift—*humility*—reinforced her understanding that we can neither understand nor control the paradoxical tides of life.

"The source of suffering is wanting things to be different than they are. We are all up against the elements of earth, air, wind, and fire," she says. "They control us; we don't control them."

Acknowledging our vulnerability strips away the armor around our hearts. Humbled by our loss, we soften and realize there is so much we will never comprehend.

"Life is a paradox. The ocean of compassion is also a sea of sorrow. What we think is beautiful contains ugly elements and what is ugly has the potential to become beautiful."

Humility and Spirituality

Whether you call it an act of nature or an act of God, any event that ends in violence and death is a disaster of the soul. Your life just hurts.

Needing relief from that inner pain that affects your entire body can bring you to a crossroad you were not expecting.

"We may be like shattered pottery and withered grass, but there is so much more. A connection to the transcendent enables us to live a life of meaning," writes Dr. Kabatznick.[56]

In "Religion/Spirituality and Wellbeing: Implications for Therapy," Dr. David Glenwick found "religiosity, spirituality, and positive religious coping to be positively related to psychosocial adjustment and negatively related to stress and depression."[57]

The instinct to connect with a force greater than yourself is as primal as your need for food, clothing, and shelter. The first gift recognizes and honors this spiritual need. Humility is a cornerstone of faith. We can see that when watching mourners joining hands and praising the Lord outside the church in Sutherland Springs, Texas, where twenty-six people were killed in a mass shooting on November 5, 2017.

Judy Grady lost her husband on September 11, 2001.

"9/11 is a journey that just doesn't end. It's constant," she says. "You're on it whether you like it or not."

Recalling how she needed all her strength not to break down in front of her three sons, she attributes it to her faith. "I wouldn't have gotten through it if I did not have faith. Faith in God, faith in yourself, faith in human nature, faith in Mother Earth that the sun is going to rise again tomorrow whether you are sad or not," she says. "That is what will get you through."

Humility in Action

For Alan Clyne, humility means service to communities in need. As an enlisted man in the US Marines for twenty-eight years, he served on five overseas tours: Desert Storm, Kosovo, Afghanistan, and two tours to Iraq. While stationed in California in 2010, he joined a church mission trip to Honduras. It was a journey that changed his life.

"Sometimes, we think of service as being in the military, but this trip showed me service to your fellow man in a capacity that is more spiritual in nature," he says. "It takes humility, but when you reach out to people and accept them, you are able to connect with God and someone else through God."

When he retired from the marines, he met Ed Thomas, a Vietnam veteran who founded World Mission Builders in the early 1970s. Clyne had a speech all ready until Thomas said, "Your work is done here in the military. Are you ready to go to work for real?"

Clyne remembered how he came back from Honduras feeling fulfilled and with a new sense of purpose. Thomas' question moved him to discard his prepared speech and announce to the group, "I think my life has just changed."

Since retiring in 2016, Clyne has gone on six missions for Thomas' group.

"I have had a huge paradigm shift in terms of service to humanity. You go to a Third World country and you see a lot of different angles and a lot of need," he says. "The humility that people in those parts of the world bring to their lives is something I missed out on. It is something we can all learn from."

The Challenge of Humility

"Humility is a gift you have to use wisely," says Dr. Kabatznick. "It has to be managed through assertiveness, and assertiveness needs to be handled with humility. Finding the balance between humility and right action takes time. They go hand in hand. But please, keep in mind that above all, humility takes a lot of patience."

How do you know when you have received the gift of humility? Your entire being relaxes. The shoulders drop. Your breathing slows and deepens.

You might even find yourself releasing an "Aaah," the universal sound of letting go. It feels like something heavy has somehow drifted away and the air around you becomes lighter.

The Element of Water

Receiving the first gift—*humility*—is as easy as looking at a glass of water.

"The more you speak your truth, the more you build your humility," says Patrician McCarthy, author of *The Face Reader* and *In Your Element: Taoist Psychology—Everything You Want to Know About the Five Element Personalities*. She is also President of the Mien Shiang Institute in Santa Monica. Mien Shiang is the 3,000-year-old art of Chinese face reading, which developed around the same time as acupuncture to help doctors diagnose illness.

Every four years since 2008, I have interviewed Patrician and two other face readers for *HuffPost* about their analyses of the presidential candidates' faces. When she heard about the Five Gifts, Patrician generously offered to share her knowledge about the connection between the gifts and the five elements in Chinese medicine and Taoist psychology.

In Your Element describes how our personalities correspond to the five Chinese elements: water, fire, wood, earth, and metal. The spiritual and psychological aspects of each element also correspond to the Five Gifts. We can connect with each gift by incorporating its respective element into our environment. It may seem eccentric but this creative, indirect approach can instill the qualities of each gift by associating with a respective element's spiritual and psychological strengths.

In Chinese medicine, humility is linked to service and to the element of water.

"To receive *humility* as a gift, add water to your environment and offer your service to others," says McCarthy. It can be as simple as a glass of water set on a table next to a flower or a small bowl of water with a few petals.

If you are recovering from a flood or water damage, the prospect of adding water to your life is going to seem counterintuitive. (In the interest of full disclosure, it took three years before I stopped freaking out whenever I saw water on the floor. Friends and neighbors reported similar reactions. Nothing triggers a flashback to a water disaster like an unexpected puddle on the floor.)

If you are living in the aftermath of a water-based disaster, you can find the First Gift when you focus on flow instead of water. Doodle wavy, curving shapes and patterns. Wear flowing clothes. Get a small aquarium with blue or black fish and observe how they move around the fishbowl without ever getting stuck.

In Chinese medicine, *humility* is linked to service and to the element of water. A Native American elder agrees:

"Water isn't just for drinking or washing. Water has its own spirit. Water is alive," says Wabinoquay Otsoquaykwan, an elder of the Anishaabe Nation. "Water has memory. Water knows how you treat it, water knows you. You should get to know water, too."

Humbl-ing

Humility, patience, empathy, forgiveness, and growth are abstract nouns. They refer to concepts and traits without material substance—for example, love, hate, fear, and courage. Each of the Five Gifts falls into this category. It can be obtained, but not bought; experienced but not weighed. It can be grasped by the mind, but not held in our hand.

When we tweak "humility," as Tiokasin Ghosthouse explained as the Lakota way, we are now "humb-ling" as in "a state of being humble." It's like turning the word inside out so that you can hold it and walk with it at the same time.

FIVE MINUTES A DAY TO HUMILITY

Pick an activity from this list and practice it for five minutes a day for five days.

- WITNESSING: Look up at uncountable stars or the vastness of the horizon where the sky meets the sea. It is instantly humbl-ing. Witness a sunrise, an eclipse, or the rising of the moon over the ocean.

- MEDITATING: Light a candle and place it next to a glass of water. Sit quietly or listen to soothing music.

- COGNITIVE RESTRUCTURING: Choose a statement (or write your own). Write it, over and over, for five minutes a day. These new concepts form a bridge to the First Gift.

I am thankful to be alive.
I have my health, family, friends, and loved ones. What more do I need?
Even though the person I loved most in the world is gone and I feel like giving up, I am doing my best to get through the day.
My home is gone, but I am still here.

- MODELING: Think of someone who represents *humility*. Pay attention to her posture, breathing, and hand gestures. Notice her facial movements when she speaks. Is she animated or subdued? Visualize that person as a hologram, facing you from across the room. Imagine you can step into the hologram. Pay attention to subtle shifts in how you stand, move, and speak. (This is an exercise that uses NLP (neurolinguistic programming) to integrate resources, i.e., the First Gift.)

- ASKING: "Ask and you shall receive." (Matthew 7:7–8)

13

Patience, The Second Gift

No one ever wrote, "Dear Santa, Forget the iPad. Bring me *patience*." Patience is the gift you need when you realize that Dr. Phil can't solve your problems by the next commercial. It's the gift you need when processing what happened to you turns out to be a slower process than you expected.

The first gift—*humility*—helps you to accept what has happened. Patience helps you tolerate the pain that comes from asking such questions as, "Why am I still crying after so many years?" or "Why is this shit *still* happening to me?" or "When will it stop hurting?"

If humility helps you accept events outside your control, patience makes it easier to endure not knowing how long your pain will continue.

"Grief is not a short-term experience. If you don't accept grief as part of the cycle of life, you are going to be impatient," says Dr. Joseph Schippa, a clinical psychologist who has worked with children after 9/11 and the Sandy Hook massacre. "You might not like that you started to cry in the middle of the department store, but instead of being angry with yourself, *patience* helps you accept that it happened, and it's okay to feel that way."

"Grief is not a short-term experience. If you don't accept grief as part of the cycle of life, you are going to be impatient."

Even if you are not okay about breaking down in public, the second gift will help you to go easier on yourself if it happens again.

"It's important to be patient with yourself and other people when they don't know what you are going through," Dr. Schippa says. "It also helps you to make peace with the event that devastated you."

When you need more time than you thought you would need to make sense of what happened, patience is the gift that delivers.

Serenity Now!

Patience is not an all-purpose gift. It's contextual. When you call 911, you don't want a laid-back crew arriving an hour late. When survival is at stake, a little impatience can go a long way.

For more than forty years, Leslie McTyre has driven ambulances and supply trucks for the United Nations and other relief organizations in such hot spots as Rwanda, Sudan, Somalia, and Kosovo. In life-and-death situations where time is of the essence, he believes that "You have to pretend to be impatient, to be in a hurry, but every syllable needs to be carefully thought out." Appearing too calm just before, during, or right after a disaster can unsettle teammates.

"You need patience before and during disasters, but if you show yourself to be laid back, you get hell from those around you," says McTyre, who sometimes has to act hurried, rushed, and impatient to convey a sense of urgency about his assignment. "There is no real rush to madness when you've already done the planning and calculations."

Wouldn't you rather have an iPad? I would.[58] That's because despite years of meditation, I remain an impatient soul who comes from a long line of easily frustrated, impatient people. Patience was neither practiced nor valued in my family, where parents and grandparents said, "Be patient" when they meant "No, you cannot have this or go there . . ." With so little exposure, I neither knew nor did I recognize the value of patience.

When I changed careers, leaving the addictive drama and rapid pace of TV newsrooms, I was surprised how challenging it was for me to learn to sit patiently and focus 100 percent of my attention to listening mindfully. During my first group meditation, not only could I not stop squirming, I could not focus at all. My mind replayed the *Seinfeld* episode where George's father screams "Serenity Now!"

Laughing out loud would have gotten me thrown out of the zendo. On the other hand, maybe I needed to see how impatient I really was.

I'm still a work in progress and can't help thinking that my writing this chapter on patience makes as much sense as Taylor Swift singing about relationships that end happily ever after.

As I finish each chapter, I pause for a quick check of my own emotional barometer. Of course, writing about what happened to someone who survived a shooting cannot be compared to having had to live through that. Nor can writing about it be compared to the front-line work done by first responders. Yet each narrative affects me deeply and often lasts longer than I expect. I search for the patience—still elusive—to take time to think about how the stories in each chapter are relevant for you.

The Two-Second Limit

Studies on patience show that people who have fast internet connections lose patience within two seconds when downloading a video that "takes too long." If the video did not load within ten seconds, 40 percent of those participants gave up. In contrast, participants who had slower connection speeds reported higher levels of patience. This research is especially interesting because it studied the responses of millions of people.[59]

Researchers point to these and other studies as evidence that our dependence on technology raises the bar for expecting quick results. Does exposure to technology make us more impatient? A number of studies point in that direction.

An Aborigine Model of Patience

Perhaps we can learn a few things about patience from the bush mechanics of Australia, where their customary patience has become legendary. An anthropologist who has lived with these indigenous people explains:

"They are not in a hurry. If something breaks down, it breaks down for a reason that you might not understand."

Instead of becoming impatient with being stranded in the outback as you or I might be inclined to become, aborigines will hunt for berries or lizards to eat while they hang out together until the problem is fixed.

As a passenger in trucks, Jeeps, and buses that have broken down in forgotten corners of the planet, I was given many opportunities to observe patience in action. My favorite breakdown was a crank-operated bus that stopped along the shoreline of Lake Titicaca. At 15,000 feet above sea level, Titicaca is the world's highest navigable lake. Watching the driver, his assistant, and an assortment of local workers trying to crank the engine back to life reminded me of Charlie Chaplin movies. Watching them working so hard to start this retro engine filled me with humility and patience, although at the time I was distracted by a Bolivian woman who was exchanging pesos on the bus for black market rates.

A few months later, traveling in a motorized dugout canoe along a skinny, no-name river in the jungle, I got to face off with my impatience yet again when we ran out of fuel and had to stay in a rubber farmer's bamboo hut until gasoline could be found. It took a few more hours to procure a live chicken and prepare it for dinner. For someone whose experience with chicken was limited to the Perdue section of her local supermarket, this, too, was a remarkable teaching on the gift of patience.

While those experiences made a strong impression, it was much easier for me to model patience in the wild. Put me in a deli line, and in less than five minutes, I can be a world-class fidgeter.

As George Harrison is reported to have said, "Anyone can meditate on a mountain with the Maharishi. The trick is to do it on Broadway."

It Takes Time

It took Dr. Ronna Kabatznick nine years to metabolize the horror of her tsunami experience.

"Healing from being a tsunami psychologist took about nine years actually, until I really worked it out through writing my book," she says. "The process would have moved faster with support but people were too threatened. But I'm a better and wiser person because of this."

Frank Smyth agrees. The founder and executive director of the Global Journalist Security Community and a senior advisor for journalists' security at the Committee to Protect Journalists, Smyth was reporting on the Gulf War in 1991 when, according to his website, he was imprisoned for eighteen days. It took him about seven years to recognize how severe the problem was, and then it took another seven years to address it in a forthright way with mind-body techniques, such as acupuncture and yoga.

"Some pain is going to take some time," he says. "You have to give yourself patience to learn, to heal, and to grow. It's very hard."

When Diana, Princess of Wales, died in a tragic car accident on August 31, 1997, her son, Prince William, was fifteen years old and his brother, Harry, just twelve. On the twentieth anniversary of her death, they spoke publically about their loss for the first time.

In the HBO original documentary *Diana Our Mother: Her Life and Legacy,* William compares her death to an earthquake that runs through a house.

"Your mind is completely split. It took me quite a while for it to actually sink in," he says. "Losing someone close to you is utterly devastating. It spins you out. You don't know what you're doing, what's going on."

Although keeping busy for the first year helped William to cushion the shock, it took *five to seven years* before he could begin to rebuild his life.

Harry, who says he has cried only twice since his mother's death, used to wonder how those who never knew her could show their emotions so openly. He says he himself was emotionally shut down.

"Being so small, it's very difficult to understand, to communicate your feelings," he says. "There's still a lot of grief to be let out."

During his decade of military service, he programmed himself not to think about her because it would bring up a lot of hurt and would not bring her back, which would have only saddened him more.

"I dug my head in the sand until it became white noise and then went through a long time sorting myself out."

Patience in Action

While serving in Afghanistan and Iraq, US Marine Corps veteran Alan Clyne observed that in both countries, the enemy was patient.

"They are patient cultures," he says, adding that "patience and calm are essential qualities of leadership."

Clyne never considered himself patient.

"Like everyone else, I wanted instant results. If you weren't living on the edge you were taking up space," he says.

But a tour in Iraq gave him a new perspective and deeper appreciation for patience as an expression of mutual respect. Returning from a combat tour in Iraq in 2004, Clyne's men gave him a plaque that said, "Thanks for bringing us all home."

"We worked so hard, trained so hard, and we were patient with each other. Throughout that six-month period, we had guys get hurt but I didn't lose anyone," he says.

Clyne believes that modeling a patient, calm leadership style earned his men's trust.

"We brought everyone home," he says. "They had a lot of patience with me because they didn't understand why I wanted to train them the way I did. That's why that patience thing is mutually supportive."

Recognizing patience is as important as practicing it.

"It does pay dividends to practice it and to realize how patient our environment is with us. We think the environment owes us something or it's collapsing around us so we are walking on eggshells," he says, adding that "more people need to learn from how indigenous people live with their environment."

The Pace of Nature

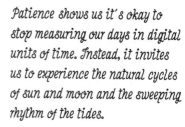

Patience shows us it's okay to stop measuring our days in digital units of time. Instead, it invites us to experience the natural cycles of sun and moon and the sweeping rhythm of the tides. In the days following a disaster, especially when there is no electricity, our bodies naturally adapt to the earth's diurnal and nocturnal rhythms. Years later, when they look back, survivors often talk somewhat wistfully about what it was like to wake up with the sun and go to sleep soon after sunset when quiet fell upon the night.

As Ralph Waldo Emerson said, "Adopt the pace of nature. Her secret is patience."

Living without electricity, water, and basic services is a crash course in patience. Every step gets thought out. How long will it take to walk to the distribution center to pick up water and bring it back? How long will it take to boil water on the small propane camping stove? Will you wash dishes tonight or wait until you have more dishes, so as not to waste water?

You begin to tell time by the light and shadow of the sun's passing and by your body's messages to eat, eliminate, and sleep. You start saying things like "It must be noon. My stomach is growling," or "It's around 4 PM. I always get sleepy around that time," or "Let's meet before the sun goes down." Through many generations of the B.I. era (Before Internet), the seasons were our calendar, and people used common expressions, such as "After the salmon spawn," "When the robins return," and "Before it snows."

Nature tells time by engaging all our senses, especially the sense of smell, which seems to store emotional memories on an olfactory palette: burning leaves in autumn; pine wreaths at the holidays; the first flowers of spring, and the smell of earth damp from a summer rain.

"A seed of prosperity is often hidden in the hulk of misfortune," tweets Scott E. McLeod, a doctor of pharmacology, who writes the blog "Dr. Scott Health." He reminds us that we cannot see the seeds' potential until they emerge after a long winter. We cannot see under the psyche's surface where our spiritual seeds incubate and germinate until they are ready to come up, into the light. They do it in their own time and their own way. We don't yell at them for being slow. Nobody can force them to grow faster. The same holds true for healing.

Patience gives us the right to say, "It's gonna take time. And that's all right."

The Element of Fire

In Chinese medicine, the element of fire corresponds to patience. That may seem counterintuitive because most of us think of fire as an element that ignites and inflames. Words like "fiery" and "passionate" connote quick surges of energy in contrast to the slowing down energy of patience.

Patrician McCarthy views patience through a different lens.

"Fire can teach patience to someone who learns by getting 'burned,'" she says. "When someone learns that lesson, they become the most patient of people."

Bringing fire into our environment can introduce us to patience (a quiet flame), and we can do that in several ways:

Wear something sparkly.
Fill your home with red flowering plants and red flowers, preferably
    with spiky petals.
Listen from your heart.

Talk to someone with whom you disagree.

Pay attention without judging his or her opinions. (This one is tough but it pays off.)

Light candles and place them around your home and outdoor space.

Sit quietly in front of a lit candle. Notice how the flame burns in its own time.

FIVE MINUTES A DAY
TO PATIENCE

Choose one statement and practice writing it for five minutes a day. Do this for five days.

(Secret key to this practice: It usually takes less than a minute to feel impatient. This may seem counterintuitive but OMG! Impatience is a good sign. Sometimes, the fastest way to the second gift is by facing our own impatience.)

Life hurts now. I don't know about tomorrow.

This too shall pass. I don't know when.

It won't be forever.

This pain is not what I want.

Let go and let God.

It is what it is. And that's okay for now.

I don't know how long this will last.

Tomorrow is a new day.

14

Empathy, the Third Gift

When everything around us is crashing and burning, the gift of empathy revives our faith in human nature. This is what carries us through the heat of chaos in a tide swell of collective goodwill right after a disaster. It's what saves us from the emotional riptide that drags us through currents of horror, helplessness, fear, and desperation. Minutes after an explosive event, individuals we never knew step up and give of themselves in that extraordinary moment when a "regular day" becomes transformed by a split-second decision.

So compelling is the gift of empathy in action that we can't help watching the ones who leap from relative safety into an unscripted theater of life and death. Coverage of the hurricane trifecta in the summer of 2017 brought us face-to-face with people escaping death by water and wind because of the kindness of strangers who rushed in to help at significant risk to themselves. Not only do these unknown heroes inspire us; they bring positive distraction from the wear and tear of daily life.

Because it is a "feel good" gift, empathy builds its own momentum. It's natural to want more of that feeling.

His Holiness the Dalai Lama describes how it works: "The more we care for the happiness of others, the greater is our own sense of well-being."

The uplift we get from empathy is immediate, available, and effective for overriding emotional states such as depression, irritability, and anxiety. It functions as a stand-alone gift, the *only* one among the five that any of us is likely to want.

In *Tribe: On Homecoming and Belonging,* Sebastian Junger cites a 1961 study by the National Opinion Research Center in Chicago, which explored the question, "Why do large-scale disasters produce such mentally healthy conditions?"[60]

Researchers hurried to scenes of disasters to interview a total of 9,000 survivors, family members of victims, and other members of the community about how they were adjusting to life after the critical incident. The authors concluded that "modern society has gravely disrupted the social bonds that have always characterized the human experience. Disasters . . . create a 'community of sufferers' that allows individuals to experience an immensely reassuring connection to others."[61]

That "reassuring connection" comes through the third gift, *empathy.*

A study of mental health soon after the Belfast riots of 1969 and 1970 and published in *The Journal of Psychosomatic Research* suggested that "people will feel better psychologically if they have more involvement with their community."[62]

It is not surprising that a study published in the *Journal of Experimental Social Psychology* in 2013 found that one effective way to increase empathy for oneself is to show empathy to others.[63]

Empathy or Compassion

"It's not about how other people handle their pain and your own struggle with pain. When you learn to empathize with others, you learn to heal yourself," says journalists' security expert Frank Smyth. "Empathy brings a grace that comes from understanding yourself."

Although empathy is essential for compassion, the two are not interchangeable.

"Empathetic means you are separate. Compassionate means you are that person," says the monk Dai-en Friedman.

Humanitarian worker Leslie McTyre finds it challenging to balance empathy and compassion. "Empathy is the gift of experiencing oneness with humanity," he says. "In relieving pain for one, we are relieving pain for all."

In order to do the grueling, demanding work of delivering medical supplies into war zones, he has learned how to empathize without feeling completely paralyzed by other people's pain.

"I'm pretty tough, except for children and women. When I see them suffering, it breaks down my shell of protection," he says, adding that it motivates him to work ten times as hard. "When the people I work with can see tears in my eyes, they say, 'Leslie, don't do that now.'"

Empathy in Action

McTyre received a heartbreaking lesson in the difference between empathy and compassion while he was working on a government project to reduce infant mortality in Bolivia. His assignment: to learn why female babies and young girls were dying at a rate four times greater than male babies and boys. One of the first women he interviewed was a mother who had just buried her baby girl because they could not afford to feed all their children. They had decided it was more important to feed the sons, and both parents let their baby daughter starve to death.

"She broke down and I broke down right with her," says McTyre. "Then I went out and raised hell."

Energized by concern and motivated for results, McTyre persuaded his boss to aggressively push for and obtain a grant from the United Nations Children's Fund (UNICEF) to provide security when distributing food to mothers and babies in need.

But nothing prepared him for the bloody year of Rwanda's 1994 civil war.

"By God's hand I was the first white man to enter Rwanda during the genocide," he says, adding that he doesn't remember many details because he worked for days without food, water, or rest. An emergency ambulance driver, McTyre transported wounded children to the only working hospital in the capital city, Kigali.

"I was about ten miles out, and all of a sudden, I knew we were getting close to Kigali because I could smell death," he says. "You became part of the bittersweet smell. It's a weird kind of communion. I was a weird white man ready to go in and help. After they realized I had no hidden agenda, they loved me for it."

One night, when his housekeeper needed a ride home, McTyre parked close to her street, which was blocked by rubble. As she picked her way through construction debris, he noticed people emerging from the rubble to follow her. Curious, he joined the back of the crowd.

"By the time I got to her, she was standing on the biggest pile of rubble in the entire community, and she was directing the reconstruction of the community at about two in the morning. She had men doing the physical work. She was directing women to take care of the children and put them to bed," he says.

He watched her give her entire salary to people to buy food for everyone.

"She was directing the spirit and survival of the community. I looked up at her and thought, 'This is what it's all about. This is how they survive.'"

Assigned to retrieve corpses from the streets and set up mass graves, he remembers, "While I was working there, we were bonded together. There was no black or white, no he or she; it was masses of humanity bonding together first for survival and then retrieving those who were close to the jaws of death."

But when he discovered a swamp in south central Rwanda where the killers had dumped 40,000 people, McTyre's life depended on the empathy of people whom he had never met before.

"They had been mauled by violence. I knew I would never see them again," he says. "It was like living in quicksand. I was a grain of sand in the universe."

Standing on the edge of the swamp, he announced, "We have to pull these bodies out and put them in body bags and identify them with the help of family members in this community."

Everybody took a step back and stared. McTyre figured they were thinking, "The white man has talked the great talk and now he has to walk the great walk." Holding his breath, McTyre stepped into the ooze.

Inspired by what he discovered in Rwanda and later in Liberia during the Ebola epidemic of 2014, McTyre believes that traumatic memories have to be released.

"You need to tell and retell your stories and learn to listen to each other," he says. "We can't get better by ourselves. We are wounded together and we need each other for healing."

Like the indigenous healers I met, McTyre believes that we, in the industrialized world, can learn about community and empathy from other cultures.

"The African people understand the concept of expanded love more easily than most Westerners. Continental identity is more developed in Africa than in other continents. It is easier for them to understand humanity's struggle for survival. Half of them live in the world of magic and intuition. We have gotten lost in this logic thing."

Empathy for Survival

I was sitting with Margie Miller at a recent memorial for those killed in the September 11, 2001, attacks on the World Trade Center when I noticed a woman sitting nearby who looked familiar. I recalled that her two older children sometimes came on baseball outings with my WTC teen group.

Ros Thackurdeen's sister-in-law, Goumatie Thackurdeen, was killed when the second plane hit the Twin Towers. Goumatie worked at Fiduciary Trust, on the 97th floor of Tower Two. When the first plane struck, she joined a group going downstairs, but by the time they reached the 78th floor they received word that Tower Two had not been struck and it was safe to go back upstairs. She called her mother to say everything was okay and was returning to her office when the second plane hit.

"Life has not been easy. It feels like we live on a cycle. When 9/11 comes around, you think about that day," says Ros. "The pain is still very raw. You do what you have to do every day. You live with it. You wait for it to explode every year. It feels like my body knows the date. It's time stamped in my cells."

Eleven years later, Ros' younger son, Ravi, was killed in a remote section of Costa Rica where he was on a premedical study abroad program. After playing soccer on the beach, he went into the water to cool off and was swept out to sea. He struggled for forty minutes but nobody came. Ravi Thackurdeen was nineteen when his mother brought his ashes home.

His parents, Ros and Raj, never got an incident report. They say that the university that organized the study abroad program refused to release it to them. Neither did their son's four-year college.

"The loss did us in. My husband and I both suffer from depression and my other son was in depression for a long time," she says.

Her daughter dropped out of medical school due to post-traumatic stress disorder and depression. She left home and was living in a homeless shelter but her family no longer hears from her.

"They say time heals but I can tell you it doesn't," says Ros. "A piece of your heart is ripped out and there's no getting better from it. Technically, I would like to stay in bed and not get up. But empathy is the only thing that gets me up."

After Ravi's death, she started to research other cases of students who died while studying abroad. Shocked to learn that there are no regulations requiring universities to fully inform students and their families about the dangers and risks at an overseas site, in 2016, she teamed up with Elizabeth Brenner, another grieving mother whose son died while studying abroad. Elizabeth's son, Thomas, fell to his death from a cliff in India, where he and his fellow students were hiking at nightfall. His body was never found.

Ros and Elizabeth founded Protect Students Abroad (*www.protect*

studentsabroad.org), whose goal is fatality prevention for students studying overseas.

"The world has become quite a different place since September 11th. As Americans, we are walking targets," says Ros. "We need to educate our students in how to travel. They need information in their back pocket."

Ros keeps a growing database of more than 3,000 families whose children lost their lives studying in foreign countries.

"When your kid dies overseas, you are left alone. Sometimes the child's body doesn't return home for months and there is no investigation," she says. "There's a sense of community because the parents know what you are going through, too. We help each other and it makes it a little bit easier.

For parents who are coping with the shock of a child's death, *Protect StudentsAbroad.org* offers practical advice from the heart. Here are some of their members' recommendations:

- "Human beings are capable of absorbing great loss. What we will not tolerate is loss of meaning.

" Human beings are capable of absorbing great loss. What we will not tolerate is loss of meaning."

- Keep paper and pen ready at all times. Write down everything, including dates and times, names, and who said what.
- All questions are valid. All feelings are valid, too. Immediately after phone contacts and meetings, make sure to review your notes to add in questions, uncertainties, and hunches.
- It will take a long time to process what has happened to your child, and these first notes—horrible as they are—will become your ally. They will be the keepers of your earliest impressions, and your future self will understand them in a way that gradually makes sense."

Among the community of families she serves, Ros is aware that very few people get answers but some get clarity.

"Getting answers can help you deal with what you have to deal with," she says.

In the meantime, she is committed to putting one foot in front of the other, reaching out in a personal way to other grieving parents.

"The gift we need to rebuild our support systems is empathy," she says. "We must create new institutions founded on empathy because we need them for our survival."

Empathy and Evolution

Dr. Jonas Salk, inventor of the first polio vaccine, believed that empathy is essential for our survival as a species. In his book, *Anatomy of Reality: Merging of Intuition and Reason*, he wrote that for our species to continue to evolve successfully, "the evolution of the human mind . . . depends upon the evolution of intuition and reason."

Recent neuroscientific research suggests that intuitive intelligence may be more complex than was previously understood but, traditionally, intuition is considered a right-brain intelligence while reason originates in the left brain. Dr. Salk's call for integrating left- and right-brain thinking has never been as important as it is now.

We need to become a species that is conscious and respectful of our interconnectivity; thus, the third gift will get us through these troubling times together.

The Three C's: Contagious Connectivity & Community

After the first few months following a crisis, when friends and family start drifting away or perhaps become more remote, possibly shaming you for "not being over it already," empathy becomes critically important. In times of hardship, it's the gift that promises and delivers *The Three C's: Contagious Connectivity & Community.*

The warm, good feelings generated by empathetic choices are contagious. Empathy equals connection in action and is integral and necessary for community resilience. According to government studies, empathy gets expressed in behaviors concerned with other people's needs.

According to the US Department of Health and Human Services Public Health Emergency website, "A resilient community is socially connected and has accessible health systems that are able to withstand disaster and foster community recovery. The community can take collective action after an adverse event because it has developed resources that reduce the impact of major disturbances and help protect people's health. Resilient communities promote individual and community physical, behavioral, and social health to strengthen their communities for daily, as well as extreme, challenges. Building social connectedness can be an important emergency preparedness action."[64]

Researchers from Johns Hopkins Bloomberg School of Public Health and the University of Delaware Disaster Research Center have been studying emergent collective behavior in a disaster.

"We think about community resilience like an ecosystem. The same is true for a community," writes the lead researcher Jon Links. Emergent collective behavior grounded in empathy brings together "a group of everyday people . . . to aid the formal emergency response." They are developing a quantifiable model called the COPEWELL project (Composite of Post-Event Well-Being) to help predict how well a community will bounce back after a disaster.[65,66]

Trending #Empathy

Seven months after Superstorm Sandy, when piles of moldy debris higher than the rooflines still lined the streets of our Long Beach neighborhoods, Moore, Oklahoma, was destroyed by a tornado. Twenty-five people, including seven children, were killed and 377 people were injured. Property damage was estimated at $2 billion.

The sight of families having lost everything touched many of my neighbors, including people who attended the weekly group meetings in the courthouse. The path to empathy runs through the heart, and ours opened instantly when we saw the devastation in Oklahoma.

Sandy sensitized us to the hurt and suffering of tornado survivors. Not only did the City of Long Beach respond with a call for donations of essentials, such as toilet paper and cleaning supplies, a few groups of neighbors took up their own collections.

Long Beach City Manager Jack Schnirman told the *Long Beach Patch*, "Here in Long Beach we know the devastation a storm can bring, and we know how critical it was for so many agencies and kind people from across the country to come to our aid, and that's why we are again paying it forward."

The #Empathy trend continues to build.

Recently, Long Beach residents opened hearts and wallets to help new survivors rebuild after events like Hurricanes Harvey, Irma, and Maria. In response to Harvey, Long Beach first responders collected donations from all around the island. One local family set up a GoFundMe page to raise $5,000 for a rental trailer and a driver to bring the donations to Houston. Within a few hours, they had raised the money they needed.

Empathy and the Starfish

As he took his morning walk along a beach, a scientist came to a stretch of sand between two jetties covered in starfish. Hundreds, possibly a few thousand starfish had been coughed up by the high tide. Now, they lay dying in the sun.

But there, in the middle of all the starfish, a young boy was picking them up, one at a time, and gently tossing each one back into the sea.

"What are you doing?" the scientist asked.

"I'm saving the starfish. They're dying," said the boy.

"That's nice," said the scientist. "But as you can see, there are thousands of starfish. Surely you don't think what you're doing can make a difference?"

Smiling, the boy picked up another starfish, and as he was preparing to return it to its home, he answered, "To this one, it does."

Catastrophic events can be so overwhelming that the desire to step back and say, "That's too much for me," is natural and understandable. That makes it exceptional when someone steps in with a similar intention, as the young boy did with the starfish.

If anyone deserves a Starfish award for stepping up for the forgotten, it would be Sue Hecht. Sue had recently moved to her mother's home in Island Park, the town facing Long Beach on the north side of the Reynolds Channel/Intracoastal Waterway. Two months prior, she had undergone spinal surgery and was on disability leave when Hurricane Sandy destroyed everything she owned.

Depressed, angry, and broke, Sue teamed up with a group of women in Rockaway, Queens, to organize free flea markets. Held in open parking lots, the flea markets gave people recovering from Sandy a place to pick up cartons of water, canned goods, bathroom products, first aid, and household supplies. The local fire departments donated cases of drinking water and Meals Ready to Eat (MREs). CVS and Walgreens donated travel-size shampoos, talcum powder, and toothpaste. People brought in kitchen implements, cooking ware, pots, pans, and cutlery.

"Sandy gave me sustainable empathy," says Sue. "It's more wired into my personality than it was five years ago." Looking at her Facebook posts before the storm showed her that her interests were "going out with my friends and what kinds of shoes people were buying."

The Oklahoma tornadoes were a turning point for her. Even though she was still unable to work due to complications from spinal surgery, Sue organized donations from medical supply houses. Her empathy was contagious. Our support group chipped in to help pay storage fees for the commodes, wheelchairs, walkers, nebulizers, oxygen concentrators, and baby formula.

After a few false starts, Sue rented a truck and found someone to help her drive the supplies to a church in Moore, Oklahoma, which served as a distribution hub for the tornado survivors.

"If I was able to do something for other people, it made me feel a little bit better," says Sue. "Today, I am no longer consumed with myself like a twenty-year-old. I am more connected to what's happening in the world, not just with what's happening in my life."

Look Out for Starfish

When you are walking through your day, look for a "starfish" situation where something as simple as making eye contact or saying hello can show

The more you give, the more empathy you receive.

another person she matters. Empathy is a renewable resource. You may be surprised to find that the more you give, the more empathy you receive.

The Element of Metal

The Chinese element associated with empathy is metal. At first, that made no sense to me. Metal is rigid; empathy requires flexibility. The mind cannot hold onto two apparently contradictory concepts at the same time, and the resulting confusion produces cognitive dissonance. Facing into contradictions with logic always lands me in the lost terrain of analysis paralysis. While meditating on the contradiction, a strong and flexible gold chain came into my mind's eye.

Empathy as metal, metal as empathy.

Bringing empathy home can be as simple as wearing beautiful jewelry and white or neutral beige clothes. The element of metal can be a catalyst for connecting with others by allowing your grief to show and permitting them to express their empathy. This interconnection is reflected in the symbol of a metal chain.

Rx: Empathy

When a patient declared her plans to commit suicide, her doctor, the late Milton Erickson, came up with a prescription that saved her life. When he asked about her hobbies, she mentioned her love of growing violets in her home greenhouse. He suggested that the woman give violets to her neighbors for special events, such as weddings, births, or even someone's death. If she still felt suicidal after a month, he wanted her to come back. But he never heard from her again.

More than two decades later, an obituary in the local paper caught his eye: "The Violet Lady" had died at the age of eighty-three. It was his former patient. She had filled the prescription and spent the rest of her life giving away what she loved. In return, she was loved for the empathy she expressed through her violets. (Unbeknownst to her, violets are traditionally associated with the gift of humility.)

If you are curious about what it can be like to look, sound, and feel empathetic, try Dr. Erickson's prescription: *Give away what you love. The more you give, the more you receive.*

FIVE MINUTES A DAY
TO EMPATHY

Choose one activity and practice five minutes a day for five days.

- ASKING: "What do *YOU* need?" is the magic key that unlocks the third gift.

- EXTENDING: "Do unto others as you would have others do unto you." Practice the Golden Rule and empathy will flow.

- REACHING OUT: Think of someone you know who is having a tough time. Reach out by email, text, or voice to let him or her know you are sending good thoughts.

- OFFERING: Offer empathy with this simple prayer and it will come back to you:

    "May you be happy. May you be healthy. May you be safe. May you live with ease."[67]

- EMPATH-ING: You may not feel like it, but when you open up to someone who truly cares for you, the third gift is strengthened by the exchange of empathy. Don't leave home without it.

15

Forgiveness, The Fourth Gift

When it comes to recovering emotionally from a violent event, forgiveness is the elephant in the room. We know we "should" forgive, but many of us cannot, or simply do not, want to go there, even though years later, our hurt and anger have not eased. We justify those feelings in a misguided belief that they preserve

Forgiveness is the elephant in the room.

loving memories or keep us strong. However, when we see our situation through a *forgiving* lens, it softens the pain by releasing at least some of the anger that we have been carrying around since the traumatic event.

Relax. There is no rule that says you must forgive or that you will be punished if you do not. Nor does it mean, "forgive and forget." That's for fairy tales.

"All situations are basically teachings. Not everybody is ready," says Buddhist monk Daie-en Friedman.

If forgiveness does not feel right for you, or you are simply not open to it, that's your choice. If the idea of forgiveness makes you uncomfortable, you are under no obligation to read this chapter.

The Five Gifts are available to you but accepting all of them, or perhaps one or two, is completely up to you. You have free will and the right to choose whatever you need from these offerings:

Humility. Patience. Empathy. Forgiveness. Growth. Although each gift serves as a booster for the next one, you don't have to take them in sequence or all at once. Or at all. They are *gifts*, not *regulations!*

> *Humility. Patience. Empathy.*
> *Forgiveness. Growth.*
> *Although each gift serves as a booster*
> *for the next one, you don't have to take them*
> *in sequence or all at once. Or at all.*
> *They are gifts, not regulations!*

A Gospel of Forgiveness

Alan Clyne takes exception to that idea.

"I do believe that forgiveness is a requirement for peace and healing," he says. "For a Christian like myself, Christ's death made forgiveness possible for everyone. This, for me, gives hope."

According to Clyne, "The word 'forgiveness' is mentioned in the New International Bible (NIV) exactly 14 times—once in the Old Testament and 13 times in the New Testament. Forgiveness, as a concept, is mentioned more frequently. For example, the word 'forgive' appears 42 times in the Old Testament and 33 times in the New Testament. The word 'forgiven' appears 17 times in the Old Testament and 28 times in the New Testament. And the word 'forgiving' appears six times in the Old Testament and once in the New. As for self-forgiveness, we do punish ourselves if we cannot forgive or be forgiven here on earth, and God only knows how much I need to be forgiven. Thank God I am."

Empathy and Forgiveness

Though interrelated, the third and fourth gifts are not interchangeable. You can receive the gift of empathy without forgiveness, but you cannot forgive without some degree of empathy for the perpetrator, and, ultimately, for yourself.

"Forgiveness is a gateway," says journalists' security expert Frank Smyth. "It requires humility and patience to develop the empathy where you understand forgiveness on a core level, not just conceptually. It's very hard to forgive yourself, but it's essential."

Healing after Genocide

Soon after his arrival in Rwanda, Leslie McTyre was put in charge of burying more than a million victims of genocide.

"My boss told me that I should get started and he would get the financing," he says. "Many communities were empty because people did not want to return to hometowns where three-quarters of the population were dead."

McTyre organized teams to go to the main villages where between forty and fifty-thousand people were in mass graves.

"We had these incredible burial ceremonies of thirty, forty, fifty-thousand people at one time," he says, "and Rwandan television broadcast the ceremonies. In my bad French I said, 'Those of you who are still guilty and running around, you have to repent and come into the communities and offer to help undo the harm you have done. Those who are victims and who have survived death threats, you have to forgive. You have to forgive if you saw anything that upset you or if someone in your family died.'"

His formula for forgiving was simple.

"If you saw it, remember it in detail and take it into your heart. And in your heart you say the word 'love' to the person who did the bad thing. And from your heart you send love to the person who did the bad thing, and you say consciously and sincerely in your heart, 'I forgive you' three times."

McTyre cautioned that it might take time for forgiveness to take hold.

"You are not going to feel like you have forgiven them right away, but eventually it will sink into your brain, and your brain will make you realize you have forgiven them."

Choosing Forgiveness

After her husband, Orlando, and his aide Ronni Moffett were killed by a car bomb on the streets of Washington, DC, in 1976, Isabel Morel Letelier struggled for years with post-traumatic stress disorder. Her friends and family became afraid that associating with her made them a potential target, and many turned away or simply refused to get in a car with her. (During my visits with Isabel after Orlando's death, it never occurred to me that riding in a car with her could be dangerous.)

As if losing him was not harsh enough, the Letelier family was punished by a social stigma that attaches to anyone who has gone through a catastrophic event. This layer of trauma is like pouring salt into the trauma wound. Isabel's four sons were ostracized when friends were forbidden to visit them because their friends' parents were afraid that associating with the Letelier boys could be dangerous.[68]

Over the next decade, Isabel channeled her grief into empathy. In El Salvador, Nicaragua, and Honduras, she worked with a priest to help women who had lost loved ones to political violence.

"I was not focused on my pain, my loss," she says. "There were so many who had terrible losses that it helped me overcome the lack of Orlando."

In 1988, twelve years after the car bomb claimed the life of her husband and his research associate, Ronni Moffett, Armando Fernandez Larios was convicted of the charge of accessory to murder.

An agent of the Chilean secret police, Fernandez Larios was responsible for surveillance on Orlando Letelier. It was Larios who informed the lead assassin about Letelier's daily route from his home to the office and back.

On the stand, Fernandez Larios professed not to speak English, but the judge refused to believe him.

"You were here in this country because your father was an attaché to an embassy here and you went to primary school in this country," Isabel recalls hearing the judge say in court. "I am going to charge you in English and you have to answer in English."

In court, the attorney for Fernandez Larios produced a letter from his client, expressing his sorrow for the pain he had caused the Letelier family. Remorse notwithstanding, Fernandez Larios confessed in English and pleaded guilty. Having informed on his Chilean bosses, he worked out a deal to avoid jail time by living and working in the United States. Fernandez Larios' plea deal included a non-extradition clause protecting him from being returned to Chile to face criminal charges.

After the trial, the defendant's lawyer caught up with Isabel and Orlando's sister, Fabiola, a respected human rights lawyer in Chile. Ronni Moffett's father and several colleagues from the Institute of Policy Studies, where Orlando, and later Isabel, worked, stopped to listen.

"Mrs. Letelier, I have a question. My client wants to know if you will ever forgive him," Fernandez Larios' lawyer asked her.

Recognizing the question as a profound test of her belief in God and her Roman Catholic faith, Isabel responded, "Sir, I am a Catholic. I know you are not but we have a sacrament called penance."

Isabel told him that if you are genuinely sorry for your sin and confess your sin in order to accept the punishment, the Catholic religion believes that God forgives you.

Speaking to Fernandez Larios through his attorney, she said, "You wrote a letter and confessed your sin and accepted your punishment and said that you repented," she told Fernandez's lawyer. "I forgive your client with my personal pardon, but I am not pardoning him for my children or for the Moffetts."

According to Isabel, Ronni Moffett's father took offense.

"It is not possible; I am a Jew, and I think that an eye for an eye. There is one thing worse than sinning and that is to cry 'I am sorry.' We don't forgive."

Isabel's sister-in-law was shocked.

"I cannot believe what you have just done," Fabiola told Isabel.

Their anger had no effect on her.

"It was like I had a huge building on my shoulders, and all of a sudden, I was totally light. The feeling of forgiving him was so wonderful, so positive that I felt enriched myself. I have done the most selfish thing of my life, forgiving Fernandez Larios," Isabel said. "He is a criminal. I cannot forgive him for all the other things he has done in his life. But from that day on, I am ready to forgive anybody that asks for forgiveness."

That's not an easy task, even when you practice every day.

Isabel says, "Loving your family, friends, and your children is natural.

"Loving your family, friends, and your children is natural. The tough thing is to love people who don't love you."

The tough thing is to love people who don't love you."

After the initial euphoria dies down, finding a way to stay in a forgiving state takes some practice.

"I have been saying, 'I forgive you, I forgive all of you' in my heart. You have done terrible things, but it is not my role in this life to hate you," Isabel says.

When a friend recently sent her an email signed, "No forgiving, no forgetting," Isabel tried to convince her that forgiving is the most selfish thing she can do for herself.

"*Odio* rots the soul," she says. (*Odio* means hatred in Spanish.)

Two Types of Forgiveness

Researchers have identified two types of forgiveness: decisional and emotional.

"Emotional forgiveness is the replacement of negative unforgiving emotions with positive other-oriented emotions," wrote the authors who published their findings in the August 30, 2007 issue of the *Journal of Behavioral Medicine*.[69]

They defined decisional forgiveness as a "behavioral intention to resist an unforgiving stance and to respond differently towards a transgressor."

One of the most effective ways to become more forgiving is to make a decision to model forgiving behavior. In "Hypertension Reduction through Forgiveness Training," two groups of subjects with hypertension were studied for eight weeks. One group underwent an eight-week course of forgiveness training. The control group that did not receive forgiveness training continued to show symptoms of hypertension, while the group that attended the forgiveness training showed significantly lower blood pressure than the control group.[70]

The lead researcher on the hypertension study was Dr. Fred Luskin, Director of the Stanford Forgiveness Project and author of *Forgive for Good*. Dr. Luskin's forgiveness research has taken him to Sierra Leone, where one dozen people whose families were murdered in that country's civil war found healing in forgiveness training. Soon after apartheid was abolished, he worked with a group of South Africans who were horrified by apartheid.[71]

"They needed to forgive themselves and their country so that they could be useful," he says.

Because forgiveness was a necessary step for making a helpful contribution to their society, participants in Luskin's program made conscious decisions to forgive.

Whether emotional or decisional, forgiveness can be good for your health.

"The act of forgiveness can result in less anxiety and depression, better health outcomes, increased coping with stress, and increased closeness to God and others," writes E.L. Worthington, a pioneer on the frontier of forgiveness research, who edited the 1999 classic *Dimensions of Forgiveness: Psychological Research and Theological Perspectives*.[72]

Seven years later, his conclusions gained additional validation after a study of emotionally abused women showed that those who received forgiveness training instead of anger validation and assertiveness training "showed significantly greater improvement in trait anxiety, PTSD, self-esteem, amount of forgiveness, environmental mastery, and finding meaning in suffering."[73]

Not Pass-Fail

The path to forgiveness may be blocked by old hurt, anger, and a fierce desire to protect yourself in the future by remembering how badly you were hurt in the past.

"Almost everybody has unhealed pain that limits us to a certain degree," says Dr. Luskin. "Forgiveness takes us out of a place of self-pity or rage. It says, 'You have a choice.' You can clean out the wound and be open to what comes next."

You might be thinking that if you forgive, you will forget the powerful lessons of your painful experience. But any wound, physical or emotional, cannot heal if you keep touching it. "Some people like to nurse grudges and enjoy a sense of righteousness. Long-term resentment blocks access to the healing intelligence," says Dr. Luskin. "Forgiveness is a blessing to ourselves and those at whom we are angry."

Like the other four gifts, forgiveness is not a "thing" you can measure, weigh, or buy. It's a state of mind and heart, which you can activate by switching the term from forgiveness to *forgiving*. When you step into what it is like to be forgiving, you immediately feel it begin to flow. Believing that forgiveness is an on-off switch that produces an all-or-nothing response makes receiving the fourth gift more difficult.

The Forgiveness Spectrum

Instead of seeing forgiveness as an on-off switch, try imagining it as a dial or a spectrum. When I think of someone whom I have a hard time forgiving, I might be at 20 percent. Tomorrow, it could be 80 percent or perhaps 5 percent. The spectrum model offers flexibility in forgiving, which in turn makes the fourth gift easily accessible when we cannot forgive the other by 100 percent.

When it comes to forgiving, many of us find that we go back and forth, forgiving a little more one day and then not forgiving a few days later. It's like recovering from the flu: up and down, back and forth, not quite there yet, until "Wow! I feel better." That doesn't mean we will never feel hurt or angry when thinking about it. With the second gift of *patience,* we can get there in our own time and our own way.

Liberating the Soul

The power of forgiveness to heal societies and communities as well as individuals has been demonstrated in many parts of the world. Two of the most powerful examples that can be found are the nations of South Africa and Rwanda.

"Forgiveness is the way we mend tears in the social fabric. It is the way we stop our human community from unraveling,"

"Forgiveness is the way we mend tears in the social fabric. It is the way we stop our human community from unraveling,"

writes South African Archbishop Desmond Tutu and his daughter, the Rev. Mpho Tutu, in *The Book of Forgiving: The Fourfold Path to Healing Ourselves and Our World.* One of the world's spiritual leaders, Archbishop Tutu won the Nobel Peace Prize in 1984 and has since been awarded numerous international peace awards.

An outspoken critic of apartheid, Tutu was threatened with jail for saying, "We refuse to be treated as the doormat for the government to wipe its jackboots on."

Instituted in 1948, apartheid was a series of government policies to segregate whites from nonwhites. Political dissent of any kind was against the regime's draconian regulations.

I got to witness the cruelty of apartheid firsthand when, in 1983, I led a human rights mission to South Africa and Zimbabwe for the Committee to

Protect Journalists. In the black township of Soweto, we met with families of black journalists who were imprisoned for reporting the truth and the government ministers responsible for the regulations that led to their being jailed.

Apartheid ended in 1990, after opposition leader Nelson Mandela was released from prison by then President Frederik Willem de Klerk. Nelson Mandela shares the 1993 Nobel Peace Prize with de Klerk, as their award says, "for their work for the peaceful termination of the apartheid regime, and for laying the foundation for a new democratic South Africa."

As South Africa's first black president, Mandela appointed Tutu to chair the Truth and Reconciliation Commission, a program designed to heal racial wounds by inviting all injured parties to dialogue in a safe, structured setting. Tutu's work on the Truth and Reconciliation Commission convinced him that everyone is capable of healing.

The 2009 movie *Invictus*, starring Morgan Freeman as Nelson Mandela, tells the story of how Mandela used the national sport of rugby to help South Africa recover from the trauma of apartheid. For many years, the all-white Springboks rugby team had been a symbol of white supremacy and their long-sleeved, green and ruby shirts symbolized white oppression to millions of nonwhite South Africans. When Mandela wore a Springboks shirt to the 1995 World Cup Final, he became a walking symbol of post-racial equality.

In awarding the World Cup trophy to the team's captain, Francois Pienaar (played by Matt Damon in the movie), Mandela signaled the rest of the world that South Africa was now united.

The new foundation for South African society was built on a platform of forgiving and reconciliation, which Mandela himself embodied. Not only did he have lunch with the state prosecutor who had demanded the death penalty during Mandela's trial for anti-apartheid activities, the new president invited prison guards to his inauguration and to a dinner celebrating the twentieth anniversary of his release from jail. He strongly believed that "forgiveness liberates the soul. It removes fear. That is why it is such a powerful lesson."

Forgiving the Ocean

As with any work in progress, forgiving does not happen in a straight line.

For Paula Crevoshay, the experience of nearly losing her partner, Martin Bell, created her own personal tsunami of rage toward the sea. They were swept up in the ocean-borne disaster that killed more than a quarter of a million people on December 26, 2004.

Standing on the beach near Khao Lak, Thailand that morning, Bell noticed a "racing white line that kept extending itself in dash after dash, as if it were playing an endless game of leap frog with itself."

About fifteen minutes later, the hotel staff politely told everyone to get back. After packing a few belongings, Bell was flabbergasted to see about half a mile of empty sand where all the water had receded.

"That represented a hell of a lot of water, and all of that water had to come right back where it had come from, and *fast*," Bell writes in his essay "Tsunami."[74]

As he started running to safety, he noticed a man standing on the beach and rushed over to warn him of the danger. That moment of empathy was nearly fatal. Seeking shelter on a temporary stage constructed for the previous evening's Christmas show, Bell was soon "lifted and carried away with sudden great force and speed."

"I was battered by tables and chairs and umbrellas and chunks of coral . . . my greatest difficulty was in navigating through big sheets of plywood and scaffolding from the stage," he remembers.

Pushing up for air, Bell was sucked down and swept towards a wooded area near the resort. After a failed attempt to grab hold of a tree, he managed to hold on while continuing to get battered by debris. About twenty feet away, a small group of people were calling out names in many different languages. A Thai man stepped across a logjam to pull him to safety. When a woman wiped Bell's face, he realized it was covered in fresh blood.

"I was covered in scratches and wounds and dirt and muck from the sea," he wrote.

Paula Crevoshay was doing morning yoga with a friend at the resort when she noticed something different and said, "Oh my God, look at the ocean. It's a different mood."

The tide was high, and she noticed spiral patterns in the sea, which she had never seen before. As they began their meditation, Crevoshay said, "We are here today to experience the power of the sea and take it back and share it with others."

Little did she know . . .

A few minutes later, the jangling sound of her friend's bracelets caused Crevoshay to open her eyes.

"What happened to the sea?" her friend asked.

Fifteen minutes earlier, the tide had been full, but now a vacuum force seemed to have sucked out all the water. At the horizon line, she noticed a white line, whiter than anything she had seen in nature. She witnessed fishing boats drifting into the white, never to return. Then she knew.

"Tsunami! We have to go now," she urged her friend.

They rushed to the top of a sixty-foot mountain, twenty feet above the tsunami line.

"People were screaming. Thais sound like cicadas when they scream," she remembers.

Because she could speak some Thai, one of the hotel staff asked if Crevoshay could save her baby. The Thai men were putting on sea gear so they could go out looking for survivors, and she asked one of them to look for the baby.

Standing in the middle of chaos, Crevoshay and her friend spread out their arms and projected that they were throwing out a net to bring people to safety. Then they mentally envisioned a mental compass to guide them back. Intuitively sensing that Bell was alive, she kept shouting his name until she heard him call out "Over here!" Crevoshay found her partner covered in blood. Her friend's husband was shaken, but safe.

Concerned that his wounds could become infected, they joined thousands of people heading to the nearest hospital.

"We saw lines of trucks filled with body bags high above the sea beds. It was bedlam," she says, adding that Bell refused treatment because everyone around was close to death and he did not want to take anyone's place. He received emergency medical care in Bangkok where they were able to let their families know they had survived.

"I knew if I could not forgive the ocean I would never heal from this impact," says Crevoshay.

For several years after, she planned every business trip to include a few days near the water. A few years after the tsunami, Crevoshay and Bell went back to Thailand. One morning before sunrise, she gathered big bunches of jacaranda and bougainvillea, which she carried to a rock jutting out to the sea.

During meditation, she told the ocean, "I forgive you. I know that you know what you do and where you are going. You are a blessing to humanity. I don't like what I had to accept because there were thousands of deaths that I witnessed, but I forgive you."

As she inhaled a surge of forgiveness, Crevoshay exhaled waves of forgiveness to all beings who were suffering similar losses.

Breathing in to feel forgiveness within us, and releasing it to all living beings, is a Buddhist practice called *metta*.

More than a decade later, Crevoshay's life is informed by her respect for nature and its power to give and to take life.

"We must never underestimate the force of Mother Nature," she says. "Wind, rain, fire, and ice can create life or annihilate it. I know that well, more than most."

So does tsunami psychologist Dr. Ronna Kabatznick.

"It takes a lot of strength to be humble, to forgive, because we realize these things are out of our control," she says. "We need to forgive the water, the rain, the universe. What are you going to do?"

After speaking to so many people affected by natural catastrophes and considering the incontrovertible evidence that we humans have done tremendous hurt to the world of nature, I can't help thinking perhaps we, too, need to ask forgiveness of the water, the rain, the earth, and the universe itself.

Forgiving Yourself

Soon after the third anniversary of 9/11, I was leading a journaling workshop at a day-long retreat for family members who had experienced direct loss. Journaling gives you a chance to reflect privately on your thoughts, feelings, and actions. They do not have to be directly related to the event. Writing whatever comes into your mind or heart frequently releases something you were not aware that you were holding onto all this time. Letting words take shape through your hands frees up images and impressions too deeply held for words. Sitting quietly with a journal can prove surprising when you read your thoughts later on.

Sitting in a circle, we began introducing ourselves: Wives, mothers, fathers, husbands, and siblings of men and women who died that day spoke about what it looked like, sounded like, and felt like three years later. One of the common themes was getting used to the constant sensations of loss, often an empty or tight feeling in the upper abdomen. About two-thirds of the way around the circle, two women started arguing.

"You have to!" one said to her companion.

"I can't," replied her friend.

"It's time."

We waited for maybe ten seconds. Apparently, being watched by us was more uncomfortable than having to talk about the most painful event in her life.

"I told him to go to work," she said, breaking down in tears. "We were going on vacation, leaving on Wednesday. I told my husband that if he went to the office on Tuesday he could finish some paperwork so his mind would be clear to enjoy the trip."

It was hard holding back tears. Rocking back and forth, she kept repeating, "It's my fault. I told him to go."

Her friend held her shoulders.

"You are not being fair to him," said a woman to my right. Her husband was also among the dead.

"What do you mean?" asked the crying woman.

"You are making him feel bad. It would hurt him to know that you hate yourself for what happened to him. He wouldn't want you to suffer anymore," she said, smiling gently.

"Can you forgive yourself?" she asked.

No longer crying, the woman looked stunned. The idea of forgiving herself had probably never occurred to her. She sat quietly for a while as we finished going around the circle. During the first writing exercise, she looked at us through her tears and nodded. She disappeared quickly as we were closing, and I never learned her name.

When people asked me why we were still providing support for the community of 9/11 families, I would ask myself, What would have happened to that woman had she not released her guilt? Some of us hold pain inside until it becomes unbearable, while others feel better talking it out. A concerned community of people with similar losses can provide the emotional safety needed for the gentle, slower process of long-term mourning.

A Self-Forgiveness Spectrum

Most of the time, forgiving is a conscious choice whether we say, "I forgive you" out loud or internally. Occasionally, we see flashes of spontaneous forgiveness, as when Isabel Letelier forgave Fernandez Larios for his role in her husband's assassination.

Forgiving ourselves takes work. As with forgiving someone else, it does not have to be a yes/no or on/off decision. If we picture a spectrum of self-forgiveness with an *ombre* progression of dark to light shades, where on the spectrum of forgiving yourself would you be right now? Where would you like to be? What stops you from being as self-forgiving as you would like? (Please save that answer.)

Write an affirmation:

"I am not the best. I am not the worst. I am doing my best. I ask for humility, patience, and empathy, so that I can learn how to begin forgiving myself."

Write that statement for five minutes a day for five days.

"It's very hard to forgive yourself but it's essential," says Frank Smyth. "Once you realize you are deserving of forgiveness, growth becomes the fruit of the whole process."

Smyth says that learning the Five Gifts is "the most important journey of my life . . . they have helped me in ways I couldn't have possibly imagined before embarking on that journey."

Gratitude Guilt

"Thankful for what?" a friend asked after her home flooded and her husband was diagnosed with stage III cancer. The house had to be gutted. When the wet Sheetrock came down, the contractor couldn't help noticing that most of the plumbing had survived since the Victorian era. Nothing was going right, but she was fighting exhaustion while keeping her chin up and putting one foot in front of the other.

But another friend implied there was something wrong with her because, "it's not like you're living in Syria."

The implied judgment that she wasn't feeling exactly grateful at that very moment was troubling. I couldn't help asking myself why anyone who was doing her best to get through each day, while caring for her husband

and dealing with both medical and homeowner's insurance, while managing a major construction project, was being shamed for not expressing gratitude. In that situation, would your heart be overflowing with thanks?

More distressing to me was the implication that my friend had no right to be upset because people in Syria had it worse. This was a variation on the Auschwitz argument often used to "persuade" survivors that they are not entitled to feel pain because people in Auschwitz had it worse.

I wish I could say this was an anomaly, but unfortunately I've heard too many accounts like these to regard this as somehow unusual. My friend felt better after learning that, sadly, this type of comment to someone who is struggling through significant hardship occurs all too frequently.

I explained that Holocaust survivor Viktor Frankl admonished those who demeaned or discounted someone's pain by comparing it to life in a concentration camp. Just because other people have it worse did not mean she wasn't entitled to feel miserable.

I told her, "Some people have it better. Some have it worse. It doesn't matter. You are entitled to what you feel."

In speaking about the Five Gifts, I am often asked why gratitude is not one of them. First, gratitude is embedded in that sense of release that comes when you bring each gift home. Second, no one needs to feel ashamed or guilty about not feeling grateful for having her heart ripped out. Forcing yourself to keep a gratitude list when that's not where you are in your emotional process is an express route to "gratitude guilt."

Seriously, aren't you going through enough? Do you really need a dose of guilt? Or can you learn to forgive yourself a little bit at a time?

"I live my life and that's all I can do," my friend told me.

Isn't that enough for any of us?

The Element of Earth

In Chinese medicine, earth is the element associated with forgiveness. It is easy to see why. Just lie back on the grass, looking at the sky on a summer's day, and you can feel tension, worry, and sorrow releasing from your body. It's as if Mother Earth cradled you in infinite compassion, absorbing and absolving your pain.

In the southern hemisphere, her name is Pachamama, and the mother of the sea is Iemanja, also known as the mother of compassion. When you go to the beach to unwind or relieve stress, the sea also absorbs and absolves heartache.

We need water in the form of humility to be ready to receive the fourth gift. If you meditate and/or journal, place a glass of water next to a small vase with a white flower and invite earth and water to open the way for humility and forgiveness.

Incorporating elements of earth and water can open the way for a more forgiving environment at home. The soothing presence of flowers and plants can soften and cleanse your space so that you can experience calm in every one of your senses. When your mind and body are calm, unhealthy stress levels drop. Angry thoughts and feelings begin to resolve.

If you do nothing else for five minutes a day, do something that makes you aware of the connection between earth and the fourth gift. Earth is associated with nurturing, grounding, supportive, and giving traits, all of which pertain to forgiveness as well. You can also bring earth into your home with vanilla, cinnamon, and nutmeg scents.

Still not in a forgiving space? Nurture yourself. That path from the stomach to the heart might just do the trick.

Taking the Next Step

For Scarlett Lewis, whose six-year-old son, Jesse, was among the twenty young schoolchildren shot by twenty-year-old Adam Lanza at Sandy Hook Elementary School in Newtown, Connecticut, forgiveness is a core component of a social education curriculum she has developed to honor her dead son. Six adult staff members and the killer's mother were also murdered that day before Adam Lanza died after shooting himself in the head.

The Jesse Lewis Choose Love Movement distributes The Choose Love Enrichment Program™, a free, downloadable, pre-K through twelfth grade, evidence-based social and emotional (SEL) classroom program, which focuses on four important character values: Courage, Gratitude, Forgiveness, and Compassion in Action, which cultivate optimism, resilience, and personal responsibility. Elements include positive psychology, mindfulness, neuroscience, and character values. That means learning how to identify and manage our emotions, how to make a conscious choice, to be kind in the face of anger, cut the cord that binds us to hurt, and harness the power of post-traumatic growth.

While Scarlett and Jesse's older brother JT have dedicated their lives to forgiveness in action, reactions among townspeople in Newtown remain mixed. Both the site of the massacre and the home where shooter Adam Lanza lived were demolished in 2013 and 2014, but Dr. Joseph Schippa says that the jury is still out on whether demolishing these visual reminders of horror goes deeper than a Band-Aid.

He says that people in Newtown don't talk about how they are still affected years later.

"I think many were relieved to have the school and Adam Lanza's house destroyed, although I am not sure that 'erasure' like that is entirely helpful," says Dr. Schippa. "Some people have been silent, some have been vocal about changing gun laws, some have pursued working with schools to become kinder places, some have forgiven, and some will never tell you that they haven't forgiven."

But for Scarlett and JT Lewis, the takeaway message is clear: Forgiveness brings hope. It is a way of cutting the cord between you and the person who hurt you.

Phyllis Rodriguez lost her only son, Greg, on September 11, 2001. An IT specialist, he worked on the 103rd floor of the north tower of the World Trade Center.

"We realized very early the morning of the 12th that our government, given its history, was going to do something military and violent in the name of our son," she says. "That wasn't going to do any good."[75]

Phyllis and her husband, Orlando Rodriguez, became vocal opponents of the death penalty for Zacarias Moussaoui, the man known as "the 20th hijacker." In the spirit of forgiveness, Phyllis reached out to Moussaoui's mother, Aicha el-Wafi.

"We realized that what we had in common was our common humanity," she says. "We were human beings. It is a very valuable part of my life and my healing."[76]

Forgiveness does not make her miss her son any less. Nor does she condone the attackers. But in the aftermath of 9/11, Phyllis Rodriguez has dedicated herself to forgiveness projects and human rights causes.

"I don't think it happened for a reason," she says. "But it did happen and I feel fortunate that I had the inner resources to respond in the way that I did."[77]

The Star of Hope

In Greek mythology, when Pandora opened a secret box, which she had been forbidden to touch, she released all sorts of evil into the air. Only one thing remained behind: Hope. The star of hope that hovers over Pandora's Box shines bright when we acknowledge the healing power of the Fourth Gift.

Practice. Practice. Practice.

In one of my favorite teaching tales, a concert violinist is asked how she got to perform at Carnegie Hall. Her answer was simple: "Practice. Practice. Practice."

So it is with forgiveness.

FIVE MINUTES A DAY
TO FORGIVENESS

Choose one activity to practice for five minutes a day for five days.

- DEFINING: What does forgiveness look like, sound like, and feel like to you? How would you know if you were forgiving?

- IDENTIFYING: Make a list. Whom do you feel you might want to forgive? From whom do you want to ask forgiveness?

- ACTUALIZING: Pick one person or institution you would like to forgive. If possible, find a picture of that person. Write "I forgive you" on the picture. Meditate, or reflect on this, for five minutes.

- ASKING: Pick someone whose forgiveness you seek. If possible, find a picture of him or her. Write "I am sorry. Please forgive me." Meditate, or reflect on this, for five minutes.

- EMERGING: Picture yourself standing on the far side of your space, having already forgiven this person or having been forgiven. Observe your facial expression. Do you look more or less relaxed? Do you look more comfortable or less?

Imagine that you can step inside this emerging version of yourself. Look out through your own eyes, listen to your thoughts, and feel what it's like in your body to have already forgiven someone, or what it's like to have forgiven. Yes, it's you. Any time you want to access a forgiving (or forgiven) state, repeat this process.

16

Growth, the Fifth Gift

*U*nlike the other four gifts, growth is biological, mental, emotional, and spiritual. It happens in its own time and its own way, whether you want it or not. Just as when we plant a garden, we add "nutrients" to the soil—humility, patience, empathy, and forgiveness—enabling us to create a more favorable environment for positive growth and optimal conditions.

Sometimes, it feels like a dream: You're in an empty field with a burnt smell. Nothing is alive or growing, at least nothing you can perceive with your physical senses. On the surface, it appears as if nothing could flourish again. But in the psyche, seedlings of ideas are nourished by the power of the first Four Gifts: Humility. Patience. Empathy. Forgiveness.

Signs of Growth

With the gift of growth we can say, "While we would never wish that type of loss on anyone, as a result of what we have been through, we have gained knowledge, strength, and hope. Our lives have meaning. We know what—and who—truly matters to us, and we appreciate them."

We are surprised when our first waking thoughts are not about the loss.

"You stop pretending that this day isn't different from the day before everything important went missing," says a friend, whose twenty-year-old son was killed crossing the street.

"When you wake up, it's the first thing you think about," he says. "It goes on for years. It's the shattered lens through which you see the world."

When we have grieved and prayed and fought, and have arrived at a place where we no longer define ourselves by our connection to that mega-event, we grow stronger and more resilient.

"I don't tell people I work with that my father was killed on 9/11," says Ian Grady. "I don't want to be prejudged based on that way. I want to be treated the same. I don't want or need a special break."

Many of the teenagers from my World Trade Center program are now adults with children of their own. Seasoned by losing a parent in a terrorist attack has strengthened their commitment to being there for their own young families.

"God forbid anything like this happens again. But you know there's a big possibility that it will," says one young man, who recently became a father himself. "Anyone who says they're not scared is either lying to themselves or stupid. I'm scared. But there's a choice where you let it rearrange your life or you can say, 'I'm not going to let it shape me.'"

He says his dad's legacy, which he plans to share with his own son, goes beyond the story of 9/11.

"The world is scary, not just with terrorism. A lot of things are scary," he says.

And as his own father taught him, "If you give in to what's scary, you're not going to get anywhere."

Ian now looks back at who he was and who he has become.

"So many people did so many things for me, I find myself a more giving person. I'm drawn to veterans," he says.

Ian finds that he spends more time with two friends recently returned from combat in Iraq and Afghanistan.

"When they have rough times, I sit there and talk to them," he says. I wasn't overseas fighting a war and can't compare their PTSD to mine."

There is no reason to compare traumas. Facing his PTSD led Ian to empathy and growth. He sees himself as their big brother.

"I feel terrible that they went through what they went through, but I feel good that I can be there to provide them with some sort of support," he says, adding that having lost his dad on 9/11, meaningful friendships are even more important.

This was brought home to me one summer afternoon when I stood in the ocean as a young father who had led our baseball mentoring program, where the older kids whose fathers were killed on 9/11 coached the younger boys to get them ready for Little League. As the man carried his two-year-old son into the water, a pod of dolphins surprised us by swimming a few yards away. People had been telling me about the dolphins for years but I had never seen them until now. I couldn't help but marvel at the perfect timing! If there was ever a message from Spirit about growth, hope, and healing, this one shining moment said it all.

Breaking News

In the year that I have been focused on writing this book, every day brings additional news about how painfully out of control the world around has become. I started this chapter on Sunday, October 29, 2016, the fifth anniversary of Hurricane Sandy. Two days later, when I wrote about the young men of 9/11, another terrorist attack took place not far from the site of the World Trade Center attacks. (Carl Jung would describe this confluence of events as "synchronicity," a meaningful coincidence.)

Watching Hurricanes Harvey, Irma, and Maria with layers of sadness, I was reminded of why I believe this book is needed.

The face of every mother clutching a child made me wince. As uplifting as the images of people being carried to safety were, I felt sad knowing that so many of those rescued would look back at that moment as the high point of their post-disaster lives. Looking at the moldy debris inside people's homes, it was hard not to feel empathy for the ordeals they would be going through for the next several years.

One basis for this book was research projections that human and natural disasters would increase in frequency and intensity through the coming decade. At least one of those reports was published in 2010, which means we are at mid-decade, and guess what? These are no longer projections. We are in a turbulent cycle in which disasters of all kinds are happening more often and inflicting more damage.

According to weather.com, "a new record for the number of billion-dollar natural disasters in the United States may be set this year (2017), with 15 such events already confirmed through September."

The first half of 2017 wrought $12 billion in weather damages.

"Since 1980, there have been 218 weather and climate disasters in the US that have reached at least $1 billion in damage or cost. The total cost of these 218 events exceeds $1.2 trillion. This cost, however, does not include Harvey, Irma and Maria. The current costliest US weather disaster . . . since 1980, adjusted for inflation, is Hurricane Katrina at $161.3 billion." [78]

There has been a 44 percent increase in the number of extreme-weather events since 2000. [79]

Intentional (human-to-human) disasters are on the rise, as well. Speaking at a press conference after the Halloween terrorist truck attack, former New York City Police Commissioner William Bratton said that vehicle attacks have been occurring around the world with increasing frequency. Between 2015–2017, there have been six acts of terrorism by vehicle in Europe.

It's a sobering reminder that life—the ultimate gift—can be taken at any time, but we can choose to live a loving life. The victims of New York City's Halloween truck attack were loving life at the moment it was taken. Knowing this can inspire us.

Growth Never Fails

With every breath, your body absorbs new atoms, which in turn, become new cells. Researchers say virtually all of your body's atoms get replaced every year. [80,81]

"A human being is not a 'single' living entity; we are actually a community of upward of 50 trillion sentient cellular citizens," says *New York Times*' best-selling author, Dr. Bruce Lipton, who notes that "the total number of cells in a human body is equal to the total number of people on 8,000 Earths!" [82]

These trillions of cells are continually renewing themselves. Your liver replaces itself approximately every six weeks; red blood cells, every four months; white blood cells, each year; bones, every three months; and your skin, monthly. [83]

When you cut your finger, your mind-body knows how to produce precisely the right number of healthy new skin cells and arrange for their transportation and distribution through the bloodstream to the exact location where they are needed. The GPS is preprogrammed into the operating system.

If I were to ask you, "How many healthy new skin cells does it take to heal that paper cut on your left index finger?" you probably would not be able to answer. But you do know your paper cut will heal. There is an operating system for cellular regeneration and healing—in other words—*growth*.

Waking and sleeping, dancing and sitting, laughing and crying, we are growing. We do not have to be conscious of how, nor do we need to memorize the code. We do not even have to think about whether or not it is going to work or how to fix it. The ability to grow naturally, safely, and organically is a biological birthright, programmed into our DNA.

Post-Traumatic Growth

A new science of post-traumatic growth has come up with some controversial findings. In a 2016 study of 240 individuals with direct exposure to the July 22, 2011, bomb in Oslo, Norway, which killed eight and wounded 209, participants who reported a high level of post-traumatic growth ten months after the bombing reported high levels of PTSD one year later. But those who reported a high level of PTSD ten months after the bombing reported high levels of post-traumatic growth one year later.

The authors of the study concluded that "post-traumatic growth (PTG) may be both a consequence and antecedent of post-traumatic stress."[83]

Writing in psychologytoday.com, Anthony Mancini, PhD, observed that "In this framework, post-traumatic growth isn't growth at all. It's a 'motivated positive illusion' whose purpose is to protect us from the possibility that we may have been damaged."[84]

"Post-traumatic injury and post-traumatic healing can be done, but you need to recognize that if you have symptoms of PTSD you have to address it," says Frank Smyth. "It is by no means a permanent condition."

Resilience: Bouncing Forward

Growth and resilience are intertwined like strands of a fiber optic cable. Resilience is defined by *Merriam-Webster's Dictionary* as:

1. the capability of a strained body to recover its size and shape after deformation caused especially by compressive stress

2. an ability to recover from or adjust easily to misfortune or change[85]

Resilience also refers to materials, such as memory foam or elastic, which recover their shapes after compression.

When it comes to psychological resilience, we can never bounce back. We can only bounce *forward*.

Nurse Sarah Cohen was on her way home after a double shift when a delivery truck ran onto a sidewalk. The impact threw her up into the air and across four lanes of traffic. In the ambulance, she slipped into a coma and remained in that state for nearly a month. When she awoke, Cohen could not move her eyes.

"I saw people's faces in pieces, which made me nauseous," she says. "My body felt like a sack of potatoes."

A decade later, she calls herself "the luckiest woman in the world" and says the accident was the most positive thing that ever happened to her.

Dr. Mona Greenfield, founder of Metropolitan Communication Associates in Greenwich Village, has been working with traumatic brain injury patients for more than twenty years. Like Sarah, most of Dr. Greenfield's patients live on Social Security Disability (SSD). Many were high-functioning professionals before their car accident, physical violence, or fall. Dismissed by doctors because medical opinion believed their conditions were incurable, these traumatized individuals often struggle with PTSD flashbacks, severe anxiety, and hypervigilance.

Programs like Dr. Greenfield's offer traumatized patients a chance to meet regularly with others like themselves, which is the best antidote for the isolation that develops with long-term PTSD. Not only do her patients receive training in cognitive skills and mind-body relaxation techniques, they receive support for relearning social skills so that they can function more effectively.

"TBI is not a death sentence. Our patients deserve to have hope," says Dr. Greenfield. "If you work on the skills and strategies while offering support, they will get better. They may not be exactly how they were before, but their skills and feelings about themselves will improve."

Sarah Cohen agrees.

"You can work it through and see things completely differently, but you cannot avoid pain in the beginning. You have to learn not to share the loss with everyone, but it can make a world of difference to have people who get what you are going through," she says.

In her case, it meant searching her soul to find strength so that she can now be there for others like herself.

"I want to show my daughter that she doesn't have to wait until seventy to get where I am," she says. "If I can serve as an example, this is my mission, and I can tell you, it's not easy. With the right emotional and mental support, and the right guidance, you cannot be who you *were*, but you can be the maximum of who you *are*."[86]

Letting Go

It has been more than half a decade since Sandy. I am no longer afraid of hurricanes, and I evacuate well ahead of their arrival. Living on the coast for most of my life, maritime storms never fazed me. Seriously, I enjoyed them. As the "On the Water" reporter for the *New York Times* Long Island section, I covered the Around Long Island regatta in a nor'easter. Conditions were rough and everyone on board got seasick. I bruised two ribs getting tossed across the cabin, but fear never entered the picture. An avid windsurfer for many years, I loved flying across the water the day after a hurricane passed.

It took time, but after four years, the flashbacks and hypervigilance resolved on their own. Giving up my home of nearly two decades was a survival decision I don't regret. Had I stayed, I would have been haunted by fears of a more expensive construction project should the house flood again. Leaving home has been complicated, but coming out as a soul in transit has freed me up to focus on balancing work, health, love, and friendship. If I could put the words of the poet Masahide on a bumper sticker, it would read as follows:

"Barn burned down. Now I can see the moon."

As much as I hate to admit it, the chaos and friction of the first two years made me grow up. No question: I liked myself better as an innocent. Before getting wiped out, I held a tourist visa to the Land of Financial Reality. Now I have a green card. It can only get better.

Were it not for the Five Gifts, I might not see it that way. They continue to inform my life in innumerable contexts. The first gift, humility, opened my eyes to the fact that mine was just one of a million lives that was damaged by that one natural disaster. Now, I am humbled every morning when I wake up to a clean floor—or for that matter, any floor. It might sound over the top, but at least once a day, I stand in awe at the miracle of clean water. I don't talk about this much because my friends roll their eyes, and at one luncheon, someone asked me if I had been living under a rock. Without humility, I could take offense, but the first gift, coupled with a sense of humor, lets their comments roll off like flowing water.

Patience has never been my strong suit, and it continues to be a challenge. Maybe New Yorkers have impatience in our DNA, but the second gift, unwanted though it is, never fails to take the edge off frustration.

Empathy strengthens the foundation for friendship, support, and ongoing concern for others suffering through the aftermath of climate change and intentional disasters.

Forgiveness? Well, that's a work in progress, too. It is hard for me to forgive the widespread institutional cruelty toward people suffering through no fault of their own, but Dr. Redelfs keeps reminding me to have compassion for individuals working in a broken, corrupt system. They, too, have been traumatized. It's going to take some time for me to metabolize that lesson.

Sharing the Five Gifts has accelerated my own growth by giving me a way to help others find their center of gravity as they struggled to get back on their feet.

But when the rug got pulled out from under me again, my own growth stalled.

Darvo'd!

Thanks to Sandy Denicker and his indefatigable crew, the house passed inspection with flying colors. Everything was up to code. But taxes and insurance premiums now made the cost of living there too expensive. With kids no longer running in and out of the house, the neighborhood no longer felt like home. After Sandy, it was impossible to ignore the reality of rising seas as monthly high tides fully covered beaches and marsh. It was time to sell.

Two weeks before we were ready to go on the market, I received a letter stating that FEMA had devalued my property by 50 percent. No one from FEMA had stepped foot on my property since the week after the storm, when I was told to rebuild. According to the letter, FEMA had based its devaluation on the county's tax assessment. We had been compliant with all regulations and had submitted and resubmitted the same documentation whenever requested. Although I had not wanted to rebuild, I did what I was told despite my reservations.

Now, due to the new "valuation" of my home, the cost of rebuilding as submitted to the building department was now worth more than 50 percent of the new devaluated value of my property. As a result, FEMA declared my brand-new, up-to-code house as "substantially damaged" and demanded that I raise the house in order to get a Certificate of Occupancy. Without a C of O, I couldn't sell, rent, or legally live in my own home.

Drowning in a flood of bills, I managed to tread water, but I was terrified every second of every day. All that work and more than $100,000—all for nothing? I couldn't stop thinking about a man in town who, like me, had obtained every permit, rebuilt according to code, and passed inspection—only to receive a letter telling him that the government had devalued his property by 50 percent and now he was required to raise his house. Word around town was that he had attempted suicide but survived. I got it. Every night before heading to bed, I prayed not to wake up.

It seemed like a waste of time trying to find out why my property had been arbitrarily devalued. I didn't care. My dream cottage had morphed into a financial nightmare, one that was about to vacuum my life's savings. To encourage myself, I whispered throughout the day, "There has to be another way. There has to be another way."

Meanwhile, my jaw and gut were in a clenching competition. I tried every mood-boosting strategy I could think of, and the only one that worked was an old joke: "There's nothing wrong with you that reincarnation won't cure."

Hopefully, things wouldn't lead to that. Instead, they led to "The Big Cheese."

In the interest of full disclosure, I never met the gentleman known as The Big Cheese although I think of him fondly as a Will Ferrell kind of guy. The Big Cheese had the authority to issue a certificate of occupancy by rescinding the substantial damage order and acknowledging that all construction had been preapproved and successfully inspected by the town's building department.

Getting to The Big Cheese took more than a month. After several attempts, I channeled my inner Olivia Benson and hired a lawyer. It took about five weeks, but after The Big Cheese reviewed the paperwork and found that everything was in order, the FEMA order was rescinded.

It took several months of real estate drama before I am happy to report that the beach cottage became home to a beautiful young family. The night we closed, for the first time in more than a year, I slept through the night.

In the words of Chinese dissident author Ma Jiang: "Everything I was I carry with me. Everything I will be lies waiting in the road ahead."

The Element of Wood

The element associated with growth, wood embodies the cycle of life—from a tiny sapling to full maturity.

Patrician McCarthy, author of *In Your Element: Taoist Psychology: Everything You Want to Know About the Five Element Personalities*, writes that "Wood represents the birth of energy, new growth, beginnings, patience, focus, vision, power, decision-making, clear direction, and benevolence." [87]

"Wood symbolizes how we put roots down and how we grow. It is a focused, not random, process," says McCarthy.

The element of wood is also associated with a strong sense of justice. We can see this connection in the stories of those who through their own loss become committed to helping others get needed services following a tragedy.

But McCarthy notes a potential downside: "The challenge is that you can become very self-focused and too righteous."

To soften these traits, add water for humility.

Cultivating the fifth gift can be as simple as planting a seed and caring for it as it grows. Bring growth into your environment by adding trees, shrubs, and hedges to your garden. Bring potted trees and tall, strong plants into your home. Use wood furniture and accessories, such as picture frames, throughout your home and on your deck. Incorporate a palette of dark greens and blues into your wardrobe and your living space to further facilitate growth. Become a mentor or coach who motivates others to stand tall. Feed your passion for justice by joining organizations whose missions you support.

Wood is not a static element. Try activities like walking, running, or hiking outdoors. Your story doesn't end with a flourish of background music or a drumroll. As long as you are alive, you will continue to grow.

FIVE MINUTES A DAY
TO GROWTH

Choose one to practice for five minutes a day for five days.

- TAKING STOCK: Meditate, reflect, walk, or journal on the following:
  What is the most important lesson you learned from the disaster?
  How has your life changed for the better?
  How has it changed for the worse?

- SEEING AROUND THE CORNER: Picture or imagine yourself a
  year from now. Notice what looks different. Step into your future self
  and experience what it is like to have already accomplished some of
  the changes you have wanted to make.

- RESEARCHING: Google an issue about which you feel passionate. Watch and listen to videos. Read as much as you can. Inform
  yourself on how you can help others prepare, cope, and heal from
  disasters.

- CREATING MEANING AND PURPOSE: Join a group or
  organization whose mission resonates with your beliefs.
  Educate people about the mental health dangers of climate
  change and/or gun violence; demonstrate for causes you
  care about.

- SHARING THE FIVE GIFTS: Please join me in giving
  away what we love. Try getting together with friends, family,
  coworkers, and neighbors who are going through tough
  times to spread the heart-based wisdom of the Five Gifts.

  Let's make it a movement.

CONCLUSION—TOP 10 SECRETS TO FINDING HOPE, HEALING, AND STRENGTH

*L*ike it or not, a life-shattering event can be our greatest teacher. Here are my secrets to hope, healing, and strength. Remember the second gift. It takes patience and time for your silver lining to appear.

10) *Expect the unexpected.*

Don't be surprised by the depth of your reactions. It's human to be moved when disaster strikes.

9) *Stay connected. Avoid isolation.*

In the best of times/worst of times, we see extremes of behavior from selfishness to generosity. Isolating after a disaster can lead to depression and unhealthy behaviors. Overall, we see more "best" behaviors during and soon after a tragic event, but when things settle down, it's important not to isolate. Spend time with people who accept you as you are. Being judged or shamed for how you feel is not helpful.

8) *"My calamity is my providence."*

This proverb is a tough one, but the ultimate power of the Five Gifts is to give us a foundation for accepting ourselves and where we are now because of everything that happened: the good, the bad, and the absolutely horrendous. This doesn't mean we no longer hurt, nor have we forgotten that others are still hurting. Living through a calamity can give us a visceral understanding that from the survivor's perspective there is no such thing as too much help.

7) Take stock of your strengths, your values, and what matters to you.

Appreciate love, friendship, and stepping up for yourself and others in need. Make a list of your inner resources and carry it in your wallet. Read them when you feel like all is lost. They have the power to rejuvenate.

6) Laugh once a day. Especially when nothing seems funny.

It's hard to joke when life hurts but nothing heals like laughter. Take a new washing machine that sprays water in all directions the first time you turn it on. (Yes, that really happened.) Ask "How funny would this be if this was a movie starring Lily Tomlin (or *your* favorite comedienne)?"

5) Take your soul vitamins. Just five minutes a day.

Rest. Hydrate. Exercise as best you can. Spend time outdoors. Connect with friends. You can do it!

4) You are not the disaster.

Yes, it takes over your life for several years, but this is not the whole movie of your life. You will get through it. The replays will stop and one morning you will wake up thinking about the day ahead instead of that one.

3) "There has to be another way."

This has turned out to be the most important tool in my psychological go-kit. There are many blockages, obstacles, and delays in the aftermath of a disaster. Right now, it may feel like it will go on forever, but reminding myself that there has to be another way has never failed me. Even when it seemed like all was lost, the flip side of obstruction has always turned out to be freedom.

2) *Appreciate yourself.*

It's not easy, but like my friend Pepi says, "This life is not for the chickens." Take stock of what you have learned about yourself and the people who really count. Thank them and yourself. Ask, "What else can I be learning?" Appreciate yourself for putting one step in front of the other.

1) *Surprise yourself.*

With the best of intentions, I leave this last one for you to determine. After all, the most authentic gift is the one you give yourself.

APPENDIX A:
DR. LAURIE'S POCKET GUIDE
TO SELF-CARE FOR ACUTE STRESS

Rip out this page and fold into quarters. Keep it in your pocket or travel bag. WITHIN THE FIRST 24–48 HOURS AFTER THE EVENT:

Keep moving. (Maintain your regular exercise routine.)

Alternate exercise with relaxation. (This lowers stress levels and helps you stay grounded.)

Hydrate. Drink lots of water. (Goes without saying but here's a reminder.)

Avoid alcohol and caffeine. (Don't try to numb your emotions.)

Eat healthy, regular meals. (This is important even when you don't feel like eating.)

Pay attention to your body and your emotions. (Don't be surprised when physical symptoms [fatigue/agitation] and emotions [anger/shock] are overwhelming.)

Flashbacks, recurring thoughts, and disturbing dreams are normal. (They will subside.)

Talk to people. (Help friends, family and colleagues by sharing your feelings.)

Reach out. (Ask others who were affected how they are doing.)

Give yourself permission to feel miserable. (It's appropriate under the circumstances and it will pass.)

Keep as normal a schedule as possible. (Eat at normal times.)

Make everyday decisions. (Choosing what to eat can give you back a sense of control.)

Put off major decisions. (Moving, changing jobs, and lifestyle modification decisions can wait until life calms down.)

Keep notes. (Keep a log of phone calls with names/dates. Spend 15 minutes a day writing about your physical/mental/emotional reactions.)

Stay in places where you feel safe. (Reassure others that they are safe.)

Help out. (Everyday tasks like cleaning up and taking out the trash give a sense of normalcy.)

DON'T ASK: "How do you feel?"
ASK: "What can I do to help?"

ACCEPT YOURSELF. YOU ARE A NORMAL PERSON HAVING NORMAL REACTIONS TO AN ABNORMAL SITUATION.

STRESSED OUT?

Contact
drnadel@laurienadel.com
Call: 212.560.2333
CONFIDENTIAL 24/7 ACCESS

STRESSED OUT?

Contact
drnadel@laurienadel.com
Call: 212.560.2333
CONFIDENTIAL 24/7 ACCESS

If you are reading this . . .

You have probably been through a critical incident (CI). A CI is any event that causes strong reactions which can potentially interfere with your ability to cope.

Even though the event may be over, you may experience emotional aftershocks after a horrible event. Aftershocks can appear days, weeks, or months after the CI.

The good news is that most acute stress reactions subside within a month. If they persist, please seek professional help. It means the event was too powerful for you to process on your own. It doesn't mean you are crazy.

DO:
Alternate exercise with rest.
Stay busy.
Follow your normal schedule.
Hydrate.

DON'T:
Numb out with booze/drugs.
Isolate.
Make major life decisions.

APPENDIX B:
HOMEOPATHIC REMEDIES
FOR ACUTE STRESS:
SAFE, NATURAL, AND EFFECTIVE

Acute Stress Reactions:

Acute stress reactions occur within the first month of exposure to a traumatic event. Symptoms are similar but not identical to PTSD, and include anxiety, sadness, irritability, mood swings, difficulty sleeping, poor concentration, exaggerated startle response, withdrawal from people, and recurring dreams about the event, or spontaneous, intrusive flashbacks, in which you re-experience the event kinesthetically.

Homeopathy for Acute Stress Reactions:

Used by millions of people around the world for more than 200 years, homeopathic remedies are safe, natural, non addictive, and effective. They work without side effects or interactions and can be taken safely with conventional medications, supplements, and herbs. In the United States, the FDA regulates homeopathic medications, but they do not require a prescription.

Homeopathic remedies can be purchased in pharmacies around the world, via amazon.com or in the US at Whole Foods or Vitamin Shoppes. The standard dilutions are 30c for behavioral/emotional issues and 6c or 9c for physiological symptoms. The 6c dilutions are more readily available.

Unlike pharmaceuticals, homeopathic remedies do not treat a disease. They treat the individual. There are numerous specific treatments for symptoms of acute stress.

Homeopathics for Acute Stress:

(Dosage: 5 pellets under the tongue every 20-30 minutes; as needed.)

Gelsemium 30c (performance anxiety; diarrhea before a deadline/event)

Argentrum nitricum 30c (agitation; diarrhea; fear of flying)

Therideon 30 c (sudden loud noises)

Phosphorous 30c (thunder/lightning; fear of sun going down)

Arnica 30c (physical/emotional trauma)

Staphysagria 30c (repressed anger/betrayal/"stabbed in the heart")

Ignatia amara 30c (grief/loss)

Ignatia amara 6c (irritation/annoyance)

Aconitum 30c (panic)

Sleep issues: Caffea cruda 30c (insomnia due to racing thoughts)

Stramonium 30c (night terrors)

Homeopathic First Aid Kit
(Dilutions of 6c if 9c is not available)

(Dosage: 5 pellets under the tongue hourly as needed unless otherwise indicated.)

Arnica 6c (bruises/cuts)

Apis 6c (swelling/redness/itching; insect stings, poison ivy, painful scratches)

(Apis is fast-acting; take 5 pellets every 10 minutes and place ice on the affected area. When swelling goes down, switch to Arnica 6c every half hour for 2–3 hours; continue with Arnica6c twice a day until area heals.)

Arsenicum album 6c (food poisoning)

Cinchona 6c (fluid loss/dehydration)

Phosphorous 6c (loss of blood)

Rhus tox 6c (joint pain)

Ruta grav 6c (tendons/ligament pain; sprained ankle)

Aloe 6c and Phodophyllum 6c (diarrhea)

Magnesium phosphoricum 6c (stomach cramps)

Hypericum 6c (nerve pain; to prevent sunburn, take once a day starting a
   week before sun exposure and then once a day)

Urinary Tract Infections:

Staphysagria 6c +

Cantharis 6c +

Hepar sulphuricum 6c (Hepar Sulph is a homeopathic antibiotic)

APPENDIX C:
ONLINE RESOURCES

Chapter One:

www.massshootingtracker.org

For information on Acute Stress and PTSD:

www.cdc.org
www.nimh.org

Chapter Two:

"Hey, NYC: Here's What to Do If We Get Nuked"
https://patch.com/new-york/new-york-city/hey-nyc-heres-what-do-if-we-get-nuked
www.nuclearsecrecy.com/nukemap/

For emergency planning and go kits:

www.fema.gov
www.ready.gov
http://nation.time.com/2013/02/21/
    youre-a-seal-stranded-in-hostile-territory-whats-in-your-survival-kit/
https://www.nytimes.com/2017/07/03/smarter-living/packing-emergency-kit-
    disaster.html
(includes interview with Frank Smyth, Executive Director of Global Journalist Security)

Chapter Three

www.icisf.org
www.chariscenter.com (Paul Schweinler)

Chapter Four

www.PTSDUnited.org

www.Sidran.org for PTSD fact sheet and referrals to PTSD professionals

https://www.ptsd.va.gov/

"The National Center for PTSD is dedicated to research and education on trauma and PTSD. We work to assure that the latest research findings help those exposed to trauma."

https://www.istss.org/ International Society for Traumatic Stress Studies/research

Chapter Five

www.AnnetheListener.com

www.cpj.org Committee to Protect Journalists

Chapter Six

www.ivoh.org Images and Voices of Hope in Media

Chapter Seven

http://drlaurahaigh.co.uk/

Chapter Eight

www.gobankingrates.co

www.lynnrobinson.com

www.chelliecampbell.com

https://ameripriseadvisors.com/edie.haughney

Credit Stacker app

Considered the most powerful and engaging financial education app in the country, Credit Stacker teaches young people about credit and personal finance issues. In the first two weeks of its launch, Stacker was downloaded by 200,000 people. Forbes.com calls Angel Rich, the young entrepreneur who developed the app "the next Steve Jobs."

Chapter Nine

www.nickarnett.com

www.SoundsTrue.com *The Roots of Buddhist Psychology* by Jack Kornfield.

www.globalmeaninginstitute.com

Chapter Ten

www.indigenousvoicesradio.org

Chapter Eleven

www.mienshiang.org

Chapter Twelve

www.franksmyth.com
www.journalistsecurity.net

Chapter Thirteen

www.protectstudentsabroad.org
http://www.centerforhealthsecurity.org/our-work/current-projects/CoPE-WELL
    %20model

Chapter Fourteen

www.theforgivenessproject.com
www.learningtoforgive.com

Chapter Fifteen

http://www.nytimes.com/2012/03/25/magazine/post-traumatic-stresss-surprisingly
    -positive-flip-side.html
http://time.com/3967885/how-trauma-can-change-you-for-the-better/

NOTES

Chapter One

1. Mooney, Chris and Brady, Dennis. "Extreme hurricanes and wildfires made 2017 the most costly US disaster year ever. *Washington Post*, January 8, 2018. https://www.washingtonpost.com/news /energy-environment/wp/2018/01/08/hurricanes-wildfires-made-2017-the-most-costly-u-s-disaster -year-on-record/?utm_term=.fdc5ebc5c044

2. National Institutes of Health, Department of Veteran Affairs, and the Sidran Institute. "PTSD STATISTICS." *PTSD UNITED, INC.* http://www.ptsdunited.org/ptsd-statistics-2/

3. MASS SHOOTING TRACKER: an unfunded, crowd-sourced effort. "U.S. Mass Shootings, all years." (2013–2017.) www.massshootingtracker.org

4. Hauser, Christine. "Gun Death Rate Rose Again in 2017, CDC Says" *The New York Times*, November 2017. https://www.nytimes.com/2017/11/04/us/gun-death-rates.html

5. Coyle, Kevin. "Global Warming Will Mean Mental Shock and Adversity for Nearly 200 Million Americans." *National Wildlife Federation's Blog.* (March 24, 2012.) http://blog.nwf.org/2012/03/nwf -report-global-warming-will-mean-mental-shock-and-adversity-for-nearly-200-million-americans/

6. Nadel, Laurie. *Baseball, Hope, and the Children of 9/11.* HuffingtonPost (September 11, 2011.) http://www.huffingtonpost.com/laurie-nadel/baseball-hope-and-the-chi_b_953075.html

7. Comforto, Bobbie and Rob (producers); Nadel, Laurie (writer); Rather, Dan (narrator). *After the Fall: The Rise of a 9/11 Community Center* (documentary) (2004.) www.laurienadel.com

Chapter Three

8. Johnston, Mark C. *FBI and an Ordinary Guy: The Private Price of Public Service.* Page Publishing, Inc. (2015), p. 45.

9. Ibid., page 416.

10. Waite TD, Chaintarli K, Beck CR, Bone A, Amlôt R, Kovats S Reacher M, Armstrong B, Leonardi G, Rubin GJ, Oliver I.. "The English national cohort study of flooding and health: cross-sectional analysis of mental health outcomes at year one." https://www.ncbi.nlm.nih.gov/pubmed/28129752

11. Medscape.com "Acute Stress Disorder" http://emedicine.medscape.com/article/2192581-overview#a6

12. Schallhorn, Kaitlyn. "What to Do During an Active Shooter Situation." FOX News, November 17, 2017.

Chapter Four

13. Wilson, Simone. "Hey, NYC: Here's What to Do If We Get Nuked. You Know . . . Just in Case." www .ChelseaPatch.com, April 17, 2017. Updated August 9, 2017.

14. Pearce, Keith. *How to Survive a Nuclear Emergency.* Katwab Ltd., 2017. p. 27.

15. Willingham, AJ. "The CDC wants to gently prepare people for (an unlikely) nuclear war." CNN.com, January 5, 2018. (The briefing was postponed on January 15th and will be rescheduled.) http://www.cnn.com/2018/01/05/health/cdc-nuclear-preparedness-trnd/index.html

16. Wikipedia, https://en.wikipedia.org/wiki/2001_anthrax_attacks#The_letters

17. Wikipedia, Ibid., https://en.wikipedia.org/wiki/2001_anthrax_attacks#The_letters

18. "Anthrax diagnosed in two more people," *CNN.com*. Last modified October 16, 2001, http://www.cnn.com/2001/HEALTH/conditions/10/15/anthrax/

19. Swain, Kristen Alley. "Outrage Factors and Explanations in News Coverage of the Anthrax Attacks." *Journalism and Mass Communications Quarterly.* June 1, 2007.

20. Swain, Kirsten Alley. Ibid.

21. Federal Bureau of Investigation. "Amerithrax or Anthrax Investigation. https://www.fbi.gov/history/famous-cases/amerithrax-or-anthrax-investigation

22. 16. "How to Drink Water Through a Gas Mask" https://www.youtube.com/watch?v=QuAJhmwQPC0

23. Wikipedia. *https://en.wikipedia.org/wiki/Hurricane_Andrew*

24. Richter, Larry. "Down to the Basics: Hunting for Food, Clothing and Shelter." *New York Times,* August 25, 1992. http://www.nytimes.com/1992/08/26/us/hurricane-andrew-down-to-the-basics-hunting-for-food-water-and-shelter.html?pagewanted=all

Chapter Five

25. Statistics published at www.PTSDUnited.org
PTSD United, Inc. is a 501(c)3 non-profit organization that provides free information and resources about PTSD. (www.huddl.org is an anonymous support network for people to connect with others living with PTSD.)

26. DSM V Criteria for PTSD. https://www.ptsd.va.gov

Chapter Six

27. Hypervigilance definition: http://www.brainworksneurotherapy.com/neurofeedback-trauma-PTSD

28. Marcetek, Branko. https://www.jacobinmag.com/2016/09/orlando-letelier-pinochet-nixon-kissinger/

29. Simon, Joel. *Muzzling the Media: How the New Autocrats Threaten Press Freedom. World Policy Journal,* September 2006. Pp. 51–61

Chapter Seven

30. National Public Radio, *Here and Now* with Robin Young and Jeremy Hobson. October 29, 2013.

31. Vesely, Alexander and Cimiluca, Mary. *Viktor Frankl and the Search for Meaning: A Conversation with Alexander Vesely and Mary Cimiluca. Parabola. Spring 2017. pp. 60–61.*

Chapter Eight

32. Mosendz, Polly. "Las Vegas Victims Must Now Wrestle With Bills, Banks, and Bosses." Bloomberg News. October 6, 2017. https://www.bloomberg.com/news/articles/2017-10-06/las-vegas-shooting-victims-must-wrestle-with-bills-banks-bosses

33. Jones, Stephanie K. "*Hurricane Katrina: The Numbers Tell Their Own Story.*" *Insurance Journal.* August 26, 2015.

34. Nadel, Laurie. "Triage in a Trolley." Lifenet, the Journal of the International Critical Incident Stress Foundation. Spring, 2013.

35. American Bankruptcy Institute Law Review: *The Category 5 Crisis: How Hurricanes Katrina and Rita Exposed Deficiencies in the Bankruptcy Abuse Prevention Act of 2005*. Spring 2007.

36. Warren, Elizabeth. *Natural Disasters and Bankruptcy: A Perspective*. Communities and Banking. Fall 2005.

37. Keenan, Sandy. "Dark Water: A Year After Hurricane Sandy." *The New York Times*. October 2, 2013.

38. "'Bag lady' fears persist among even the most successful women." Allianz Life Insurance Company of North America. 2013. https://www.allianzlife.com/retirement-and-planning-tools/women-money-and-power/bag-lady

39. https://blogs.chapman.edu/wilkinson/2016/10/11/americas-top-fears-2016/

40. Freyd, Jennifer. *Betrayal Trauma*, p. 76. *The Encyclopedia of Psychological Trauma*. Editors Reyes, Gilbert, Elhai John, and Ford, Julian. John Wiley & Sons, 2008. http://pages.uoregon.edu/dynamic/jjf/articles/freyd2008bt.pdf

41. Arnett, Nick. *Stress Management and Crisis Response*. http://nickarnett.net. p.6

Chapter Nine

42. Lappin, Linda. *Your Journey to Hell and Back: The Greek Concept of Katabasis Can Provide Analysis and Structure for Creating Strong Narratives*.

43. Siege of Sarajevo (April 5,1992 – February 29, 1996). https://en.wikipedia.org/wiki/Siege_of_Sarajevo

44. Kornfield, Jack. *The Roots of Buddhist Psychology*. Sounds True. 1995.

Chapter Ten

45. Kalweit, Holger. *When Insanity Is a Blessing: The Message of Shamanism*. Grof, Stansilav and Grof, Cristina. *Spiritual Emergency: When Personal Transformation Becomes a Crisis*. p. 85, Tarcher/Perigee 1989.

46. Diamond, Jared. *The World Until Yesterday: What Can We Learn from Traditional Societies?* Viking/Penguin 2012. p. 291.

Chapter Eleven

47. http://www.ptsdunited.org/ptsd-statistics-2/

48. Nena, PhD.,Yuval; Bravova, Margarita; Halper, Jessica. *Trauma and PTSD Among Civilians in the Middle East*. PTSD Research Quarterly. National Center for PTSD. Vol. 21, Issue 4. Fall 2010.

Chapter Twelve

49. Seriously, if you picked humility, please email me at thefivegifts@gmail.com. I would appreciate the opportunity to connect.

50. Exline, Julie and Hill, Peter. "Humility: A consistent and robust predictor of generosity," *The Journal of Positive Psychology* (May 2012): 208–218.

51. Kabatznick, Ronna. *Who by Water: Reflections of a Tsunami Psychologist*. Ronna Kabbatznick. Berkeley, CA. 2014.p. *ix*.

52. Kabatznick, ibid. p. 5.

53. Kabatznick, ibid. p. 5.

54. Kabatznick, ibid. p. 27.

55. Kabatznick, ibid. p. 86.

56. Kabatznick, ibid, p. 86.

57. Glenwick, Ph.D., David. "Religion/Spirituality and Well-Being: Implications for Therapy." *NYSPA Notebook*. Spring 2014. Pp. 8–9.

Chapter Thirteen

58. Seriously, if you picked patience, please email me at thefivegifts@gmail.com.

59. Sutter, John. D. "Online viewers ditch slow-loading video after 2 seconds. CNN. November 12, 2012. http://www.cnn.com/2012/11/12/tech/web/video-loading-study/index.html

Chapter Fourteen

60. Junger, Sebastian. *Tribe: On Homecoming and Belonging* (New York, NY: Twelve/Hachette Book Group) 2016. Pp. 52–53

61. Junger, Sebastian. Ibid., p. 49.

62. Breines, Juliana G. and Chen, Serena. "Activating the inner caregiver: The role of support-giving schemas in increasing state self-compassion." Journal of Experimental Social Psychology. Vol. 9, Issue 1, January 2013. Pp. 58–64.

63. Saez, Ignaco; Zhu, Lusha;Set, Eric; Kayser, Andrew; Hsu, Ming. "Dopamine Modulates Egalitarian Behavior in Humans." *Current Biology*. March 30, 2015. Volume 25, Issue 7. Pp. 912–919.

64. "Community Resilience." Department of Health and Human Services Public Health Emergency website: https://www.phe.gov/preparedness/planning/abc/pages/community-resilience.aspx

65. Links, Jon. "Predicting Community Resilience and Recovery After a Disaster." August 7, 2017. https://blogs.cdc.gov/publichealthmatters/2017/08/predicting-community-resilience-and-recovery-after-a-disaster

66. Norris, Fran H; Stevens, Susan P; Pfefferbaum, Betty; Wyche, Karen F.; Pfefferbaum, Rose L. "Community Resilience as a Metaphor, Theory, Set of Capacities and Strategy for Disaster Readiness." *American Journal of Community Psychology* (2008). Vol. 41, pp. 127–150.

67. "May you be free from suffering" is an alternate ending. There are many versions of this Tibetan Buddhist prayer which invokes empathy and kindness of all living beings.

Chapter Fifteen

68. Mine, Douglas Grant. "The Assassin Next Door." *New Miami Times*. http://www.miaminewtimes.com/news/the-assassin-next-door-6357449

69. Worthington, E.L., Jr; Witvliet, CV; Pietrini, P; Miller, AJ. "Forgiveness, health, and well-being: a review of evidence for emotional versus decisional forgiveness, dispositional forgiveness, and reduced unforgiveness." Journal of Behavioral Medicine. August 30, 2004. Pp. 291–302 www.hcbi.nlm.nih.gov/pubmed/17453329.

70. Tibbits, D; Ellis, G; Piramelli, C; Luskin, F.; Lukman, R. "Hypertension Reduction Through Forgiveness Training." Journal of Pastoral Care and Counseling, Vol. 60, Issue 1-2, pp. 27–34. www.learningtoforgive.com/research

71. Fred Luskin interview on *The Sixth Sense with Dr. Laurie Nadel* on www.webtalkradio.net aired the week of February 18, 2009.

72. Worthington, E.L. Dimensions of Forgiveness: Psychological Research and Theological Perspectives. New York: Templeton Foundation Press, 1997. Introduction.

73. Reed, G.L., et al. Women's Forgiveness Study. *Journal of Clinical Psychology*, October 2006. Pp. 920–929.

74. Bell, Martin. "Tsunami!" Privately published. Quotes reprinted with permission from the author.

75. Hadavi, Tala. "9/11 Victim's Mother Expresses Forgiveness 10 Years After." VOA News. September 13, 2011. www.voanews.com/a/article-911-victims-mother-expresses-forgiveness-10-years-after.com

76. Hadavi, Tala. Ibid.

77. Hadavi, Tala. Ibid.

Chapter Sixteen

78. Lam, Linda."15 Billion-Dollar Disasters Have Impacted the U.S. This Year; 2017 Tied for Second -Most All-Time" . www.weather.com October 17, 2017. https://weather.com/news/weather/news/2017 -10-17-billion-dollar-weather-disasters-united-states-record-pace

79. Meyer, Robinson. "A Contested Finding in a Major New Climate Change Report." *The Atlantic*. November 3, 2017.

80. Kestenbau, David. "Atomic Tune-Up: How the Body Rejuvenates Itself" on "All Things Considered." NPR. July 14, 2007.

81. Fraser, Carly. www.livelovefruit.com. August 3, 2015. https://livelovefruit.com/how-your-body -rebuilds-itself-in-less-than-365-days

82. Baird, James, Ph.D., Nadel, Laurie, PhD. *Happiness Genes: Unlock the Positive Potential Hidden within Your DNA*. New Page Books/Career Press. 2010. pp. 16–20.

83. Blix, Ines; Skogbrott Birekeland, Marianne; Bang Hansen, Marianne. "Posttraumatic Growth—An Antecedent and Outcome of Post-traumatic Stress: Cross-Lagged Associations Among Individuals Exposed to Terrorism ." "*Clinical Psychological Science*. January 12, 2016. Volume: 4 issue: 4, page(s): 620–628.

84. Mancini, Ph.D., Anthony. "The Trouble With Post-Traumatic Growth." https://www.psychologytoday. com/blog/rethinking-trauma/201606/the-trouble-post-traumatic-growth June 1, 2016.

85. Merriam-Webster definition of resilience. https://www.merriam-webster.com/dictionary/resilience.

86. Nadel, Laurie. "Healing the Forgotten: New Hope for TBI Patients." *Huffington Post*. April 1, 2014. https://www.huffingtonpost.com/laurie-nadel/healing-the-forgotten-new_b_5045967.html

87. McCarthy, Patrician. *In Your Element: Taoist Psychology: Everything You Wanted to Know about the Five Element Personalities*. Tao House Press, 2017. p.70.

BIBLIOGRAPHY

Arnett, Nick. *Stress Management and Crisis Response.* http://nickarnett.net, 2017.

Bro, Harmon Harzell with Bro, June Avis. Charles Thomas Cayce, Editor. *Growing Through Personal Crisis.* San Francisco, CA: Harper & Row, 1988.

Campbell, Chellie. *From Worry to Wealthy: A Woman's Guide to Financial Success Without the Stress.* Naperville, IL: Sourcebooks, Inc., 2015.

Campbell, Chellie. *The Wealthy Spirit: Daily Affirmations for Financial Stress Reduction.* Naperville, IL: Sourcebooks, Inc. 2002, 2009.

Chevalier, Jean and Gheerbrant, Alain. *The Penguin Dictionary of Symbols.* London, UK: Penguin Books, 1996.

Chodron, Pema. *When Things Fall Apart: Heart Advice for Difficult Times.* Boston, MA: Shambhala Publications, Inc., 1997.

Clarke, Robin and Hindley, Geoffrey. *The Challenge of the Primitives.* New York, NY: McGraw-Hill Book Company, 1975.

Crockett, Tom. *Stone Age Wisdom: The Healing Principles of Shamanism.* Gloucester, MA: Fair Winds Press, 2003.

Diamond, Jared. *The World Until Yesterday: What Can We Learn from Traditional Societies?* New York, NY: Viking, 2012.

Frankl, Viktor. *Man's Search for Meaning.* New York, NY: Beacon Press, 2001.

Grof, Stanislav. *Spiritual Emergency: When Personal Transformation Becomes a Crisis.* New York, NY: TarcherPerigee, 1989.

Hall, Edward T. *The Dance of Life: The Other Dimension of Time.* Garden City, NY: Anchor Press, 1973.

Hall, Edward T. *Beyond Culture.* Garden City, NY: Anchor Press, 1976.

Hill, Michael Ortiz. *Dreaming the End of the World: Apocalypse as a Rite of Passage.* Putnam, CT: Spring Publications, Inc., 1994, 2004.

His Holiness the Dalai Lama: *The Dalai Lama's Little Book of Buddhism.* New York, NY: MFJ Books, Fine Communications, 1999, 2015.

Hott, Ph.D., Rachel and Leeds, Steven A. *NLP: A Changing Perspective.* New York, NY: Rachel Hott and Steven Leeds, 2014.

Ingerman, Sandra. *Shamanic Journeying: A Beginner's Guide.* Boulder, CO: Sounds True, 2004.

Johnson, Robert A. *Inner Work: Using Dreams and Active Imagination for Personal Growth.* New York, NY: HarperCollins, 1986.

Johnston, Mark. *FBI and an Ordinary Guy: The Private Price of Public Service*. New York, NY: Page Publishing, Inc., 2015.

Junger, Sebastian. *Tribe: On Homecoming and Belonging*. New York, NY: Twelve, 2016.

Kabatznick, Ronna. *Who by Water: Reflections of a Tsunami Psychologist*. Berkeley, CA: Ronna Kabbatznick, 2014.

Le Maistre, Ph.D., JoAnn. *After the Diagnosis: From Crisis to Personal Renewal for Patients with Chronic Illnesses*. Berkeley, CA: Ulysses Press,1985, 1993, 1995.

Lodu, Lama. *Bardo Teachings: The Way of Death & Rebirth*. Ithaca, NY: Snow Lion Publications, 1982, 2010.

Luskin, Dr. Fred. *Forgive for Good*. New York, NY: HarperOne, 2003.

McCarthy, Patrician. *Taoist Five Elements: Finding Balance Workbook*. Santa Monica, CA: The Mien Shiang Institute, 2017.

McCarthy, Patrician. *In Your Element: Taoist Psychology—Everything You Want to Know About the Five Element Personalities*. Santa Monica, CA: Tao House Press, 2018.

Mehl-Madrona, M.D., Ph.D., Lewis. *Coyote Wisdom: The Power of Story in Healing*. Rochester, VT: Bear & Company, 2005.

Mercree, Amy Leigh: *The Compassion Revolution: 30 Days of Living from the Heart*. Woodbury, MN: Llewellyn Publications, 2017.

Mindell, Arnold. *Working on Yourself Alone: Inner Dreambody Work*. London, UK: Penguin, 1990.

Mitrell, Ian. *Smart Thinking for Crazy Times: The Art of Solving the Right Problems*. San Francisco, CA: Berrett-Kohler Publishers, Inc., 1998.

Morehouse, David A. *Nonlethal Weapons: War Without Death*. Westport, CT: Praeger Publishers, 1996.

Nadel, Laurie with Haims, Judy and Stemson, Robert. *Sixth Sense: Unlocking Your Ultimate Mind Power*. Indianapolis, IN: ASJA Press, 1990, 1992, 2006.

Pattakos, Ph.D. Alex and Dundon, Elaine. *Prisoners of Our Thoughts: Viktor Frankl's Principles for Discovering Meaning in Life and Work*. San Francisco, CA: Berrett-Kohler Publishers, Inc., 2017.

Pearce, Keith. *How to Survive a Nuclear Emergency*. England and Wales: Katwab, Ltd., 2017.

Piley, Orrin H. and Cooper, J. Andrew G. *The Last Beach*. Durham, NC and London, UK: Duke University Press, 2014.

Pinkola Estes, Ph.D., Clarissa. *Women Who Run with the Wolves: Myths and Stories of the Wild Woman Archetype*. New York, NY: Ballantine Books, 1992, 1995.

Santina, Peter D. *Fundamentals of Buddhism*. Carmel, NY: The Buddhist Association of the United States, 2007.

Solnit, Rebecca. *A Paradise Built in Hell: The Extraordinary Communities that Arise in Disaster*. New York, NY: Viking, 2009.

Tutu, Desmond and Tutu, Mpho. *The Book of Forgiving: The Fourfold Path for Healing Ourselves and Our World*. New York, NY: HarperOne, 2014.

Viorst, Judith: *Necessary Losses: The Loves, Illusions, Dependencies and Impossible Expectations That All of Us Have to Give Up in Order to Grow*. New York, NY: Fawcett Gold Medal, 1986.

ABOUT THE AUTHOR

Photo credit: Neal Bredbeck

Laurie Nadel, PhD, is an expert on mental health and climate change. She has been interviewed in the *New York Times*, National Public Radio, Reuters, and NBC-News.com. A specialist in acute stress, she is a member of a critical incident stress management team working with first responders.

During her 20-year career in journalism, she recognized a need to help people whose lives were shattered by violence. After earning two doctorates through independent study and completing training in mind-body medicine, she pioneered emotional first aid tools to help lower acute stress after catastrophic events. After losing her home during Hurricane Sandy, Dr. Laurie ran long-term support groups for survivors. From 2003 to 2005, she directed a program for teenagers whose fathers were killed in the 9/11 World Trade Center attacks and wrote the script for *After the Fall: The Rise of a 9/11 Community Center*, narrated by Dan Rather.

Her four-time bestseller, *Sixth Sense: Unlocking Your Ultimate Mind Power,* was featured twice on *Oprah*. A journalist for twenty years, Laurie reported for *Newsweek* and United Press International in South America, wrote TV news for CBS, ABC News, and Reuters Television, and was a religion columnist for the *New York Times* Long Island section.

The Five Gifts: Discovering Hope, Healing, and Strength When Disaster Strikes, is her seventh book. Please visit her at: *www.laurienadel.com* and *www.mindbodynetwork.com.*

INDEX